EVELYN UNDERHILL

Artist of the Infinite Life

Miss Evelyn Underhill, from a drawing by Howard Smith,
appearing in the Supplement to *The Bookman*, Christmas, 1932.

EVELYN UNDERHILL

Artist of the Infinite Life

Dana Greene

CROSSROAD • NEW YORK

1990

The Crossroad Publishing Company
370 Lexington Avenue, New York, N.Y. 10017

Printed in the United States of America

Library of Congress Cataloging-in-Publication Data

Greene, Dana
    Evelyn Underhill : artist of the infinite life / Dana Greene.
      p. cm.
    ISBN 0-8245-1006-2
    1. Underhill, Evelyn, 1875–1941. 2. Anglicans — England —
Biography. 3. Spirituality — Church of England. 4. Spirituality —
History — 20th century. 5. Church of England — Doctrines —
History — 20th century. 6. Anglican Communion — England — Doctrines —
History — 20th century. I. Title
BX5199.U53G74   1990
248.2'2'092 — dc20
    [B]   89-77843
                                                             CIP

TO THE WOMEN OF SPIRIT
WHO NURTURED ME

CONTENTS

ACKNOWLEDGMENTS

RESEARCH AND WRITING are solitary activities, but in making this book I have been buoyed up by a community of support, both living and dead, which extends to both sides of the Atlantic and around the world. It was the work and belief of many that brought this book to completion.

Financial support was given by the Virginia Foundation for the Humanities, the Earhart Foundation, the National Endowment for the Humanities, and St. Mary's College of Maryland. Permission to quote unpublished material was extended by Sir William Wilkinson. Archival materials were supplied by King's College, London; St. Andrews University, Scotland; and the House of Retreat, Pleshey.

Special thanks goes to friends of Evelyn Underhill who shared their recollections of her: the late Agatha Norman, Lady Laura Estaugh, Mrs. Renée Tickell, and Miss Daphne Martin-Hurst.

For long discussions on the work of Evelyn Underhill I thank A. M. Allchin, Christopher Armstrong, Grace Brame, Terry Coutret, Dolores Leckey, Joy Milos, and Gail Ranadive. The advice and suggestions of the staff and fellows of the Virginia Foundation for the Humanities and the Washington Biography Group, particularly Marc Pachter, have made this a better book. Rose Chioni offered gracious hospitality, Chris Bazemore his expertise. I owe an enormous debt of gratitude to Fay Campbell, who read and critiqued the manuscript several times, and to Lin Ludy, who gave me invaluable encouragement.

Friends at Communitas, Shalem, and Good Shepherd endured my preoccupation with Evelyn Underhill as did my family, Richard Roesel, Kristin, Justin, Lauren and Ryan Greene-Roesel, and Jackie Leclerc. The importance of their love and respect is incalculable.

INTRODUCTION

I<small>F ONE COMES UP CHURCH ROW</small> in London's northwest section of Hampstead, one sees the red brick church of St. John, surrounded by trees with a cemetery on its south side. On the right, just before the church is another cemetery enclosed within a wrought-iron fence; the gate is on Holly Walk. To enter is to find oneself among the many headstones now obscured by long grass and brambles. The stone path that leads down between the rows is mostly overgrown. One's eye is drawn to the far corner of this cemetery, not by the upright gray stone marker that is like the others that share the same untended ground, but by a small clearing which has been made around it. Some of the dead grass has been hacked away with a sharp rock that lies nearby. A small bunch of white wild flowers, picked from a nearby plant, lies near the headstone. The name on the stone is visible now — EVELYN, 1875–1941. She is identified as "wife of Hubert Stuart Moore" and "daughter of Sir Arthur Underhill." The obscurity and neglect of the marker are challenged by the attention given by someone who had searched it out and claimed it from the natural course of grass and weeds. The act demanded some physical strength as well as the knowledge that the beauty of wild flowers would have pleased the woman buried there.

What brings a visitor to this private, out-of-the-way unkempt shrine? Evelyn and Hubert Stuart Moore had no children. Most of those who had known Evelyn Underhill personally would be too old to make this pilgrimage, too weak to chop away long grass from the packed, hard dirt. Yet someone has found her grave and tended it. Does this suggest that the life of Evelyn Underhill has some meaning that still reaches out a half century after her death? The wild flowers suggest, "Yes." Yet the dead grass, the weeds, suggest that probing for that meaning will take persistence and some intuitive sense that the search itself is worthwhile.

1

The beginning of the search reveals that Evelyn Underhill was a woman acclaimed in her own time. She was acknowledged as a writer and a scholar and was the recipient of many honors: she was the first woman to be chosen as an outside lecturer at Oxford and the first laywoman to give retreats within the Anglican church; she was both a Fellow at King's College, London, and a holder of an honorary Doctor of Divinity degree from the University of Aberdeen. Her thirty-nine books and more than three hundred fifty articles won her the respect of both ordinary people and great ones. Her friend T. S. Eliot hailed her as a writer attuned to the great spiritual hunger of her times. "Her studies," he wrote, "have the inspiration not primarily of the scholar or the champion of forgotten genius, but of the consciousness of the grievous need of the contemplative element in the modern world."[1] At the time of her death the *Times Literary Supplement* confirmed this judgment: Evelyn Underhill "possessed an insight into the meaning both of the culture and the individual gropings of the soul, that was unmatched by any professional teacher of her day."[2] The French philosopher Henri Bergson called her work "remarkable"[3] and Michael Ramsey, late Archbishop of Canterbury, attested to her importance for her contemporaries. She did more, he said, than anyone else to keep the spiritual life alive in the Anglican church in the period between the wars.[4]

Who was this remarkable women who was claimed by those both inside and outside of Anglicanism? The outline of Evelyn Underhill's life is simple. She was born in 1875, the only child of Arthur Underhill and his wife Lucy Ironmonger. She was educated first privately and then for a few years at Sandgate House near Folkstone. She attended King's College, London, where she studied botany, languages, philosophy, and history. In her early twenties she began to make annual trips with her mother to the continent, especially Italy. She published her first book at age twenty-seven and three novels in the next few years. At age thirty-two she married a childhood friend, Hubert Stuart Moore, a barrister. They lived a comfortable life in London close to her parents. She wrote at home and participated in an active social life. At the time of her marriage, Evelyn Underhill had hoped to become a Roman Catholic, but she deferred this because of her husband's opposition. The subsequent condemnation of Modernism by the Vatican convinced her that she could not join the Roman Catholic church. Only many years later did she place herself within the Church of England, the church in which she had been baptized and confirmed as a youth. In 1911 she published her pioneering book *Mysticism*, which saw numerous editions and reprintings and established her reputation as a religious writer. For the next ten years she published a variety of articles, translations, and biographical works related to mysticism.

During World War I she worked in naval intelligence and actively supported the war effort by both lecturing and writing. In 1921 she gave the Upton lectures at the Unitarian-affiliated Manchester College and in so doing became the first woman to be chosen as an outside lecturer in religion at Oxford University. During that same year she sought the guidance of Baron Friedrich von Hügel, the best known Roman Catholic theologian in England, a layman and writer on mysticism. Von Hügel served as her spiritual director until his death in 1925. In the mid-1920s, Underhill began to serve as a retreat director and to shift her writing toward an exploration of the spiritual life. Many of her retreat addresses were published, and her work as religious book review editor for the *Spectator* and later *Time and Tide* kept her name before the public. The major work of the last years of her life was *Worship*, a study of the nature, principles, and chief expressions of the human response to and relationship with the Eternal. In the late 1930s she became a pacifist, and until her death in 1941, she continued to support that position. She preceded her husband in death by ten years.

Evelyn Underhill's life was "quiet"; it was not marked by adventurous acts and deeds. Although her life circumstances are important in that they provide the raw data for her development, a biography that focused on them rather than on the development of her mind and spirit would miss the meaning of her life. The adventure here is the inner one, the conflict and reconciliation of mind and heart, the development of individual consciousness and its ultimate transcendence.

Biography, like portraiture, has as its goal the illumination of person.[5] Like the artist, the biographer begins with a blank canvas, the materials with which to paint, some "facts" about a physical entity, and clues about the inner self. Through a combination of the artist's skillful craft, intuition, and persistence, the picture emerges; it succeeds or fails to the degree that it draws one in and illuminates that which is other. The obstacles to its realization are sometimes formidable. In the case of Evelyn Underhill, there are several that pose particular problems.

Like most of her contemporaries Underhill believed in a separation between public and private life, and she and others went to great lengths to ensure this. With very few exceptions, she refused to state her personal views on a variety of subjects lest she alienate those she wanted to serve. In addition, since she believed that "will" was much more important than "feeling," she frequently did not record the latter.

Those who have preserved her memory have tried to protect Underhill and her friends and acquaintances. The originals of most of her letters have apparently been destroyed and those that remain have been "cleaned up"; names have been changed, passages deleted. For an important decade in her life, her forties, there is only scant archival material.

A more general problem, but one that presses heavily upon the writer is that although Underhill dealt squarely with some of the conflicts in her life and thought, there are others she was incapable of resolving. Biography, both to explain the life and to evaluate its significance, must deal with these conflicts. Its merit is that it presents a life not as an intellectual problem fraught with contradictions but as a lived process in which the person is forced to a more primary level where contradictions are held in tension and deeper growth is possible. While exploration of contradiction points up the limitations of the person and her culture, it also provides a way to understand her development. Like the fifteenth-century philosopher Nicholas of Cusa, Underhill could say of her life: "And I have learnt that the place wherein Thou art found unveiled is girt round with the coincidence of contradictories; And this is the wall of Paradise wherein Thou dost abide."[6]

The principal focus of this biography is the development of Underhill's thought as expressed in her writing. As intellectual biography, her "quiet" life becomes the context for inner growth. In order to understand that growth, it is important to notice not only what happened to Underhill but what did not happen. For instance, what were the consequences of not being brought up in a religious home; of not having siblings; of not being able to join the Roman Catholic church; of not having children; of not living in peaceful times; of not being a man in a male-controlled world? Stated positively these become the what-if questions: What if the Underhill family home had been orthodox and pious? What if she had been showered with the affection of siblings? What if she had become a Roman Catholic? What if she had had children? What if her times had been serene? What if she had been a man rather than a woman?

Does Evelyn Underhill want a biography? Does she want to be a subject of "portraiture," to be "interpreted"? All the evidence would suggest that, yes, she does. She "wants" this not so that she might be remembered or aggrandized, but because she was convinced that it was through the person that we come to know mystery. "We most easily recognize spiritual reality," she wrote, "when it is perceived transfiguring human character, and most easily attain it by sympathetic contagion."[7] She made frequent reference to the fact that the life of the spirit was not "taught," but "caught"; one learned about it through encounter with others.

Underhill would argue that her life/work was a medium through which spiritual reality was revealed; and if that could be shown to be helpful to others, she wanted it made available.[8] Although she would put the emphasis on her work, she was fully aware that the lived experience provided the context for her ideas to emerge. It was the ordinary, the daily, which was the theater in which the infinite broke through. Her writing was her attempt to articulate those breakthroughs as she encountered them in her own life and that of others.

The function of biography is to answer the question: Who is this person and why is she significant? Charles Williams in his introduction to the letters of Evelyn Underhill claims that she was not primarily a writer, that she was something more and something less.[9] On its face this is a startling statement given the fact that she produced over four hundred published pieces. If not a writer, who *is* Underhill? The plaque on her home at Campden Hill Square commemorates her as a Christian philosopher. But that designation does not serve either; it is too narrow and imprecise. While clearly a Christian, she was initially an agnostic and a theist, and her sympathies went beyond Christianity. Her religious sense was of the broadest sort. Neither was she a philosopher except in the most ancient meaning of the word as a seeker after wisdom. Philosophy connotes an occupation that is more abstract and more systematic than the one she undertook. Others have called Underhill a mystic. She denies the designation and redefines the word so as to demythologize it. The mystic way is the spiritual way, open to all, participated in by the many, fully realized by the few. Neither does the definition of ecumenist capture her central contribution. Although she always had a clear understanding of the unity shared by all religions, and although her last major work is a brilliant, intuitive defense of the validity and uniqueness of a variety of religious traditions of worship, the word "ecumenist" allies her too closely with institutional religion. She recognized the importance of institutional and corporate religious expression, but her principal contribution lies elsewhere.

Evelyn Underhill was certainly a writer in the sense that writing was the vehicle she used to put forth her ideas. As early as her seventeenth year one can see her choice is set: "When I grow up I should like to be an author because you can influence people."[10] But this vehicle does not explain who she was but merely the means she used to influence others. Williams is correct. Writing for Underhill was not an end; it was a means to an end, and that end is only revealed by examining her voluminous corpus with its varied themes.

One finds clues early on as to how Underhill carved out her sphere, her terrain, her field for examination. In the subtitle to *Mysticism*, "the study of the nature and development of man's spiritual consciousness," she determined the perimeters of her subject. Although she studied history and art and was influenced by developments in modern psychology, philosophy, and science, her focus was on human experience and the possibility it offered for the development of a consciousness of the transcendent, the eternal, the absolute, the infinite. Underhill asked the question so often ignored: What is the deepest human longing? She found her answer first in the experience of Western mystics who claimed that it was to behold love itself — that is, God — and second, in the experience of ordinary life that offers the opportunity to respond with awe and gratitude to that love.

It was this subject matter that made her work significant for her contemporaries. Speaking in ordinary language to ordinary people about the deepest human realities, Evelyn Underhill served as a beacon to an age that contested and obscured those realities. For the late twentieth century her function is a different one. Grounded in the cultural assumptions and theological worldview of an earlier time, Evelyn Underhill is a bridge between her own times and ours. Firmly planted in her own class and station, she reaches over into ours; never one of us, she is nonetheless not a stranger to us. The persistence of her vision and the passion and single-mindedness with which she searched for the infinite life speaks across generations. Through her, past and present meet. Yes, Evelyn Underhill was a writer, one whose work was elegant, immediate, powerful, and accessible. Her significance rests, however, on the fact that she used this craft in the service of a particular subject — the universal human experience of and response to the infinite.

Yeats wrote that there is some one "myth" for every person, which if we knew it would make us understand all that the person did and thought.[11] For Evelyn Underhill that "myth" was the search for infinite life; it dominated all her life and work. In its service she became more than a beacon or bridge; she became an artist of the infinite life.

1

ROUTES TO THE UNSEEN

THE LANDSCAPE OF EVERY LIFE has a particular character and like the natural landscape it stretches out before us revealing its contours. When one surveys the sixty-five years of Evelyn Underhill's life, it is not heights and depths that dominate, but broad expansiveness. Like a plain, it extends in all directions joining sky and mountains and the very edges of the land itself. It is open terrain across which the eye travels toward the outer boundary of vision where the visible and invisible meet.

The life of Evelyn Underhill points to this outer boundary and seeks to know what lies beyond. It is here at this edge that she camped out and took up her work, attesting that just beyond the seen lies the infinite, which when discovered is immediate and accessible to all. Hers was a distinctive work.

Evelyn Underhill's work was to search out the infinite "in a landscape so rich and great that no one person can explore, apprehend, still less live in all of it."[1] She did live in that landscape, and she made it her particular vocation to mediate what she found there to others. Such mediation demanded "a drastic process of translation" before the infinite could be apprehended by the human mind. This translation was the work of the artist who through the "power of perceiving in any object a range of reality and beauty to which the common eye is blind,...give[s]...an inkling of...other reaches of reality and beauty."[2]

Evelyn Underhill was an artist of the infinite life; her distinctive work, pursued for many years and expressed in many different forms, is remarkable in itself. What makes it more so was that it was accomplished without formal religious training, without early benefit of church affiliation, without family encouragement, without academic or ecclesiastical support.

One searches in vain for indications in Evelyn's childhood of specifically religious influence. Little is known of her early life in any regard; she was unwilling to talk about it publicly or privately with friends.[3] Although she was born in Wolverhampton, her family moved to London soon after her birth so that her father could move on in his career. Established there, Arthur Underhill was to become a successful barrister and an authority on torts and private trust. He was knighted in 1922. He apparently gave little attention to his daughter until she was in her late teens, and Lucy Underhill, whose interests were in philanthropy, seems not to have been particularly close to her either. Typical of many socially well-placed families, the Underhills provided security for their daughter, but not much affection or intimacy. Evelyn, a frail child, was educated at home until about age thirteen, then was sent to Sandgate House, near Folkstone, to continue her education. As she had few friends at school, this was not a particularly happy time in her life. At home in London, however, she had two neighbor friends, Jeff and Hubert, who lived with their father, Archibald Stuart Moore, around the corner from the Underhill's large home on Campden Hill Place. Like his colleague Arthur Underhill, Mr. Stuart Moore was a bencher and avid yachtsman. His sons, who experienced the death of their mother at an early age, were given special attention by Lucy Underhill and Evelyn. The family friendship continued over many years, and Hubert, the elder, ultimately became Evelyn's intended.

The Underhill household was not particularly pious, and Evelyn herself claimed that she "was not brought up to religion." Arthur Underhill was a deist at best, although one of his brothers, Ernest, became a priest in the Church of England.[4] At sixteen, while she was still at Sandgate House, Evelyn was confirmed, and the first record of her religious inclinations is found in a diary entry she made on the eve of her seventeenth birthday:

> I believe in God and think it is better to love and help the poor people around me than to go on saying that I love an abstract spirit whom I have never seen. If I can do both, all the better, but it is best to begin with the *nearest*. I do not think anything is gained by being orthodox, and a great deal of beauty and sweetness of things is lost by being bigoted and dogmatic. If we

are to see God at all it must be through nature and our fellow men.

I don't believe in worrying God with prayers for things we want. If he is omnipotent he knows we want them, and if he isn't, He can't give them to us. I think it is an insult to Him to repeat the same prayers every day. It is as much as to say He is deaf, or very slow of comprehension.

I do not believe the Bible is inspired, but I think nevertheless that it is one of the best and wisest books the world has ever seen.[5]

Although Evelyn shared her father's deist view, she believed that the experience of beauty and nature led to an understanding of an infinite love that guided the universe. In one of her first published articles, "A Woman's Thoughts About Silence," she wrote,

Go out under the solemn stars and strive to think of the infinite love which guides and governs them in their courses from the least to the greatest, which is also guiding these poor human lives of ours, each to fulfil a Divinely appointed purpose.[6]

In both life and politics, her worldview was expansive and inclusive. At odds with the beliefs of her Mugwump father, she proclaimed: "In politics I am a Socialist.... I think it is the only fair form of government, and it gives every class an equal status, and does away with the incentive to many sorts of crime."[7] She practiced what she preached and tried to convince one of her father's deckhands to join the socialist cause.[8] But politics were never a central interest for her; the drive toward inclusivity was expressed in other ways. By her seventeenth birthday she would wish that "my mind will not grow tall to look down on things, but wide to embrace all sorts of things during the coming year."[9] This inclusivity naturally put her at odds with institutional religion that she found narrow and constricting. As early as 1891 she recorded in her "Dialogues with Nesta":

"Do you see that sky lark?", said Nesta, as a morsel of feathered music rose from the field and darted, trilling melodiously into the heavens. "He rises up and up and up, sings louder and even louder as if he would like to hit himself against the sky; but he cannot because it is elastic. And I always think that you clergy act in much the same way. You go higher and higher, and pray louder and louder, as though you hoped to hit God Himself, but you cannot, because He too is elastic." "Then you do believe in a God?", the curate inquired tentatively. "Oh yes!", she replied. "But you would not acknowledge Him to be the same as yours, because He is so much more stretched out."[10]

In another dialogue between Nesta and a clergyman, she shows her irritation with religious exclusiveness. "It seems to me," said Nesta as they left St. Paul's,

> that domed architecture is peculiarly symbolic of religion in general. After permitting you to struggle, with infinite pains, to a high spiritual elevation, it makes things easy for you to slide down again to earth by the very structure which first assisted you to rise." "Yes," he replied, "but the architecture of spires and points is even more appropriate. With that, you see, the higher you rise, the narrower you become until at last you find yourself at a truly heavenly altitude, looking down on all the rest of the world." "How true that is," she remarked; "I do so detest exclusiveness."[11]

These adolescent writings reveal a young woman who was intelligent, lively, and interested in the world. She was also exacting toward herself and relentless in her self-scrutiny. At age fifteen she drew up a list of faults that illustrates the tendency toward self-criticism that would plague her continuously. She accuses herself of "[s]elfishness, pride, conceit, disorder, moral cowardice, self-deceit, scepticism, thoughtlessness, revengefulness, exaggeration, want of truth, changeableness, double-dealing, teasing, unkindness, disobedience, dishonourableness, profanity, idleness."[12] In fact, she was probably much like the female ideal toward which she aspired; one who was "clever, vivacious and accurately but not priggishly informed, gentle, truthful, tactful and tolerant, and... [with] a due sense of proportion."[13] While this was an ideal that conformed closely to many of the typical Victorian attitudes toward her sex, it was not an abstraction, but one she attempted to internalize. In an early article entitled "How Should a Girl Prepare Herself for a Worthy Womanhood," she defined the most important womanly virtues to be sympathy and self-control. This choice of values is instructive because it contains in incipient form her basic methodology for approaching both persons and learning in general. "In order to become widely and generally sympathetic," she wrote, a girl should try to cultivate a habit of observation and interest in everything, not only in her fellow-creatures but in all the beauties of nature and art.... If she gets no further than this she will at any rate have made herself a pleasant and sociable companion; but she must, if she wishes her life to be good and beautiful, acquire what Watson called *a sense of oneness* with our kind, which helps us to remember that A may be stupid and B tiresome, yet they are just as worthy of our tact and consideration as other more brilliant or pleasing people.[14]

In the same article she discussed the importance of practical competence in women:

A girl who can converse on every subject from metaphysics to penny novelettes but cannot darn a stocking or boil a potato, is not, in my opinion, a worthy specimen of womanhood. Nothing fosters helplessness so much as an education which gives all its attention to the brain but utterly neglects the hands.[15]

Although Evelyn probably never needed to boil a potato, her competence as an excellent bookbinder and yachtswoman (she ultimately gained a Master Mariner's Certificate) illustrate her commitment to be physically engaged with her world. As for occupation, her early reflections are telling: "My favourite occupations are literature and art, though I do not think I have much taste for the latter. When I grow up I should like to be an author because you can influence people more widely by books than by pictures."[16]

These early notes and essays, all of which were written by the time Evelyn was eighteen, show the ideals toward which she aimed. Her motto sums them up: "Be noble men of noble deeds, For love is holier than creeds."[17] She wanted to be noble, balanced, tolerant, and to seek truth through sympathy. Her ideal was the largest one, and the way toward it was through inclusivity. Already at age eighteen Evelyn's life had the contours of a broad plain, one which caught up all within it, and directed the eye outward toward the edge.

In 1893 Evelyn enlisted in the recently opened Ladies' Department of King's College, London. The building at 13 Kensington Square was a short walk from home through the lovely streets of Kensington. There she studied history, languages, botany, and art, each of which was to have great importance in her life. Ultimately, she came to appreciate most the modern history courses with Professor Samuel Gardiner. The importance he gave to human character and small facts was, she wrote later in life, "priceless training for anyone whose natural inclination is to float about in the air."[18] At King's she improved her competence in languages (Latin, French, and Italian) and learned to draw and paint.[19] It is unclear whether her love of nature, particularly flowers, caused her to study botany or resulted from it, but she left King's with some scientific appreciation of the natural world. Theology was offered there as well, but she paid little attention to that.[20] She was interested in philosophy, however, particularly Plotinus and Augustine, and although she had no philosophical training, she read from her father's ample library. In fact Arthur Underhill claimed that his daughter's interest in philosophy was gained from him.[21] She also read poetry. Dante and Blake, discovered during these years, would come to have great influence in her life.

Her intellectual studies were supplemented by practical ones, particularly bookbinding. The knives she used to cut leather were kept sharp for her by her friend Hubert Stuart Moore, with whom she spent more time. Their companionship deepened during this time, but marriage was still a long way off.

In 1898 Evelyn left her insular world of Kensington to accompany her mother on a trip to Italy. There she discovered not only beauty but herself. "Italy the holy land of Europe," she wrote, "the only place left, I suppose, that is really medicinal to the soul.... There is a type of mind which must go there to find itself."[22] "The place," she wrote to Hubert about Florence, "has taught me more than I can tell you: a sort of gradual unconscious growing into an understanding of things."[23] This was the first of sixteen trips that Evelyn made to the continent, usually with her mother, sometimes alone.

Evelyn Underhill claimed that she first came to God through philosophy,[24] and certainly her reading of Plotinus and others ignited in her a sense of the Divine. But she found more powerful and evocative access to the Divine in the art, architecture, and landscape of Italy. Her travel notebooks are filled with watercolor drawings, sketches, and written descriptions of the place, all concrete evidence of her engagement with a new reality. It is true that the quality of Italian light illuminates differently and that beauty there was free from the constraints of Victorian morality, but neither of these facts explains her response. She had encountered something new. Italy changed her life; it taught her that beauty was a way to the infinite life for which she longed.

The attraction was not merely the beauty of nature and art but of religious ritual as well. Describing a religious procession through a crowded piazza in Florence, she wrote that it

> brought old Florence forcibly before one's eyes. Then came numbers of acolytes, then priests in crimson and white. Then others in purple vestments, all bearing candles and chanting. Then came the great white and gold canopy with priests under it in lovely vestments of rose and white brocade....After came more priests...then a crowd of worthy-looking citizens with candles, remnants of the medieval societies of *Flagellanti*. It was a most moving sight.[25]

Beauty was a lure, drawing her to an object and then through it to the spirit of a former time, a time in which the Divine was palpable and near at hand. Of Santa Maria Novella in Florence she wrote:

> [T]he loveliest thing of all was the Spanish Chapel, standing in the beautiful, quiet old cloisters. It is one enormous fresco in praise of the Dominicans, the glory of St. Thomas Aquinas as he sits above the prophets and apostles: the earthly and heavenly sciences, is a vision of loveliness; colour, composition, feeling, all there. The other side, the church militant and triumphant is almost as good and contains exquisite groups of figures. I could have lingered for hours. It was so peaceful, so filled with the best medieval spirit; learned yet pious, stern but loving.[26]

For Underhill the medieval world intimately linked matter and spirit, the inner and the outer, the natural and the supernatural. At shrines and in medieval towns in Italy and later in France she found that same sense of unity. Of Rocamadour she wrote later:

> [T]here was an odd sense of seclusion, intimacy and silence about it all. The chapel itself was soaked with the sense of prayer and adoration: had an atmosphere one could not mistake. Above it, a steep path wound up the cliff past the Stations of the Cross. At the top of all, a large bare cross made of wood brought from Jerusalem. There is a sense of clambering effort, quest and of quiet havens suddenly reached in the midst of the travail. The effort of approach, the secret chapel, the close communion of the supernatural haven with the actual structure of the earth, the lifting of it above the homes of men — all these things contribute to the wonder of Rocamadour.[27]

As she made her pilgrimages through various medieval towns, she always looked for this unity of matter and spirit. Capturing the walls of Carcassone in a photograph, she wrote that it

> is not a place but a picture: a pure image of the old ideal of an ordered town.... one goes through streets of cobble-stones... on to an old Gothic bridge. Then suddenly the city leaps up ahead of you, high on a very green hill, the shadow of its walls on the grass...the donjon of the castle, the tower and the long ridge of cathedral are the main masses of the place: church and state, an intense aspect of unity, spiritually and materially achieved, *secure.*[28]

Her travels to Italy and France began when she was in her mid-twenties, and continued for years. Not much is known of her life during that time. As a proper young Victorian woman she lived at home and was dutiful toward her parents, a characteristic she retained throughout her life. Her days were spent in study, in time with Hubert, in sailing and bookbinding, and in helping her father. Her circle of friends at this time came to include J. A. and Alice Herbert, Arthur Machen, Arthur Waite, Margaret Robinson, Ethel Ross Barker, and Robert Hugh Benson. This was a diverse group of persons: each had an intense interest in religion and would play an important role in subsequent decisions in her life. She took an interest in law, the profession of both her father and her fiancé, and began gathering materials for an entertaining and clever satirical poem about that world. *A Bar Lamb's Ballad* was published in 1902; she was greatly pleased by its warm reception. That same year, when she was twenty-seven, she began work on her first novel, *The Grey World.*

It was clear at this point that she and Hubert would marry, even though they would wait for another five years to do so. Their relationship as intendeds, based on many years of childhood friendship, was a strong one — respectful, familiar, and sometimes playful. In letters Hubert addressed her as "my dearest little one," "my dearest love and companion," and "my dearest treasure." She wrote to "Nicko," "my dear Laddie," and signed herself "Nursie."[29] Her protective and motherly attitude toward a boy without a mother took the form of concern about his health and happiness. Her letters to him are jaunty, solicitous, and undemanding and must have been meant to bolster a sometimes depressed fiancé.[30] They are guarded documents; unrevealing, with few exceptions, of the enormous intellectual and emotional growth she was experiencing in Italy. This guardedness, so characteristic of her, stemmed from both her desire not to bother Hubert with things not of interest to him and fear of his rejection and mockery of her growing religious interests. Responding to his query about why she had not shown him some photographs of religious subjects she explains, "You always used to mock at those sort of things."[31] It was only on the eve of their marriage in 1907 that differences over religion drove them to explore their relationship more deeply. Hubert gave her balance, support, concern, and devotion; but hers was an ardent nature, one that desired both transcendence and intimacy. These desires had been ignited in Italy, but in England there was little to sustain them. Her devotion to Hubert was unquestioned; yet that relationship could not nurture her at the most basic level. Her growing friendship with a group of people who shared her interests provided nourishment at this critical point.

J. A. Herbert was Keeper of Manuscripts at the British Museum and it was he who introduced Evelyn Underhill to the treasure trove of medieval manuscripts in his keeping.[32] Herbert and his wife, Alice, a well-known novelist, were both devout Roman Catholics, and while Underhill owed a professional debt to Jack Herbert, to Alice Herbert she owed a personal one. Evelyn's dedication of her first novel, *The Grey World*, is to Alice Herbert, as "a small acknowledgement of a great debt." One can only surmise that as J. A. Herbert opened up the world of medieval mystical literature to her, Alice Herbert sustained her in a personal quest to understand its truth.[33]

While the visual arts gave Underhill access to the medieval spirit and Herbert's medieval manuscripts deepened her understanding of that world, her first attempt to express that understanding took fictional form.

As one who knew from an early age that she wanted to be an author, Evelyn Underhill was impressed by the work of the Flemish writer Maurice Maeterlinck, whose *Treasures of the Humble* and *Wisdom of Destiny* she read in 1899 soon after they were translated into English.[34] In these works Maeterlinck, who was deeply influenced by Plotinus and by the Flemish mystic Jan van Ruysbroeck, captured the mystery of the ordinary. Maeterlinck's acknowledgment of the importance of mystical writing for humanity, his emphasis on symbol, and his theme of life in two worlds, were to have an important impact on Underhill. This last theme was to become the subject of *The Grey World*.

The Grey World was widely and positively received. *Bookman* announced it as "the book of the week" when it appeared. Hubert, obviously proud of his fiancée's work, saved the more than eighty reviews and pasted them in a notebook. This first novel is valuable not as great literature but as popular literature of the early twentieth century and for what it reveals of its author. It is above all a discussion of philosophical idealism, a fictionalized exploration of the world beyond the senses.

The principal theme of the novel, life in two worlds, is examined through the story of Willie, a young English boy, who has been reincarnated as a member of a suburban family, the Hopkinsons. He finds them trivial, materialistic, and totally uncomprehending of his former life in the unseen world. Bewildered and misunderstood, Willie stumbles through life, falls in and out of love, and decides finally to retreat from the world to nature, to the humble craft of bookbinding, and to art.

The central message of *The Grey World* is that beauty points to a world beyond. Those who guide Willie in his search for the real make these claims: "It seems so much easier in these days to live morally than to live beautifully. Lots of us manage to exist for years without ever sinning against society, but we sin against loveliness every hour of the day. I don't think the crime is less great."[35] "Beauty is the only thing really worth having,"[36] "It is after all the visual side of goodness."[37]

The importance of process is emphasized throughout the book. Willie is described as "[p]ossessing the deliberation of the idealist who looks to process, not to completion for his pleasure, and knows reality to consist in anything rather than material results, [one who] found each stage of the work as important as its end."[38]

Ultimately for Willie, everything in the world becomes lovable because it is a symbol or sacrament of the world beyond. The woman in the woods tells him: "You must love everything, don't you see, because everything in the whole world is being offered to you as a symbol of an adorable idea that is beyond."[39] And Willie "learned to treat his work as a sacrament which bore some mystic relation to truth."[40]

It was in Italy that Willie searched for the world beyond. Like Underhill he found venerable, old Roman Catholic churches charged with a kind of holy magic. "He had been, of course, in Protestant churches, but they had left no mark on his spirit, and gave him no clue to this experience — to the hush, the awe, the weight of a new form of life."[41]

Willie's access to the world beyond also came through the poets and mystics. "Poets see further than most people," says Willie. "They don't get the dust of daily life in their eyes, as practical persons do."[42]

Mystics like Plotinus, Blake, Swedenborg, the Indian philosophers are like "contemplatives all over the world who have looked beyond the shadow of the earth and seen another reality, some as a dim reflection, some as a perfect truth."[43] Like the poets, "they all speak a different language, but what they are trying to say is substantially the same."[44]

In Roman churches, in the writings of poets and mystics, and in nature, Willie found a route to the beyond. "Eternity was here and now: and he, wondrous immortal, saw through the grassy symbol which is nature, the glory of the spiritual flame."[45]

It was in the here and now, in the world of symbol and sacraments, that Willie chose to live. The ecstasy and sense of awe that he longed for came in many ways, but its source was the same. "The inarticulate ecstasy which came to him in the presence of all beautiful things was the same in essence as that emotion which he felt in our Lady of Pity [chapel]... another approach to the same God."[46] Beauty, which was Truth, came to Willie in many ways, but in each case it brought him to communion with the beyond.

The autobiographical elements of *The Grey World* are obvious. The search for the world "over the border," the importance of Italy, the significance of symbol, the role of beauty, nature, the poets and mystics, dominated Evelyn Underhill's thought during this period of her life.

The novel ends with Willie alone in the woods, living with nature and art. His quest, like that of his creator Evelyn Underhill, is an individualistic one. His isolation is never dealt with; hers would be confronted soon.

The publication of *The Grey World* in 1904 came at the same time that she joined the Hermetic Society of the Golden Dawn, a fellowship dedicated to ritual spiritualism. In turn-of-the-century London interest in magic, spiritism, theosophy, and astrology was high. Underhill's preoccupation with the supernatural drew her to others who shared these views. Although the Golden Dawn began in 1887, Evelyn joined a branch founded by Arthur Waite in 1903.[47] She was introduced to Waite probably by their mutual friend Arthur Machen, who was a member of Waite's branch of the Society.[48] This branch differed from the rest of the Society in that under Waite's leadership it abandoned traditional use of ritual magic and astrology and focused exclusively on Christian mysticism and ritual. Although she was only minimally involved in the Society for a short period of time, the influence on her was probably substantial.[49] Italy introduced her to the rituals of Roman Catholicism, but she was excluded from full personal participation in them. In the Golden Dawn, she experienced for the first time a communal search through ritual for a world beyond the senses.

It was from Arthur Waite, who had been influenced by the French occultist Eliphas Lévi,[50] that Underhill learned of the power of magic and ritual to awaken one to a deep desire for the unseen. Waite also provided her with useful contacts. In 1904 five of her stories appeared in *Horlicks Magazine,* a short-lived publication edited by Waite and to which Arthur Machen contributed.

These stories focus on many of the themes of *The Grey World,* particularly the relationship between beauty and truth and forms of access to the invisible world. Unlike her novel, the stories all transmit an eerie sense of the power of the supernatural world. Her more extensive probing into the world of the occult revealed its danger as well as its power.

"The Death of a Saint" is a story about the relationship of art to beauty and goodness. Father John is a priest known for his sanctity and his daily retreat, supposedly for prayer, behind closed doors. One day after he does not emerge from his retreat, his followers break through locked doors and find his dead body in what is an art studio. Assembled are paintings representing years of his work, art which is not ennobling and uplifting, but grotesque and bestial, the outpouring of a tormented soul. Father John's followers raise the question: was this saint only an artist, or was he a saint because his art allowed him to purge himself of his bestiality?

The relationship between beauty, truth, love, and knowledge is raised in "The Ivory Tower." The story here follows the quest of young men for a princess, the perfection of beauty and truth, who lives in an ivory tower in the sea. Most who seek her despair. They lose their way, smash into the rocks, drown, or return home and give up the quest. One of the young men perseveres, only to find that she (truth) is not beautiful. The lover can only embrace truth with eyes shut; he says: "Oh, truth, blind me for ever, I had rather love than know."[51] The relationship between loving and knowing and the priority of the former over the latter will become central not only to all of Underhill's subsequent writing, but to her personal life as well. "The Ivory Tower" is her first treatment of this subject.

The quest for the perfect is also examined in "Mountain Image," the haunting story of a sculptor who retreats to a mountain to carve on its cliff an image of the great Madonna. Disdaining the imperfections of ordinary art, Nicholas seeks in his monumental creation the realization and possession of his perfect idea. His first attempt yields a cold and lifeless Lady; but driven on by the perfect that torments him, he creates another Madonna, this one imperious and vital. Lured on by his desire to possess her, he lunges forward at her and smashes his head on the hard rock. His search for "joy," for the "satisfaction of all longing," leads to death and mockery by his own creation. To seek the perfect in and of itself, independent of the ordinary, and as an object of individual possession, is to confront the demonic face-to-face.

"The Green Mass" and "Our Lady at the Gate" were the last two of her stories to appear in *Horlicks Magazine*. The former is a paean to nature, in which a spectator watches as all aspects of nature combine to produce a mass in which sacrifice, praise, and thanksgiving are offered. "Our Lady at the Gate" is set in Umbria where Father Porter encounters the Madonna as one of the pilgrims at the monastery gate. His difficulty is how to explain her appearance to others. While the woman reveals herself as a mother who has come to visit her son, Father Porter insists that Our Lady was at the Gate, that the holy was present to him.

These five stories carry forward Underhill's preoccupation with the supernatural; with that which is sought and loved but not known and possessed; that which is beyond, but embodied in the ordinary; that which is most accessible in beauty and nature. These are stories meant for those who, as Blake said, are born crying, "I want," "I want." They are stories of desire, yet they offer no consolation to those who seek the perfect. In fact, they tell of despair and evil. They are stories of warning.

The *Horlicks* short stories and *The Grey World* were both published in 1904; that year also brought Underhill two friends, Margaret Robinson and Ethel Ross Barker, each of whom would have an important part in her life and the choices she would make.

The long friendship between Margaret Robinson and Evelyn Underhill began with a letter from this Scottish Presbyterian after she read *The Grey World*. Seeking the counsel of Underhill on spiritual matters, she initiated a correspondence that would last for many years. Underhill's letters, even at this early stage, show a deep sensitivity and understanding of the spiritual needs of others. Although hesitant to guide others because of her own confused state, she nonetheless responded to Margaret Robinson's queries. Before she knew what she was doing, she was involved in what she came to call "the care of souls."

Robinson wrote to Evelyn as a kindred spirit, one attuned to beauty as a way to truth. One of her concerns was a fear of the sensuous side of beauty, which she believed could be both dangerous and distracting. Underhill's response reveals her fundamental trust that the visible and invisible are linked and that the one leads inevitably to the other. On the dangerous and distracting side of beauty she wrote:

> This is true at first: but when once it has happened to you to perceive that beauty is the "outward and visible sign" of the greatest sacraments, I don't think you can ever again get hopelessly entangled by its merely visible side.[52]

Underhill, seeing the anxiety and strain of Margaret Robinson, consoles and reminds her that her efforts will not produce the end she longs for. "The light comes," she writes, "when it does come, rather suddenly and strangely I think. It is just like falling in love; a thing that never happens to those who are always trying to do it."[53]

While she encourages Margaret Robinson to be open to "the light," and to trust that there is a link between the visible and the invisible, she also offers this warning: "The perfect accomplishment of the quest is impossible; we can only come to the edge of the sea that separates us from the city of Sarras. Few get so far: but for those who do, it seems that there is a certain hope."[54]

As a natural counselor, Evelyn Underhill grasped the psychological needs of each individual. Aware that Margaret Robinson veered toward a contemplative and solitary life, she urged her toward balance and communion with others.

> What struck me about you was, not that there was any danger of your relapsing into "comfiness," but that your tendency was to make your religion a *tête-à-tête* affair. The communion of Saints and all that is implied by that does not occupy a sufficiently prominent place in your creed, I *think*.[55]

Evelyn Underhill's friendship with Margaret Robinson would provide her not only with her first opportunity to guide another person in the search for an infinite life, but also with practical help. Unable to read German, Evelyn would rely on Margaret Robinson as a translator of German mystical literature.

As friendship with Margaret Robinson provided Evelyn with new opportunities, friendship with Ethel Ross Barker opened up still others. The two met shortly after the publication of *The Grey World* and became cherished friends whose intimacy was cut short only by the early death of Barker in 1921. Barker, the daughter of a canon of St. Paul's Cathedral, was an extramural lecturer in ancient history and archaeology at the University of London who later published *Buried Herculaneum*. Like Underhill, Barker experienced a period of estrangement from religion, but at the time of their meeting she too felt drawn to Roman Catholicism. Ultimately they made divergent choices; Dominica (Barker) would become a Roman Catholic, but Thomasina (Underhill) would not. Their affectionate names point to what was central in their friendship — the search for the truth and their love of Roman Catholicism. It was to Barker, the faithful Dominic, that Evelyn, the doubting Thomas, would turn for help during the next difficult years of her life.

The year 1904 brought the publication of *The Grey World*, her participation in the Golden Dawn, the friendship of Margaret Robinson and Ethel Ross Barker, and the opportunity to work on her first scholarly book, *The Miracles of Our Lady, St. Mary*, a translation of twenty-five medieval legends about the Virgin Mary. These melodramatic and mystical legends, dating from the fourth through fourteenth centuries, were buried in Old French and Latin manuscripts of sermons and histories of religious orders that were in the care of J. A. Herbert. Through them Underhill had access once again to that religious world she had discovered in Italy. Although she would publish two more novels, *The Miracles of Our Lady, St. Mary*, is the first indication that she would move from fiction to a more scholarly genre. The fact that Herbert, who introduced her to these legends, and Arthur Machen, who critiqued her manuscript, were both Roman Catholics should not be overlooked; the lure of Roman Catholicism through literature and friendship had become powerful for her.

While drawn to Roman Catholicism, she nonetheless considered herself an outsider. In early 1905 she wrote of being at Easter Sunday High Mass at San Marco in Venice. She had the sense "of being in the heart of a great and traditional spiritual household, ordered and coherent, overpowering to the miserable outsider, but a strong tower for her sons."[56] Her attraction to Catholicism, yet her inability to claim it, would be of dominant concern for the next two years.

During 1905 through 1907 she traveled to the continent each spring with her mother, a ritual carried out by many mothers and daughters of their station. During these decisive years she made choices which would influence the course of her life. The decision to withdraw from the Golden Dawn was probably made in 1905. In July 1906 she and Hubert formally announced their intention to marry. In April 1907 she decided to convert to Roman Catholicism, a decision she discussed extensively with Ethel, her greatest friend and confidant.[57] Her writing during this period focused on her second novel, *The Lost World*, which appeared in 1907. It is this novel that provides the few available clues to the conflict between her two loves — that of this world and of the one beyond.

The themes of *The Grey World* — the search for "the beyond" and the importance of beauty — reappear in this second novel, but they are handled differently. The protagonist is not the solitary ghostlike Willie Hopkinson who retreats to nature and art, but the architect Paul Valéry, whose single-minded goal, the construction of a magnificent church, consumes him body and soul. The novel is about Valéry's pursuit and loss of this perfect achievement. It is in the loss of the perfect that he is given a "substitute word," "sacrifice," and a commitment not to an ideal realized in stone but to the ordinary life of a married, professional man. At the end of the book Paul leaves the church he had hoped to finish. He locks up the door and heads toward home, " . . . setting his face, once for all, towards the steady years of professional duty, domestic affection, material profit, and spiritual loss which lay between him and the journey's end."[58] Paul Valéry's route was not the direct quest for the perfect, but the ordinary way of commitment and sacrifice. "[H]is programme, however strange it might appear from the point of view of artist or mystic, could not fail to be satisfactory to the honest, wholesome sentiment of the British race."[59]

Unlike Willie Hopkinson who forsook the ordinary and communal for the solitary pursuit of the perfect, Paul Valéry chose to embrace an ordinary life with others. This choice was a reflection of his new understanding of the relationship between matter and spirit. He

> was snatched from the false dualism of matter and spirit to the mystical union of the shadow and the idea. No longer with the single eye of the determined visionary, but rather with the same outlook of an immortal spirit that has learned, not despised, the lesson of the flesh, he perceived the life of the body also to be holy, needful, consecrate. It was . . . no foul miasma from which one must escape, but a firm and friendly highway which led by difficult places to the mystic city of the Quest.[60]

The Lost Word is not a good novel. It is too long and has none of the suspense and adventure of *The Grey World*. Nonetheless it offers a restatement of Underhill's principal concern, the relationship between the visible and the invisible worlds, both real worlds that are linked together. Paul lives in the world of shadows, but the shadow exists because of the perfect itself. In the life of the shadows the quest

for perfection is lived out. This is the low road, the route of ordinary
life, but it leads nonetheless to the same end. In addition to redefining
the route to the perfect, *The Lost Word* also offers a reconsideration
of the nature of the religious quest. In *The Grey World* Willie found
beauty and ecstasy in the chapel of Our Lady of Pity, but he remained
solitary in his quest. Paul, on the other hand

> felt exalted by their [the saints'] presence, lifted from earth; trou-
> bled but no longer alone. He understood something of their
> language, for these were aflame, as he was, with some great de-
> sire: something that possessed them, pushed them on, as his
> new-found marvel did, towards a secret consummation. The
> restlessness, the agony, the adoration: all these he shared with
> them. He stood in the midst of a ring of great lovers, who called
> on him to justify his state: was brought to the bar, arraigned
> before an actual and eternal court of Love.[61]

What is new here is that the quest is defined in terms of love
and the consequence of pursuing it is communion with other lovers.
These seminal insights, expressed first in fiction, will reappear in different forms throughout Evelyn Underhill's life.

Underhill used Paul Valéry both to redefine the nature of the religious quest and to discuss its various institutional expressions. In
clearly autobiographical expression she has Paul defend Roman Catholicism in this way:

> It's not the name or the outside meaning that matters; it's the
> turning of its symbols to the service of an inner truth. And in
> the long run, Catholic forms are the loveliest and the rightest;
> all the better because they are so incredible. They were made
> by people who understand symbols, knew that they were living
> things; nerves, by which we apprehend the other side. Nothing's
> true this side the veil; but the Catholic faith is a hint worth
> taking. In a sense I stay outside the church; but I use it as a
> lens through which I can focus reality for some of the others to
> see.[62]

Yet her ambiguity toward institutional religion remains. Through
one of her characters she speaks her mind:

> I think sometimes that the Church is like a London snowstorm;
> it only shows its pure and poetic side to those who are not in it.

To the others it gives muddy roads and blinding confusion and
the defilement of whiteness. A steady fall from the white sky to
black earth; that's the history of an organized faith.[63]

It is, however, with the help of the symbols of organized religion
that both Paul and Catherine, the woman he marries, come to find
their understanding of love and of sacrifice. Catherine goes through
her own torture regarding her impending marriage to Paul. Fearful
that his love for her will diminish his artistic quest, Catherine decides
that real love mandates that she not marry him. She wrestles with the
meaning of sacrifice, visiting churches that present her with images of
the wounded madonna. Rejecting these symbols she finds her solace
in the Pietà. It was Mary, "full of sense and full of sadness, who had
looked life between the eyes, and yet preserved a vulnerable heart."[64]
In Mary, who took on the pain of her son, Catherine discovers the
meaning of real love; she marries Paul, and in love, bears his suffering.

While *The Lost Word* redefines love and holds it out as the ordinary route available to those who are not mystics and artists, the
novel also contains abundant evidence of Underhill's awareness of
the limits and struggles of married life. For example, Emma, one of
her characters, asks about marriage:

[D]oes one want it;...? ...[A] plain woman of thirty-two has
not a great choice, you know. At that age we still attract —
some of us — but it is the attraction of a weak magnet whose
field can be avoided at will. We are good comrades. Men find
us safe. I am safe. Can you bear a safe wife; and I an inevitable
husband?[65]

In discussions of marriage with her suitor, Emma goes on to
say: "Promise first,...that you will never imprison me in a dainty
drawing-room, with lampshades and cushions and things."[66]

What is clear from *The Lost Word* is that Evelyn Underhill, a
woman of thirty-two, was well aware of the nature of love and its
illusions. Within the year she would marry, yet that decision would
be challenged by another love.

The year 1907 was a crucial year in her life. In that year she
married and both decided and then postponed entry into the Roman
Catholic church. It was the year as well that having abandoned her
interest in the occult she began in earnest to work on the subject of
mysticism.[67] It was, however, the decisions of religious affiliation and
marriage that dominated her consciousness.

In February of that year, at the invitation of Ethel and probably without her family's knowledge, she made a retreat at the French Franciscan convent, St. Mary's of the Angels, in Southampton. She clearly wanted to be there, but fearful of the self-suggestion she found rampant in convent life, she left the place after the fourth day lest she make some hasty decision to convert.[68] She returned home, and the following day she had an experience, of which she gives almost no detail, in which she "was converted, quite suddenly, once and for all by an overpowering vision which had really no specifically Christian elements, but convinced [her] that the Catholic religion was true."[69] Always fearful of self-deceptive experience, she was nonetheless deeply attracted to Roman Catholicism with its powerful communal ritual and rich symbolic life. Although she wanted to join the church and believed she should, there were many obstacles to this commitment. She turned to someone who seemingly would understand her plight during this very difficult time — Robert Hugh Benson, son of the Archbishop of Canterbury, a convert to Roman Catholicism, a priest, and a writer on mysticism, whom she had met socially and heard preach at the Carmelite Church in Kensington. Her letter to him points up the difference she saw between admiring Catholicism and actually embracing it.

I have got half-way from agnosticism to Catholicism, and seem unable to get any farther.... I feel that you know all that there is to be known about this borderland, and the helpless sensations of those who are caught in it. I want to get out, but without sacrificing intellectual honesty, and each struggle only sends me back again with renewed sensations of unreality.

As I understand the matter, before one can become a Catholic, and for me Catholicism is the only possible organized faith, one must get into the state of mind which ignores all the results of the study of Comparative religions, and accepts, for instance the Ascension, in as literal and concrete a spirit as the Spanish Armada. Is this really so?

Of course innumerable bad motives are mixed up with the muddle and indecision . . . at the same time the borderland position is horrible morally because it means losing the old idea that it was natural and justifiable to be self-centered without gaining the power of not being self-centered. Also the alternative fits of mystical fervour and critical examination lead nowhere except to complete self-contempt, and a miserable sense of the unreality of all things, and the incalculable dangers of self suggestion.

What ought I to do? It would I am sure be many months before I could take any definite steps — but if you would help me, and tell me where I have gone wrong, I should be truly and deeply grateful.[70]

As Underhill saw it, her problem was an intellectual one. She lived on a borderland between agnosticism and belief, because she could not accept as literally true the doctrines of Catholicism, the only church she wanted to join. Vacillating between a mystical and a critical view of reality, she presented her problem to Benson hoping he would understand and offer some way through this intellectual morass.

Benson proceeded to deal with the particular problem that Underhill raised in her letter, namely Catholicism's demand that dogmas be accepted as both spiritually and historically true. Her difficulty lay, he believed, in misunderstanding the relationship between matter and spirit, ideas and history. "What I think therefore is your obstacle to this," he wrote, "is that while you have tight hold of the importance of the idea, and of the transcendence of God, you have not sufficiently firm hold of the dignity of matter, or sufficient sympathy with its limitations."[71] He urged her to focus on her "incredible smallness" and to visit another convent.[72] Since Underhill saw her dilemma in terms of intellectual honesty, Benson's suggestion that she place herself in an environment in which, to her mind, self-suggestion was common, was a useless one. Benson wrote back that while he appreciated her concern over self-suggestion in the convent, this phenomenon was operative everywhere.

These intellectual concerns were shared with Ethel Ross Barker as well. Yet in spite of these difficulties, her conversion experience prevailed. By the beginning of April 1907 she had made up her mind to join the Roman Catholic church.[73] She wrote to Benson: "After Holy Week, and much time given to considering the question, I felt practically certain that I must eventually become a Catholic if I was to be true to my convictions."[74] Torn between what she could accept intellectually and what she had experienced, she realized she must eventually side with the latter. Her decision to become a Catholic, however, raised another knotty question: how would Hubert react?

While Hubert Stuart Moore had no personal interest for or against religion, he was vehemently anticlerical.[75] He apparently accepted his fiancée's growing interest in Roman Catholicism, both in her writing and in her attendance at services, because there had never been a direct suggestion that she might join. Although he must have known of her deep personal interest in Roman Catholicism and she must have known of his animosity toward it, the issue was not discussed between them. She was to marry Hubert in a few months; Benson urged her to tell him of her decision.[76]

Having skirted the issue for years, Evelyn was now forced to raise it; she was not prepared for Hubert's response. He was "heart-broken" when she revealed her intention; her becoming a Roman Catholic would mean, as he saw it, an end to the trust between them; "all hope of [their] happiness [was] at an end."[77] The source of Hubert's fear was the confessional and the specter of a priest standing between him and his wife, not an atypical concern of Englishmen who were suspicious of Roman Catholicism.

What is important is Evelyn's response. Apparently she at least contemplated breaking off the engagement. The advice of Ethel, her dearest friend, urged her against such a course. "[D]on't talk about breaking of engagements," Ethel wrote. "If I were a man under the circumstances and after all these years the marriage didn't come off I'd go to the devil. Stuart won't do this. But it's hard on a man when he has not much left on earth or heaven."[78] The needs of Hubert are echoed in Evelyn's response: He "has so little but this one thing [the marriage] in his life."[79] There seemed to be no possible reconciliation between her longtime friendship with Hubert and her decision of conscience to embrace Roman Catholicism. Unable to choose between them, she proceeded negatively, that is, to not reject what presented itself. "[T]o not marry however, would be a cruelty," she wrote, "a negation of half the spirit of Christianity for the sake of one's personal beliefs and tendencies. The sacrifice of oneself is really nothing compared with this."[80]

The decision to live with the conflict between love and belief (truth as she saw it) is telling. One might understand it as a decision typical of those imbued with "womanly sacrifice," a notion so deeply inculcated and so unchallenged in the world of Evelyn Underhill. But the decision to affirm a love and to live with the tension of unrealized truth represented a methodology for life and a characteristic of her thought, though in 1907 it was impossible for Evelyn or anyone to know the meaning of her decision to marry Hubert.

She did what seemed doable: she agreed to Hubert's request that she postpone her decision. Robert Benson supported her in this. "I think," he wrote, "you are perfectly right to wait for your own sake as well as for his — until the thing becomes clear and established."[81] After the decision was made she continued to assure Hubert of her love, to assuage his fears, and to offer hope that their communication on religious issues might enhance their relationship. She hoped that her delay would bring Hubert round to accept the fact that she wanted to become a Roman Catholic. In a letter from Italy she wrote:

> My own darling boy, I was so glad to get your letter.... I only hope you are telling me the truth and are *really* feeling purry *and* closer to one another in spite of the "depression." After all, as I have thought as I now think for many months, if it was to separate us you ought to have felt it coming on long ago and as the chief result has been to force us to talk openly to each other about all the real things which we sedulously kept from each other before, the final effect in spite of difference of opinion ought to be to make us much more real companions than in the past, when we each had a watertight bulk-head carefully fixed to prevent undue explorations. Also I do think it must be a great gain to *you*, all round, if I can make you see the real beauties of Catholicism, as well as the merely superficial corruptions on which you had been led to concentrate yourself. It is better, after all, to walk along a rather muddy path to Heavenly Syon, than not to get there at all![82]

Her decision to "sacrifice oneself" was accompanied by a frankness and a decisiveness; she would marry *and* walk the "muddy path" of Roman Catholicism. On 3 July 1907 she and Hubert married. She expected that within a year she would be a Roman Catholic. While postponement dealt with her immediate problem, it was nonetheless risky business. "I feel," she wrote Benson, "the real point is not so much whether one is inside or outside the visible church, as whether one can keep "the flame of adoration" burning bright without the sacraments when one is living under strong personal influence which sets the other way."[83]

Her desire to be part of the Roman church was at least in part born from her own self-understanding that she needed its sacramental life in order to balance what she already appreciated as her tendency toward the transcendent.

Although this desire was clear, other obstacles, inaccessible to her love, obstructed the way. Shortly after her marriage to Hubert, Ethel became a Roman Catholic. The nuns at the Southampton convent prayed that Evelyn would follow in short order, but the last months of 1907 brought with them the sobering realization that this was not to be. The papacy issued the encyclical *Pascendi Dominici Gregis*, a condemnation of Modernist teaching. Entrance into the Roman church now presented new problems. It was one thing for her to decide that she desired and could intellectually join the Roman church; it was quite another to be told that one of her persuasion was not welcome.

Underhill considered herself a Modernist and for some time had read George Tyrrell and Maud Petre. With them she supported attempts to bring together the essential truths of Christianity and those of modern science and historical criticism. The purpose of Modernism, as Underhill saw it, was to revitalize religion, and the prerequisite for such revitalization was freedom of research and discussion in the pursuit of truth. In the harshest language the papal encyclical condemned the Modernists as "audacious," "sacrilegious," "corrupting," and disdainful of all authority.[84] Modernists were "agnostics," believers in "vital immanence," "Protestants," and "pseudo-mystics" who existed within the church itself, claiming religious certitude based on individual experience and "threatening," "poisoning," and "striking at the root" of the church itself. *Pascendi* closed the door of Rome to Underhill; she could not "walk the muddy path" but would be forced to live on the "borderland," a place from which she had hoped to escape.

She continued to believe that the Roman church was her "ultimate home," that there the "mysteries" were best preserved, and that only there could she "touch-see-feel Reality," but, she wrote, "I can't get in without suppressions and evasions to which I can't quite bring myself."[85] Unable to join the Roman Catholic church, she was also unable to join any other church. "I can't accept Anglicanism instead: it seems an integrally different thing.... to join any other communion is simply an impossible thought."[86]

Her plan to marry and then join was now supplanted. Her intellectual integrity demanded that she not become a Roman Catholic, but the decision came with a price. She was depressed. A year after her marriage Benson wrote to her explaining his diagnosis:

> [W]e are made for two lives, the inner and the outer. Materialism is the ultimate end of one; spiritualism (not Spiritism) of the other. The only reconciliation of the two, if principles are carried right out, is Catholicism.... I can see nothing, anywhere, that even intelligibly *claims* to perform this function except the Catholic Church. Now it appears to me that you have been trying to do without it; to develop an individual inner life, and to project an outer religious life of *your own*...and it appears to me that the sudden blackness that you describe is a perfectly inevitable result of that attempt.[87]

While Benson could see the logical outcome of her choice not to embrace Roman Catholicism, namely, isolation and emotional and sensual deprivation, he had little appreciation of her intellectual integrity. "Honestly," he wrote,

> I think your fear of losing intellectual liberty is a dream.... Of course it is a fact that some do lose it.... But I know one need not. One does not lose one's intellectual liberty when one learns mathematics, though one certainly loses the liberty of doing sums wrong, or doing them by laborious methods![88]

Benson was unable to help Evelyn with that decision not only because he did not appreciate her intellectual dilemma but because there was a lack of sympathy between them. "I wonder how it is you don't find Hugh simpatico," J. A. Herbert wrote her. "Perhaps he is better with men than women."[89] Whatever the limitations of their relationship, after the encyclical the problem for Evelyn Underhill was not that of reconciling differences between historical and spiritual truth as she had initially proposed it to Benson, but that of joining an institution that had irrevocably closed itself off from the truth of the modern world. She could not in conscience join a church that explicitly repudiated what she believed was the way to truth. She could not reject what was at hand, what she knew to be the truth. To do so would be to reject the truth itself. Months earlier she had been forced to choose between her love of Hubert and her love of Roman Catholicism; she chose what was near — Hubert, her friend of many years. In neither case was this choice of the near, the proximate, a rejection of the distant, of the ideal, of perfection. Rather it meant that the way to that goal was through the near, through that which was present. Through these choices she articulated a method, a way of proceeding not only in life, but in thought. Such choices also meant that she would accept the difficult life on the "borderland," marginalized, outside her "ultimate home." When she wrote to Benson she said she wanted to get out of the borderland without sacrificing her intellectual honesty. There was no way out now. Although the borderland would produce despair and blackness, it would also offer her the opportunity for enormous creativity.

While 1907 was a year of crucial decision, her work continued unabated. *The Lost Word* was published by Heinemann, and "A Defence of Magic" appeared in the November issue of *Fortnightly*. In addition, her correspondence with Margaret Robinson increased tremendously. This correspondence is important for two reasons. It gives the first indications of Evelyn Underhill's abilities as a spiritual guide, a role she would assume more fully in the last years of her life, and it reveals with extraordinary clarity the assumptions that frame her thought for the next forty years.

Margaret Robinson wrote to Evelyn Underhill for her advice again in 1907, a period when Underhill herself was in great turmoil regarding her own marriage. The incongruity of someone asking her for advice at this time was evident to her. "This is a horrible responsibility," she confided to Hubert, "and rather ridiculous when I'm in as much a tangle as anyone else."[90] The tangle notwithstanding, Underhill offered to Margaret Robinson her thoughts on the primacy of spiritual experience, the purpose of meditation and ritual, the meaning of the incarnation, and the relationship between faith and love.

In the most open and direct way she shared with Robinson her own experience of what she came to call "reality."

> The first thing I found out was exalted and indescribable beauty in the most squalid places. I still remember walking down the Notting Hill main road and observing the (extremely sordid) landscape with joy and astonishment. Even the movement of the traffic had something universal and sublime in it. Of course, that does not last! but the after flavour of it does, and now and then one catches it again. When one *does* catch it, it is so real that to look upon it as wrong would be an unthinkable absurdity. At the same time, one sees the world at those moments so completely as "energized by the invisible" that there is no temptation to rest in mere enjoyment of the visible.[91]

The primacy of personal experience as the criterion by which one knows the truth is laid out here. This experience is not illusory, contemptible, or trivial; rather it presents "the dim shadow of the thought of the Real." Of course, Underhill warned, this experience would be looked on with skepticism by many others. "There are plenty of learned persons," she wrote, "saying all the time that what you have already found is not there at all. But their arguments will never be valid to you again.... Direct spiritual experience is the only possible basis; and if you will trust yours absolutely you are safe."[92]

Evelyn only gradually began to trust her own experience absolutely, but she knew that the power and vividness of that experience in one's life was connected to increased consciousness of it.

Now it seems to me that one's life only attains reality in so far as it is *consciously* lived in the presence of God. This consciousness can be attained and clung to by a definite act of the will — or rather by a series of graduated acts — once you can breathe that atmosphere, *it* will determine most questions of conduct for you — become a sort of norm or standard, by which all other propositions are judged.[93]

She suggests that this consciousness can be augmented by means of meditation. "[A]s a means of getting at this, there is the regular and systematic practise of meditation by which of course I do *not* mean thinking about a pious subject but the 'deep' meditation which tends to pass over into unitive prayer."[94]

While she recommends this "deep meditation," she admits that it is a phenomenon that is not well understood. "In spite of all the mystics have told us," she wrote, "we are in it working with almost an unknown tool."[95] Prayer, however, "is only half one's job; the other half is to love everything for and in God. This is of course only a long-winded way of saying that one has got to let faith issue in charity."[96]

The expressions of charity are many; one suggested to Margaret Robinson was to work with the poor.

Half an hour spent with Christ's poor is worth far more than half a million spent on them. It is necessary to a sane Christianity.... Do this not only as a "response," a "sacrifice," but as a natural act of friendship to your brothers and sisters. The kingdom of heaven is not a solitude *a deux*. It is the vice of false mysticism that it often produces this impression.[97]

Underhill's perceptiveness about the needs of Margaret Robinson and the nature of religious life are evident here. Thirteen years later when Friedrich von Hügel urged Underhill to make contact with the poor of North Kensington she responded positively; she had recommended such action to Margaret Robinson years before.

In Margaret Robinson Evelyn had her first directee in the life of the spirit. This work of spiritual counsel began to flourish at the same time that she began to articulate her interest in mysticism. Her article, "A Defence of Magic," reveals her assessment of both the achievements and the limitations of magic that had been of great personal interest to her. While she recognizes the importance of this phenomenon, her article marks an end to her interest in the occult; as such it serves as an important marker in her intellectual development. It is no coincidence that she published this article at the same time that she began to write on mysticism.

"A Defence of Magic" is in large part a biographical and analytical study of Alphonse Louis Constant, that is, Eliphas Lévi, a well known nineteenth-century French writer on magic and the occult. Recent criticism of him by Arthur Waite obviously prompted Underhill's piece. In it, she traces the development of Lévi's life, his initial intellectual curiosity, his search for magic practices, his mystic quest for transcendent truth, his exploration of artistic and natural symbolism, and his final reconciliation with the faith of his youth, Roman Catholicism. In the end, his life comes full circle and magic and faith are joined. "In Catholicism," she wrote,

> he found, as in magic, the same qualities of purity and detachment, faith, steadfastness, and self-control accomplishing the same task; that namely, of opening the eyes of the soul and passing beyond the flaming rampart of the world. In magic he found an explanation of those age-old mysteries which are concealed beneath the dogmas of the church; a reasonable theory of her sacraments and ceremonies: a reconciling medium between philosophy and orthodox faith.[98]

Underhill defends magic as preparation for communion with the unseen. Religion, she claims, had always recognized its power. "The appeal of religion," she wrote,

> is not to the intellect but to the soul. Its theology may or may not convince the reason; only its magic will open the inner door. Therefore Christianity, when she founds her external system on sacraments and symbols, on prayer and praise, and insists on the power of the pure and self-denying will and "the magic chain" of congregational worship, joins hands with those magi whose gold, frankincense and myrrh were the first gifts that she received.[99]

While Underhill defends the historical connection between religion and magic, she also maintains that modern magic is different from its ancient forms. One can only suspect that this insight was learned through personal experience with contemporary forms. "It is the defect of all modern occultism "that it is tainted by a certain intellectual arrogance. A divorce has been effected between knowledge and love, between the religion and the science of the Magi; and in the language of mysticism, till these be reunited the Divine Word cannot be born."[100]

Affirming magic, she nonetheless turns from its contemporary manifestations to mysticism, where knowledge and love are united. "A Defence of Magic" is an apology for magic and a warning of its limitations. It is as well a manifesto on mysticism, containing her seminal insight about the nature of mystical experience; as such "A Defence of Magic" set the course of her writing for the next fifteen years.

While she began collecting materials on mysticism in 1904, she started to work on her book in earnest in 1907. It was a labor which would last for three years and would result in *Mysticism: A Study of the Nature and Development of Man's Spiritual Consciousness*, her most famous book, and one that would establish her as the pre-eminent authority on mysticism in the English-speaking world. A project of this magnitude could not have been undertaken without great commitment. The events of 1907, no matter how draining and frustrating, brought her to a primary point of decision. Having experienced the occult firsthand, she knew of its bareness. Having been blocked from entry from what she believed was her "ultimate home" of Roman Catholicism, she found herself where she did not want to be, on the borderland. Cut off from participation in a sacramental life that she believed gave access to Reality, she sat in churches with Ethel Ross Barker who, newly converted, could enter fully into a life for which she longed. Newly married, she could not share her religious intensity with her spouse. At this crossroad, she chose what was at hand — the exploration of mysticism. This decision was unintelligible by many standards, yet everything in her life had led her to this choice. She embraced it with extraordinary intensity and energy; mysticism became her life and work on the borderland.

2

THE WORK OF THE
BORDERLAND

THE BOOK-LINED STUDY on the first floor of the Campden Hill Square row house opened into the garden which in the growing season was filled with flowers, especially Evelyn's favorites, larkspur and snowdrops.[1] Two cats, Jacob and Dickie, curled up on the chairs; and above the mantle was an embroidered plaque stitched with the single word, ETERNITY. It was given to Evelyn by a friend, and here in her study it recalled the focus she sought so consistently to maintain. The room, with its blue, purple, and silver tones, was an unlikely place to write her "serious" book on mysticism. If Italy had been holy for her, this place was pleasant and ordinary, yet it was here she traced and unlocked the great insight of the mystics, the "giants" of the human race.

By qualification and circumstance she did not seem to be the person to undertake such work. She had attended King's College but had no degree, and in philosophy and the new science of psychology she was self-taught. Neither did she have theological training, and her attraction to Roman Catholicism brought with it no systematic schooling in its history or doctrine. Although she had a certain status as a member of a well-respected professional family, she had no ecclesiastical or academic connections. At age thirty-two, she was a married woman who had produced three books of limited literary quality.

To all appearances she was a "lady scribbler" of a somewhat otherworldly bent. Her circumstances, while circumscribed, offered her freedom. As she and Hubert, who was six years her senior, had delayed marriage until their financial situation was secure, she was not preoccupied with money matters. Neither did the demands of family life overwhelm her. For whatever reason, the Stuart Moores had no children. They lived alone in their Kensington residence on a lovely quiet square that sloped down to a busy thoroughfare. Hubert inherited this eighteenth-century row house from his father, and he and Evelyn moved into it directly after their marriage. The interior was pleasant and roomy enough to provide a study for Evelyn and a workshop on the ground floor for Hubert to make jewelry and do enameling when he had leisure.

The work of Mrs. Stuart Moore and Miss Evelyn Underhill was combined in a quiet round of daily activities. In the morning Evelyn supervised the work of two servants and then began her writing about ten o'clock. She continued to work through early afternoon. Every day she had tea with her mother who lived around the corner on Campden Hill Place. She also did Health Society and Poor Law visiting twice a week and often attended Benediction at five. In the Chapel of the Assumption in Kensington Square, a stone's throw from where she had attended classes at the Ladies' Department of King's College, she found solace as the nuns, ensconced behind a large gold grill, sang their praise. By six o'clock Hubert usually returned home, and they spent the evening together in front of the fire. She would read and write letters until about nine in the evening. Their quiet life of work, care of parents, and attention to cats, which they both loved, was broken by trips to the countryside, yachting expeditions, annual continental excursions by Evelyn and her mother, and an active social life of entertaining and being entertained. A gracious hostess, Evelyn Stuart Moore easily welcomed many friends and acquaintances; Sunday afternoon tea brought together the ordinary and the famous who sought her companionship.

The Stuart Moores had a life typical of those of their station. Materially and socially secure, they were insulated from the great changes that afflicted Edwardian England. Labor strikes, the challenge to empire and aristocracy, unrest in Ireland, were all remote. Yet the constancy of this environment did not stultify, but made possible Evelyn's long intellectual and emotional effort. In this environment her intense romantic nature, her energy and discipline, were marshaled for inner work. Unlike her contemporaries Beatrice Webb and Emmeline and Christabel Pankhurst, who challenged their society, Evelyn Underhill lived within its constraints and limitations. This acceptance allowed for the possibility of an inward adventure and her dialogue with the mystics, those she called "the great pioneers" of human consciousness.

If Underhill's life is characterized by an inner search, it is also characterized by a prodigious output. In thirty-nine years she produced forty books, editions, and collections, and more than three hundred fifty articles, essays, and reviews. This was possible because she was a woman of leisure, but leisure alone does not explain her productivity; it was merely a prerequisite for it. Fear of leisure can, of course, be a prod, but in this case the need merely to "keep busy" does not explain her productivity. Her work was too costly in personal terms to have been carried out as a form of escape. Neither would she have undertaken her writing to secure fame and the accompanying material profit. The meticulous record keeping of sales of her books as well as a suggestion made subsequently by Friedrich von Hügel that an inheritance received at her mother's death might free her from the need to publish so often, suggest that Evelyn appreciated the importance of generating income.[2] But in 1907 there was no way to predict the success of a book on the mystics. Neither fame, fortune, nor fear explains why she wrote, why she wrote so much, and why everything she wrote was a variation on this first theme of mysticism.

Evelyn Underhill saw the mystic life as the life of adventure with the Real; it was to this life she was drawn and to this life she clung tenaciously in the quiet circumstances in which she lived. She must have been attracted as well to the integration of personality that she believed the mystics achieved. In them she found some wholeness in which belief and life had been reconciled. By studying their lives she could make sense of her own inner life. Of course there was the practical aim as well. She believed that the mystics, the exemplars of the highest stage of human consciousness, had something to say to every person. As a young girl she had announced that she wanted to be an author so that she could "influence people." Through her writing, the mystics could teach humanity what it most needed to know about life. This was not an entirely new goal. Her fiction had the aim of "show[ing] eternal things in and through temporal things,"[3] but now she wanted to focus more directly on the eternal, on what she came to call the Absolute, the Real, God. Arthur Waite, her mentor, claimed that "God is the proper quest of the romantic spirit." Underhill concurred not only with intellectual assent but with her life.[4]

It was through the taxing work on mysticism that she nurtured her own romantic spirit. As she kept up her round of life's activities, her principal dialogue was not with friends, but with the mystics she discovered. In her preface to *Mysticism* she thanked a number of persons for their help. While each is important, there are few with whom she shared her intellectual and emotional development.

Margaret Robinson helped her more than anyone else. She did translations of the German mystics as well as some typing. But since Robinson also continued to receive Underhill's advice on spiritual matters, it was unlikely that Underhill discussed her own inner life with her client. Their correspondence reflects both spiritual guidance and the business of completing a long, complex manuscript. May Sinclair, the noted novelist, was also a friend who critiqued sections of *Mysticism*. Underhill encouraged Sinclair's writing, shared social interests with her and a love of yachting and cats. Their correspondence however reveals that Underhill shared little of her inner life with her.[5] In the preface to *Mysticism* Evelyn also thanked Jack Herbert of the British Museum for help with manuscripts, W. Scott Palmer for help with the chapter on vitalism, Arthur Symons for his translations of John of the Cross, and the Rev. William Inge, Dean of St. Paul's Cathedral and writer on mysticism, for reading parts of the manuscript. She also commended H. Delacroix for his studies on mysticism. Although he is the only French writer to be listed in the preface, the bibliography and notes reveal a decided French influence: A. Poulain, E. Récéjac, J. Ribet, and H. Bergson are all included. Noticeably absent from the preface are Arthur Waite, her former mentor in the Golden Dawn whose seven books are listed in the bibliography, and Hugh Benson, whose lectures on mysticism are included there also. Her correspondence with Benson abated in late 1908 when his advice no longer seemed helpful. Although in 1910 she sought his assistance in securing a general audience with the pope, by 1911 she felt estranged; she said she was "disgusted and pained" at the publication of his *The Dawn in All*, "a mixture of childishness, intolerance and unspirituality."[6]

Others mentioned in her preface are Hubert, Ethel Barker, and Baron Friedrich von Hügel, the Catholic theologian. The acknowledgment of her husband not only reflects his respect for her work but also shows that their crisis over religion had subsided. His accommodation to his wife's interests is shown in his sending flowers to the convent at Southampton, the place of her retreat, on the first Easter after their marriage. He knew this would please Evelyn, who was then traveling in Europe with her mother. "You were a *darling* to send flowers to the convent for Easter — nothing you could have done would have pleased me more as you know.... I *do* love you for having done that. It's lovely to think that there is something of ours there then — 'offering the homage of their beauty.' "[7]

Underhill's acknowledgment of Ethel Barker is probably the most important since Ethel was Evelyn's closest friend and the only person with whom she discussed her inner life. Unfortunately, the substance of their relationship is not known.[8] Finally, she recognizes a debt to Baron Friedrich von Hügel whose book, *The Mystical Element of Religion*, had appeared as she was in the process of writing hers.

Underhill's acknowledgments confirm what one surmises: that with the exception of Ethel Barker, during the years she was writing *Mysticism*, Underhill did not consistently and intimately share her personal quest with anyone. Her intimates were her subjects, the mystics themselves; she was in dialogue with them, and through their obscure texts a hidden world was revealed to her. Her personal isolation from others is critical to understanding her seemingly exaggerated response to friendship with von Hügel.

The most important contact made in the course of writing *Mysticism* was with von Hügel. The first edition of the book appeared in early 1911. Von Hügel read it and returned a letter urging major revisions.

(1) Either you rest content, as far as my little help is concerned, with those corrections proposed for the first four chapters — yet with this extension — that you would carefully go thro' all the passages concerning A) the supposed identity of the deepest of man's soul and God, and B) the supposed non-necessity of institutional, historical etc. religion for many or for some, and you would strictly weigh and reconsider them all, or (2) You would get your publisher to defer the reprinting till the beginning of February, in which case *I willingly undertake to give January to a careful study of your entire book.*[9]

Von Hügel was the pre-eminent Roman Catholic theologian in England. A native German speaker, he was twenty-three years her senior. While he disagreed with her emphases, he was willing to correct and teach her. Although she generally resisted his changes, she was impressed by his person. She wrote to Jack Herbert:

I have become the friend (or rather, disciple and adorer) of von Hügel. He is the most wonderful personality I have ever known — so saintly, so truthful, sane and tolerant. I feel very

safe and happy sitting in his shadow, and he has been most
awfully kind to me.[10]

Evelyn adored this powerful German personality for his goodness,
sanity, and sympathetic understanding of her plight. In a single extant
letter to her from 1911 von Hügel discusses his attitude toward non-
Catholics like herself:

> My general rule in such cases is to do what I can to feed in such
> souls the true and deep, in their degree, Catholic instincts and
> practices that I find in them, either already active or near to
> birth, and, whilst warning them (if they show a *velleite* to come
> to Rome) as to the grave practical difficulties for *them* on the side
> of any vigorous and sincere intellectual life, that are now to be
> found in the Catholic Church, to let them feel that, nevertheless,
> in the Roman Catholic Church resides a depth and tenderness
> and heroism of Christian sanctity greater and richer than, as a
> matter of fact, is to be found elsewhere. In this way one does,
> I think, as much good and as little harm as possible. One feeds
> and encourages, and yet leaves such souls to God's ways. For
> He *may* call even such souls, and even in such times; only I
> think that such souls, in such times, ought not to be encouraged
> to come, unless they *felt for long, beyond the possibility of any
> honest doubt*, that it would be a *grave sin against the light for
> them to remain where they are.*
>   It is certainly a very real grace given you by God that you
> should so plainly see the dangers, and yet should so steadfastly
> hold the divinity, of the Catholic and Roman Church.[11]

Underhill cherished von Hügel's caution and sensitivity, capabili-
ties won in part from his own recent close escape from condemnation
as a Modernist.[12] His intellectual acumen and his knowledge of mysticism obviously attracted her as well, but it was his person, not his
intellect she adored. It was to him she would turn ten years later
when her own life was "plaited" with pain.

The personal needs of Underhill led her to write her book; her
circumstances made it possible. Its popularity is explained, at least
in part, by its appeal to prevalent intellectual currents and its offer
of an alternative worldview to both the Philosophic Idealism and the
Positivism of the Edwardian period.

Interest in mysticism was clearly evident in England by the first
decade of the century. William Inge published *Christian Mysticism*

in 1899 and William James's Gifford lectures of 1901–02 appeared as *Varieties of Religious Experience*. The causes for this incipient interest in religious experience in general and mysticism in particular are various and complex.

In England orthodox Christianity, both as an institution and as an intellectual system, had been shown to be deficient. Church attendance, particularly in urban areas, was minimal.[13] The Modernists, who were tinged with mysticism themselves, attempted to save Christian doctrine by accommodating it to secular and scientific thought. Their condemnation by the papacy showed the inflexibility of Roman orthodoxy to accommodate to modern intellectual developments. It was precisely in the gaps created by the dissolution of Christianity in England that interest in mysticism flourished.

The growth of mysticism was also supported by two developments in philosophy. One was the attack emanating from the British universities on Absolute Idealism, a dominant philosophical system and one compatible with Christian orthodoxy. The other was a more general attack on Positivism carried out by Pragmatism, Activism, and Vitalism. These "philosophies of life" shared common premises that supported mysticism. Particularly important were their emphases on process and becoming and on instinct and intuition as faculties for the apprehension of truth.[14] William James of the United States, Henri Bergson of France, and Rudolph Eucken of Germany were in vogue among the Edwardians and each, reflecting these common emphases, gave philosophical support to mysticism and the importance of religious experience.

The attacks on Absolute Idealism and Positivism, the rise of the "philosophies of life," the power of Modernism, and the failure of religious institutions all allowed for the growth of mysticism, a way of being religious independent of philosophical, institutional, and doctrinal constraints. Mysticism was also supported by interest in psychology, the new science of human consciousness, which had permeated all levels of intellectual life. The founding of the Society for Psychical Research in 1882 in England illustrates this early link between psychological research and religious experience.[15] As well, advances in comparative religion led to a search for a universal element in religious expression; mysticism seemed a likely candidate.

What is clear is that by the first decade of this century there was interest in mysticism both as a worldview and as a way of life. James, Inge, and von Hügel helped bring attention to this phenomenon in England, but it was popularized by Evelyn Underhill; historians and contemporaries alike attest to that fact.[16]

Evelyn Underhill was, of course, greatly influenced by the thought of her age. She lived outside of institutional religion, was greatly impressed by the Catholic Modernists, particularly George Tyrrell, and she borrowed heavily from the vitalistic philosophies of Bergson and Eucken. In 1912 when the former lectured in London she wrote

> I'm still drunk with Bergson, who sharpened one's mind and swept one off one's feet both at once. Those lectures have been a real, great experience; direct contact with the personality of a profound intuitive thinker of the first rank.... It was rather strange, and gave me quite a shock last night, when he gave us his final conclusions on the nature of spirit (conclusions which sounded like a metaphysical version of the Communion of Saints), to find that they were exactly the same as my mystic declares that she *saw* — her intellectual vision, and insists upon in the teeth of all arguments, as absolutely true.[17]

If Evelyn Underhill's personal development led her to work on mysticism, that work was confirmed by her times. Although she had no suspicion of its success at the outset, *Mysticism* was to become a popular book.

The manuscript was completed in November of 1910, and was published in March of the following year. She had worked on it from the end of 1907, collecting sources, hunting down manuscripts, checking translations, reading for background. This was not her only project, however. In 1908 she published her third novel, *The Column of Dust*, and a short defense of May Sinclair's *Helpmate*, which had been criticized by Lady Robert Cecil. In 1910 she published four short articles on mysticism and related subjects. During that year she was also planning a number of articles and a devotional book, *Path of Eternal Wisdom: A Mystical Commentary on the Way of the Cross*, which appeared under the pseudonym John Cordelier in 1911. She also published poems in a variety of magazines; they were collected and appeared in *Immanence* in 1912.

The most important of these writings was her novel, which was finished in March 1909 and dedicated to her friends Arthur and Purefoy Machen. Like her other novels, *The Column of Dust* was complex, symbolic, and overwritten and like them its theme was about life in two worlds. In this book however the protagonist, Constance Tyrrel, a prudent bookseller, reconciles the two worlds, not through escape as Willie Hopkinson had, or by accepting the ordinary as Paul Valéry did, but in her own sacrificial death for her illegitimate and not particularly lovable daughter Vera. The book is filled with autobiographical hints. Ruysbroeck, John of the Cross, Bergson, Blake, Eliphas Lévi, Waite, and Machen are all quoted. The mystic consciousness and the clash between knowing and being are discussed, and love is proposed as the way through to infinite life.

Early in the novel, Constance's guide Martin gives her the key to life: "Oh, learn to love! Do please, learn to love. It's such terrible waste if you don't... and this is the one thing which is worth doing well."[18] *The Column of Dust* is about love and the maturing of this ordinary woman who, in burning herself out in love, confronts the Real. The Pietà that had impressed Catherine in *The Lost Word* reappears, now in the form of the ordinary mother sharing the pain of her child. Duality is overcome, illusion is vanquished in the theater of life; the method of living is proclaimed: it is sacrificial love.

The Column of Dust was Underhill's last attempt at fiction. While she was never particularly successful in this genre, it did allow her to explore the most pressing concerns of her life. *Mysticism*, her next effort, would provide a new opportunity for this exploration.

While her daily work consisted in the laborious effort of researching and writing the eighteen chapters of her book, she continued to travel, entertain, and keep up her correspondence with Margaret Robinson and others. Her letters give hints of her development during this period.

Underhill's desire to be rooted in a community of belief was still strong, as was her sense of being thwarted by being outside it. In a brief correspondence with Hugh Benson in 1909 she wrote about the loneliness of being in what she called "the invisible church."

> I wish the invisible church had a little more substance in it; it has many conspicuous advantages over the visible one, especially in the matter of intellectual liberty, as to which I'm afraid I still disagree with you. I would like to talk to you very much, or rather let you talk. I simply cannot talk about religion, and get shy or snappy at once, sometimes both... but it's merely wasting your time. I'm afraid I'm destined to go on fidgeting away and trying to square the spiritual circle.[19]

The lure of Rome and Roman churches continued to be tremendous for her. "I do miss churches when I have not got them to run to," she wrote to Margaret Robinson.[20] As late as 1911 she wrote to another friend, "So here I am, going to Mass and so on of course, but entirely deprived of the sacraments."[21] She believed that the Catholic

church was her "ultimate home" and in 1910 she made a pilgrimage
to Rome. She found St. Peter's "hideous" and "not a bit more religious than St. Paul's cathedral," but was impressed by the historical
power of the papacy there; Rome was the pope's city. As to the person
of Pius X, the condemner of the Modernists, she wrote,

> I never received such an impression of sanctity from anyone
> before. Whatever muddles he may make intellectually or po-
> litically, spiritually he is equal to his position. I do not think
> anyone who had been in his atmosphere could doubt it.[22]

Her letters also reveal her playfulness, a quality she retained
throughout her life. This playfulness was often associated with cats,
those affectionate, beautiful, and whimsical creatures that gave re-
lease from intense intellectual and emotional life. She wrote to
Margaret Robinson:

> I nearly forgot the most important part of this letter: namely
> that Jacob [the cat] sends his best love and says that — most
> fortunately — he is, as you wished, Tabby: but emphatically not
> common. He has been told he is pure Persian, and is inclined
> to believe it. He celebrated my return yesterday by catching a
> mouse and eating it, with every circumstance of cruelty, in the
> garden whilst I was having my tea.[23]

Evelyn Underhill was, nonetheless, a typically reserved Edwardian
woman. Of her trip to France she wrote: "It was quite affecting saying
good-bye to all our friends — particularly Madame Bobelin, who for
some unknown reason loved me dearly and kissed me fervently (to
my great amazement) in the middle of the narthex."[24]
    Although she reflected the attitudes of her times, she was neither
stuffy nor pretentious. About an announcement of *The Lost Word*
she wrote:

> I was amused to find you had seen the picture in *The Bookman!*
> It is more like a nigger boy than anything else, having been
> taken in the back of the chemist's shop at Scilly, at the end of a
> day's fishing! Heinemann annoyed me by demanding a portrait
> for publication, which should be "mystical and strike a personal
> note!" Whereupon in a spirit of pure devilry, I sent him that![25]

She found pomposity of all kinds amusing. Describing the Women
Writers Dinner she wrote:

My opposite neighbour was a lady who has made herself a religion of Conic Sections, and told me that Curves were the key to the Universe and an infallible corrective of pantheism: and that Sex and Psychology were in it all — a dark saying indeed which I have not yet unravelled! Next to her sat Mrs. Tay Pay O'Connor who interrupted the discourse on Curves to ask her if she knew Mrs. Cecil Raleigh, who had done so much in Drury Lane Melodrama. Add to this a large chorus of successful Suffragists, full of Saturday's demonstrations: and the hare-and-hounds business of anxious admirers chasing successful authors in order to have the pleasure of saying, "I *do* so like your book!"[26]

Although she would be plagued throughout her life by devotees who competed for her affection, she shunned adulation of every sort. "Please don't ever talk or think of 'sitting at my feet(!)' or any nonsense like that," she wrote.[27] Likewise she found it difficult to tolerate "the ever growing crowd of bores, who have had visions and want me to tell them what they are like."[28]

As she proceeded with her work on mysticism, Underhill was simultaneously clarifying her understanding of the life of the spirit and what it meant for ordinary persons like herself and Margaret Robinson. Her correspondence reveals an attitude on the one hand passionate and on the other balanced — characteristics that marked all her writings on the spiritual life.

At the heart of Underhill's worldview was the insight she learned from the mystics and that she shared first with Margaret Robinson and then with thousands of her readers. This insight, she wrote,

is not *mine* you know. You will find it all in Eckhardt, & the Imitation & lots of other places — They all knew, as Richard of St. Victor said, that the Fire of Love *burns.* We have not fulfilled our destiny when we have sat down at a safe distance from it, purring like overfed cats. "Suffering is the ancient law of love" — & its highest pleasure into the bargain.[29]

As she wrote *Mysticism* her central idea was clarified: the mystic was one who experienced the powerful love of God. This insight was taken up into her own understanding of the spiritual life. Counter to prevailing theological opinion, she did not consider ascetical spirituality as primary; first came the lure of God and only then the willingness to take up suffering. This voluntary suffering must always be evaluated in terms of the needs of the person. Love and balance became the hallmarks of her advice. At the Communion and Confirmation of young Rose Herbert, Underhill warned her father:

> That fortnight's retreat in the Convent does sound rather drastic for one of her small size: I do hope it won't be too overpowering for her and is sufficiently tempered with fresh air. Still, as you say, it must impress her with the supreme importance of religion: I hope it will impress her with its beauty and lovableness too.[30]

For Margaret Robinson, a woman of narrow and excessive tendencies, Underhill stressed the need for equilibrium.

> I do so want your life to be properly balanced. To live alone, and be shy, and have a turn for mysticism, makes an individualistic concept of the relation between yourself and God almost inevitable. Such a concept is not untrue: it is half a truth, and when held together with the other half — the concept of yourself as one of the household of faith, related to every other soul in the household, living and dead — it becomes actually true. If this were *quite* true to you, intercessory prayer would become as natural and necessary as passing the salt to your neighbour at table instead of remaining in profound contemplation of your own plate.... "The best way of knowing God is to frequent the company of his friends," said St. Teresa, and it is just as important to keep in touch with your brothers and sisters out of the body as in the body.[31]

Underhill believed that "balanced faculties" were central for anyone involved in the active life, and life in which the greatest contemplative saints participated. Even Francis, Ruysbroeck, and Bernard lead balanced lives, she argued; they loved the birds, music, the forest. The point was not to repress the senses but to be detached from them. "As to what you say about the cloistered life,"

> I don't know whether you have ever known any nuns or monks personally? I know a good many and as a matter of fact, they live the life of the senses just as much as anyone else, only in a peculiarly simple and detached way. If you want to find the person who combines spiritual passion with appreciation of a cup of coffee — go to a convent.[32]

Again and again Underhill warned against too much introspection. She urged Margaret Robinson to "Live hard, with both hands, and love as much as you can, and don't faddle with your experience."[33] "Hold the scales level," she said and "don't do anything which lowers your all-around efficiency for life — ."[34]

In her own life Underhill sought balance too. The quiet support of Hubert, the regularity of leisure, her social commitments, the cats and garden, were all essential to keep her romantic spirit on course. She had come to the point, as Waite had said, where God becomes the proper object of the quest. It was that quest she pursued relentlessly for three years in the context of her quiet life. The intensity of this work would have broken an older woman or derailed a younger one. At this stage in her life, her body and mind were able to withstand its rigors. The borderland had become a place of opportunity.

The writing of *Mysticism* was arduous. A thousand sources were cited or listed.[35] Her letters are filled with nervousness over the accuracy of translations, of the need to locate manuscripts, of visits to booksellers, and the British Museum. She talks about "bits" and "scraps" from which she tries to make sense and her love for some of her subjects and dislike for others. Ruysbroeck, Richard Rolle, Julian of Norwich, and Gertrude More are some of her favorites. She found Madame Guyon "gushing" and Thomas Traherne too "meditative and not sufficiently contemplative." "I want [mystics] with a high temperature, at whose fires I may re-enkindle my chilliness," she wrote.[36]

As the book went on, the subject got more difficult. She considered some chapters better than others.

I am glad the Vision Chapter strikes you as imposing! Really it is rather a fraud, being easier to get up than the more elusive parts of the subject. The only difficulties were in arranging it neatly and speaking what one believed to be the truth without hurting the feelings of the pious.[37]

About one of her final chapters she wrote:

I am glad *Ecstasy* is not entirely illegible. I have done it very badly I think: it was altogether too much for me — just piecing things together and guessing in the dark. But I have been working very poorly lately and now can hardly work at all, which is a dreadful waste of time when one is shut up in the house. The book gets more and more difficult. I am past all the stages at which scraps of experiences could guide one, and can only rely on sympathetic imagination, which is not always safe.[38]

Here Underhill discloses her method and the source of her originality as a writer. Experience is the first guide in understanding one's subject. The outer edges of experience are reached by what she calls sympathetic imagination, an imagined participation with the subject. From the time of her youth she wanted "to cultivate a habit of observation and interest in everything," and to have a mind "wide to embrace all sorts of things" and a "sense of one-ness with our kind." Identifying these values with "worthy womanhood," she inculcated them so deeply that they became a way of understanding reality. Close observation, inclusivity, and a sense of oneness were the components of the methodology she applied both to life and to the study of the mystics. It was a learned methodology, one designated by societal expectations of gender and the source of her perceptiveness both as a writer and a person.[39]

Mysticism was a serious book. In the first third of it, "The Mystic Fact," she defined mysticism, set out its characteristics, and showed its relationship to vitalism, psychology, theology, symbolism, and magic. The second part, "The Mystic Way," describes the stages of mystic consciousness. A historical sketch of European mysticism and an impressive bibliography are included. The book was an introduction to mysticism and a work of scholarship. Hundreds of apt quotations from mystical literature gave the English reader direct access to a world previously closed off by language as well as by misunderstanding.

Underhill's starting point was the existence of mystical experience as described in texts, what she called "the mystic fact." This is asserted as an *a priori* and is not examined. Her aim, to describe and make intelligible that experience as it presents itself in hundreds of various expressions, leads her to reject a historical treatment of her subject. She wants to understand the mystics not in relation to their own times, but in relationship to truth. She ignores their historical context, claiming that all mystics "speak the same language and come from the same country."[40]

The language, tone, and pace of the book are all related to its object — to convince the reader of the importance of the mystics, the "pioneers" of a higher human consciousness, toward which all of the "race" aims. In dramatic, energized language Underhill, more like an artist than a philosopher, describes the mystic life. Her intent is not to win over the mind but to enlighten the understanding; to give proof of the "personal passion for the Absolute." In Italy she learned of the power of art to illuminate reality; *Mysticism* was an effort toward that same end. Although lengthy and dense, its pace was urgent, its tone compelling, its writer eager to show the riches of this uncharted world that lay within reach of everyone.

Her "point of departure" is a definite type of personality, one which "craves absolute truth" and for whom the whole meaning of life is found in this passionate quest. Straight off she warns: because the experiences of these "lovers of humanity" are remote and difficult to enter into, the reader must first "purge the intellect," and "clear away prejudice and convention."

Although *Mysticism* is a study in psychology and the highest reaches of human consciousness, Underhill begins by clearing away philosophical obstacles. Naturalism, Idealism, and Skepticism are each dismissed as inadequate philosophies to approach her subject. Vitalism is offered as an alternative scheme, although it too presents only half the truth.

Her treatment of psychology is important because mysticism can only be understood as it is embodied in personality. She focuses on the two great psychic cravings, the desire to know, which she allies with magic and science, and the desire to love, which she associates with mysticism. "In magic,"

> the will unites with the intellect in an impassioned desire for supersensible knowledge. This is the intellectual, aggressive, and scientific temperament trying to extend its field of consciousness, until it includes the supersensual world....
>
> In mysticism the will is united with the emotions in an impassioned desire to transcend the sense-world, in order that the self may be joined by love to the one eternal and ultimate Object of love; whose existence is intuitively perceived by that which we...refer to as "the cosmic" or "transcendental" sense.[41]

The distinction between the desire to know and the desire to love, first articulated in "A Defence of Magic," is central to her book. It reflects her rejection of the attempt to control reality by scientific or magical means. For her, the highest human effort must be expended not to control reality, but to participate in it.

The real strength of the first part of the book is the description of mysticism from different angles and perspectives. She defined it variously.

> It is essentially a movement of the heart, seeking to transcend the limitations of the individual standpoint and to surrender itself to ultimate Reality; for no personal gain, to satisfy no tran-

scendent curiosity, to obtain no other-worldly joys, but purely from an instinct of love. By the word *heart*, of course we here mean not merely "the seat of the affection," "the organ of tender emotion," and the like: but rather the inmost sanctuary of personal being, the deep root of its love and will, the very source of its energy and life. The mystic is "in love with the Absolute" not in any idle or sentimental manner, but in the vital sense which presses at all costs and through all dangers towards union with the object beloved.... [M]ysticism, like art cannot exist without it [passionate emotion]. We must feel, and feel acutely, before we want to act on this hard and heroic scale.[42]

About its object she wrote:

Whether that end be called the God of Christianity, the World-Soul of Pantheism, the Absolute of Philosophy, the desire to attain it and the movement towards it — so long as this is a genuine life process and not an intellectual speculation — is the proper subject of mysticism. I believe this movement to represent the true line of development of the highest form of human consciousness.[43]

As a process, a movement that could not be apprehended intellectually, mysticism was clearly distinct from philosophy.

Where the philosopher guesses and argues, the mystic lives and looks; and speaks, consequently, the disconcerting language of firsthand experience, not the neat dialectic of the schools. Hence whilst the Absolute of the metaphysicians remains a diagram — impersonal and unattainable — the Absolute of the mystics is lovable, attainable, alive.[44]

Stated differently, mysticism is

not an opinion: it is not a philosophy. It has nothing in common with the pursuit of occult knowledge. On the one hand it is not merely the power of contemplating Eternity: on the other, it is not to be identified with any kind of religious queerness. It is the name of that organic process which involves the perfect consummation of the Love of God: the achievement here and now of the immortal heritage of man. Or, if you like it better — for this means exactly the same thing — it is the art of establishing his conscious relation with the Absolute.[45]

[It is]...the science of ultimates, the science of union with the Absolute, and nothing else, and that the mystic is the person who attains to this Union, not the person who talks about it. Not to *know about*, but to *Be*, is the mark of the real initiate.[46]

The initiates, the mystics, had a power "latent in the whole race," of perceiving transcendent Reality, not in some isolated vision, or through some "fugitive glimpse of Reality," but as "a complete system of life" which "transfigures" consciousness by a relation to the transcendent world. In short, Underhill believed that mysticism was a way of life, open to all, achieved by the few whose lives were transformed by that which they loved.

One of the most important aspects of her book was the setting out and illustrating of four characteristics of mysticism. Here she proceeded to search the mystical texts in order to determine the nature of the phenomenon. She began by rejecting as unsatisfactory William James's four marks of the mystic state.[47] Mysticism, she claimed, is "active and practical, not passive and theoretical. It is an organic life-process, something which the whole self does."[48] Second, mysticism is "entirely a spiritual activity." By this she meant that it is not done in order to gain or achieve anything, but only for its own end. Third, the "business and method of mysticism is love." It is an activity, a total dedication of the will toward its source. "It is at once an act of love, an act of surrender, and an act of supreme perception."[49] But the One is always a living and personal Object of Love, never an object of exploration. Fourth, mysticism entails a definite psychological experience. It is "a definite and peculiar development of the whole self, conscious and unconscious, under the spur of such a hunger: a remaking of the whole character on high levels in the interest of the transcendental life."[50]

Before undertaking a discussion of the stages of the mystic way, she clarifies in three additional chapters the relationship between mysticism and theology, symbolism, and magic. In the first she shows how the mystics reflect diverse ideas of God. In the second she describes three types of symbolism used by them, that of pilgrimage, of life, and of a craving for perfection. Finally, the uses and limits of magical practice are discussed.

If the first part of the book is an attempt at description and definition, the second is aimed at catapulting the reader into the process of the mystic life itself. Underhill describes what she does as a kind of

"map-making" of the mystical process, of allying the self to the Absolute. She then illustrates with rich detail from mystical writings five,
as opposed to the traditional three, stages in the mystic way. These
she calls awakening, purgation, illumination, dark night of the soul,
and union. "Our business, then," she wrote,

> is to trace from its beginning a gradual and complete change in
> the equilibrium of the self. It is a change whereby that self turns
> from the unreal world of sense in which it is normally immersed,
> first to apprehend, then to unite itself with Absolute Reality: fi-
> nally, possessed by and wholly surrendered to this Transcendent
> Life, becomes a medium whereby the spiritual world is seen in
> unique degree operating directly in the world of sense. In other
> words, we are to see the human mind advance from the mere
> perception of phenomena, through the intuition...to the entire
> realization of, and union with, Absolute Life under its aspect of
> Divine Immanence.
>
> The completed mystical life, then, is more than intuitional:
> it is theopathetic. In the old, frank language of the mystics, it is
> the *deified life.*[51]

Through the use of vigorous, eloquent, and compelling language,
Underhill pulls the reader into the process as it unfolds. What is
described is a movement, a winning over, in pain and in pleasure,
of the will, an oscillation toward the Absolute and back again to the
self. The process is dynamic and only becomes intelligible and be-
lievable when entered into. Having entered, the reader participates
in the great adventure of humanity. While each person has the req-
uisite "germ," "the little buried talent," the "spring of energy," the
mystic has a genius for the Absolute, not merely an apprehension,
but a passion for it. This passion is connected to a particular psychological makeup, a natural capability of extraordinary concentration,
an intensity of love and will, the capacity for self-discipline, stead-
fastness, and courage. Although mystics vary tremendously in their
language, symbolic expression, and lives, their psychological structure
is similar.

Likewise, the stages of their deepening consciousness are similar.
The beginning of this process, what Underhill calls Awakening to the
Divine, starts by the stimulation of the will through the emotional
life. Usually abrupt and well-marked off, it is analogous to conversion. As the field of consciousness begins to shift subtly from the
self to the Divine, there is the experience of joy. The second stage,

purification, is the completion of conversion and is characterized by self-simplification and stripping. Having awakened to the Perfect, there is the desire to eliminate what stands between the self and the Divine. This stage is marked by pain. Illumination, the third stage, provides a kind of perception radically different from that in the normal experience. A joyous apprehension of the Absolute, a clarity of vision, and a developed intuition are all present in the self. This is "the first mystic life"; many artists belong here and many mystics never move beyond it.

In order to deepen alignment of the self with Reality, to awaken the deepest self, attentiveness, inwardness, and interior silence are required. Through this inward contemplation one enters into the life of Reality, not observing it, but being remade by it through participation. What might be considered abnormal psychic phenomena — rapture, ecstasy, voices, and visions — may appear at this stage. They are not central, however, to the mystic life; what is central is the movement of increasing participation with the life of the Absolute.

Beyond illumination is another stage, born of exhaustion of the former state and growth toward a new state of consciousness. This Dark Night of the Soul is filled with disharmony and strain and a sense of abandonment, sinfulness, despair, powerlessness, and temptation.

The final state, union, is only known by the great mystics. It is described as a state of vitality, of unification of personality, of freedom, of heroic activity. Here all duality is overcome. Achieving the highest, the mystics take the lowest place; possessing fullness, they become innocent. It is here that the destiny of the mystics, "to enhance life," is achieved. The result of union is their divine fecundity.

The language of life and of place is used to describe this state.

> God, said St. Augustine, is the country of the soul: it's Home, says Ruysbroeck. The mystic in the unitive state is living in and of his native land; no exploring alien, but a returned exile, now wholly identified with it, part of it, yet retaining his personality intact. As none know the spirit of England but the English; and they know it by intuitive participation, by mergence, not by thought; so none but the "deified" know the secret of the life of God. This, too, is a knowledge conferred only by participation: by living a life, breathing an atmosphere.[52]

Mysticism was immediately recognized as a remarkable book. Many thought it the work of a man, a trained theologian.[53] Within the year of issue it was reprinted, then re-edited and reprinted again. Two years later it reached its fifth edition.[54] Its popularity stemmed from the fact that it carved out a new subject, made it intelligible, and interpreted it with convincing power. Although Underhill appealed to psychology, philosophy, and theology, her contribution does not rest principally on her analysis of her subject. Above all her book is a personal defense of the achievement of the mystics that she was able to understand because she lived intimately with their texts.

Mysticism's originality lay in the fact that it redefined what it is to be human and what it is to be religious. In the language of her day, Underhill claimed that to be fully human was to be "in love with the Absolute," and to have one's character transmuted because of that love. To be religious was defined not in terms of doctrinal adherence, scriptural fidelity, or theological purity. Her book did not deal with these subjects and its language did not reflect them. Sin, grace, Christ, are barely mentioned. At the heart of all religious expression is mysticism, not a narrow, esoteric "opinion" which claims some "spiritual" aspect of the individual, but a way of life that involves the totality of the person.

Whatever its limitations *Mysticism* was — as John Chapman, the future Abbot of Downside, wrote — "the most readable... and most enlightening book on mysticism," even though it had some omissions from the Catholic point of view.[55] Von Hügel was eager to point out the nature of those omissions and the book's particularly antihistorical, anti-institutional, and monistic biases. Even a cursory reading of *Mysticism* confirms von Hügel's complaints. The mystics are presented as disembodied and without context and their independence from religious tradition is noticeable. Furthermore, the discrete identities of God and the soul are not clearly maintained. William Inge praised the book publicly but privately indicated to Methuen, the publisher, that Underhill's work was stronger on the psychological than the philosophical side, that she misunderstood Plotinus and was unduly influenced by French Vitalism, especially Bergson, which to his lights was incompatible with belief in an absolute God.[56] This clearly miffed Evelyn, who privately referred to Inge as "the old wretch."[57]

There were other problems as well. What was the mystic sense? Was it possessed by every person or was it only potentially there? Didn't she, in her effort to counteract prevailing opinion, place too much emphasis on will and feeling and actually denigrate intellect? Was she not supporting an anti-intellectualist view, "religion without thought"? Did it not make any difference if the end of union was called the "God of Christianity," "the World-Soul of Pantheism," or the "Absolute of Philosophy"? And did not such emphasis on union promote a callousness toward human suffering, an abandonment of ethics, and a blindness toward sin and evil? These were the questions not of clerics and philosophers but of a contemporary English woman writer Emma Herman whose book, *The Meaning and Value of Mysticism*, appeared four years after Underhill's.[58]

Some of the arguments raised by both von Hügel and Herman would be dealt with by Underhill in a new preface written for the twelfth edition in 1930. But the focus of her book would never change. Her central insight was fixed: the most important human experience was personal confrontation with Reality, God, the Absolute; at this point she used these words interchangeably.

Mysticism reflected the romantic, adventurous, and passionate commitment of its young author. It focused almost exclusively on the priority of union with the Absolute. In fact, Underhill originally proposed entitling the book, *The Quest of the Absolute*.[59] The Absolute came, as she suggested in her first chapter, through various experiences. "To all...who will receive it" she wrote, "news comes...of a world of Absolute Life, Absolute Beauty, Absolute Truth,...news that most of us translate...into the language of religion, of beauty, of love, or of pain."[60] In her own life she knew best the experiences and language of religion, beauty, and love; of pain and suffering she had yet to learn. Of pain, she wrote, it "plunges like a sword through creation, leaving on the one side cringing and degraded animals and on the other side heroes and saints."[61] Although she spoke of it as a "peculiarly intractable fact of universal experience," the problem of pain and suffering was hardly mentioned in her book. Yet this "grave but kindly teacher of immortal secrets, [this] conferrer of liberty,"[62] while not examined by her, would be confronted in subsequent years. The work of the borderland had been to articulate "the personal passion" of the mystics. Completed, *Mysticism* ensured her enormous success as a writer; yet the sweetness of victory was diminished by her growing understanding of a world "plaited" with pain.

3

THE CAULDRON OF WAR

THE GREAT WAR CHANGED EVERYTHING. Unexpected and protracted beyond all imagining, it caught England off-guard. She was a mighty nation with a secure empire; no one was prepared for the destruction and death war brought in its wake. Two million English soldiers died; two million more were wounded. Its effects were everywhere personal ones and it prompted a patriotic fervor that consumed every interest. In retrospect it could be seen as the beginning of the end of the old order, but in the moment it was a war to preserve a way of life and a cultural heritage. It was a war that was "for the right," for God, as well as for England. Although victorious, the England of the nineteenth century died. The war was a watershed, a divide. It reordered relationships, upset notions of social class and gender; it set colonies on the way to independence; it dealt a deathblow to the optimistic worldview that dominated intellectual life. The old way was destroyed as one Western nation clawed at another, showing for all the world to see that the patina of culture was very thin indeed.

The seeds of war had been sown decades before, but their coming to flower was unexpected. The destruction offered the possibility of reappraisal and new arrangements, but these possibilities were not immediately evident. Evident everywhere were chaos and confusion. "During the war," Evelyn Underhill later wrote to von Hügel, "I went to pieces."[1] This cryptic remark is the only direct evidence of her anguish during that time. There are few letters from the period, and Underhill, always unwilling to burden others with her own anxieties, left no clues to the cause of her confusion. What is clear is that the war, although not a direct cause of her anxieties, was the context in which she faced the limits of her ideas.

Although the war brought great suffering, the second decade of the twentieth century was a halcyon one for Underhill. This period was characterized by enormous productivity and public acclaim. *Mysticism* appeared in 1911 and was reprinted, reissued, and reprinted again. It was followed by *The Mystic Way* in 1913 and *Practical Mysticism* in 1914. She had come into her own as the popularizer and defender of mysticism. Success made her neither remote nor inaccessible. What was striking about her was her manner and appearance of ordinariness. She was not a particularly handsome woman, her dress was not fashionable, and her hair was rather dowdy and covered on top by a small lace headpiece.[2] But there was a lightness about her that endeared. One was attracted to this defender of mysticism and immediately put at ease by her.[3]

Her personal accessibility and serenity belied her single-minded and determined drive to make the mystical tradition available to her contemporaries. For the ten years preceding and including the war and its aftermath, Underhill continued to explore mysticism in essay, poetry, biography, and critical editions of original texts. What drove her was the belief that her times needed the experience of "God-intoxicated" spirits, with "the great qualities of wildness and romance."[4] She found these not only in the mystics, but in some of her contemporaries as well. When she encountered this spirit in the flesh, she responded enthusiastically. In 1912 when she heard Henri Bergson lecture in London she claimed she was "drunk" with him. She immediately dashed off an article, "Bergson and the Mystics," in which she described him as the "mediator" between "the inarticulate explorers of the infinite," the mystics, and "the map-loving mind."[5] "Drunk" with Bergson, an "adorer" of von Hügel, she hailed Rabindranath Tagore as a "seer," a "great seeker," "my beloved Indian prophet." She was first put onto Tagore by her friend May Sinclair[6] and in 1912 and 1913 reviewed three of his books in *The Nation*. Tagore, very much in fashion in London, was awarded the Nobel Prize for Literature in 1913. During that year she worked directly with him preparing a translation of and an introduction to one hundred poems attributed, unfortunately incorrectly, to the fifteenth-century Bengali mystical poet Kabir, and an introduction to an autobiography of Tagore's father, Maharishi Devendranath Tagore.[7]

Underhill found Rabindranath Tagore attractive for a number of reasons. She resonated with the positive mysticism she saw in his work. Of his book *Gitanjali* she wrote, "Coming out of the midst of life, it accepts life in its wholeness as a revelation of the Divine mind. This is not the Via Negativa of the Neoplatonists, but a positive mysticism, which presses forward to a more abundant life."[8]

Not only did his mystic vision parallel hers, but it was one that harmonized with the vitalism of Bergson, her philosophic mentor. "The flux of life," she wrote, "the living changeful onward-pressing universe of modern vitalist thought, is the stuff from which this seer [Tagore] has woven his vision of truth."[9]

What attracted her to both Tagore and Bergson, much as it had to von Hügel, was not mere intellectual or intuitive compatibility, but the person. After sustained contact with Tagore, she called him a "master." "I want so much to tell you — but it is not possible — " she wrote,

> what your kindness and friendship has meant to me this summer & will always mean to me now. This is the first time I have had the privilege of being with one who is a master in the things I care so much about but know so little of as yet: & I understand now something of what your writers mean when they insist on the necessity & value of the personal teacher & the fact that he gives something which the learner cannot get in any other way. It has been like hearing the language of which I barely know the alphabet, spoken perfectly.[10]

Underhill loved working with Tagore. After he returned to India she made sure their translation of Kabir was published; this involved a nasty battle with the India Society over publication rights that showed both her tenacity in honoring Tagore's wishes and Hubert's participation as her legal adviser in her literary efforts.[11] It was "a real joy and education" to work with Tagore, but it left little time for other things.[12] Nevertheless, the other things, particularly her writing, went on.

By 1913 Underhill opened up new ways of exploring the subject of mysticism. Poetry was one. She wrote many poems that appeared in *The Nation*, *The Spectator*, and *The Outlook*. Some of these were collected in a volume called *Immanence: A Book of Verses* published in 1912 and dedicated to her father. It opened with, "I come in the little things, saith the Lord"; probably the best line in the book. *Theophanies*, another collection, appeared in 1916 and substantiates that although she was considered a good religious poet in her time,[13] her work is not of lasting value. Suffused with philosophical vitalism and focused mostly on nature, her poetry is dated and has little power. In the poem "Nature" she wrote:

> Thou art a priest, O Nature,
> And from Thee
> All who believe
> Assuredly receive
> Enshrined in many a changeful accident,
> The substance of the only sacrament.[14]

"Dynamic Love" was one of the best poems in *Theophanies:*

> Not to me
> The Unmoved Mover of Philosophy
> Nay, rather a great moving wave of Bliss.
> A surging torrent of Dynamic Love
> In passionate swift career
> That down the sheer
> And fathomless abyss
> Of Being ever pours,
> His ecstasy to prove.[15]

Underhill said she gave up writing poetry, "because it was too easy."[16] Perhaps it came facilely; perhaps it did not challenge her adventurous and intellectual spirit. Whatever the reason, it was better that she spent her energies in other ways, lest the sentimentalism she found so abhorrent mark her own work.

If poetry was not her vehicle, neither was, at least at this point, devotional literature. She produced two books in this genre, both written under the name John Cordelier. Although Evelyn sometimes used pen names (Thomasina, Tommy, Brigid, Josephine),[17] it is not known why she used this pseudonym; but it did provide some anonymity to the author of *Mysticism* as she ventured into a new genre. The themes and objectives of the two books were similar. In both she took a devotional theme — be it the passion and death of Jesus as in *The Path of Eternal Wisdom: A Mystical Commentary on the Way of the Cross* (1911) or the fifteen mysteries in the soul's ascent to God as in *The Spiral Way* (1912) — and showed how these great dramas of the Christian church provided insight into the secrets of life. In both books her emphasis was on entering into the fullness of life with all its suffering and sorrow so that one might in the end transcend them. While the books were consonant with *Mysticism*, the restrictive format and explicitly religious language limited their appeal. Her genius as an author of devotional literature was yet to be realized.

In her search to find ways to express her convictions about mysticism, she successfully used two vehicles, biography and texts; their use followed logically from her previous work and proved to have lasting merit.[18] It was the mystical text that gave evidence of new levels of human consciousness, and it was the embodiment of this consciousness in human personality that she explored in biography.

In biography she ranged widely, producing books and articles on individuals as diverse as St. Paul and Thérèse of Lisieux. She selected her subjects and interpreted their lives according to the ideas laid out in *Mysticism*. In "St. Paul and the Mystic Way,"[19] which she wrote in 1911, Underhill traced Paul's psychological development through the states of mystic consciousness. This article was subsequently incorporated into *The Mystic Way: A Psychological Study of Christian Origins*. One of her earliest biographical pieces was on the fourteenth-century Angela de Foligno who helped spread Franciscan ideals. Underhill saw her as the paradigm of the great mystic with her strong romantic temperament, innate simplicity, power of total self-giving, endurance, and strong will. Although of unstable psychic makeup, her self-knowledge and love of poverty helped her to grow in character. Like Jan of Ruysbroeck and Jacopone da Todi, two favorites of Underhill, Angela de Foligno claimed an immediate apprehension of transcendent reality.[20]

Underhill's biographical studies of Kabir and Devendranath Tagore had a similar purpose — to show the universal development of mystic consciousness. She dealt with Kabir both in the introduction to *One Hundred Poems* and in a separate article.[21] Although she saw in him a synthesis of Moslem, Hindu, and Persian traditions, he was captive of none. He hated religious exclusivism and found creeds nonessential. He was not excessively emotional and did not identify God and the soul but maintained the separateness of each. What was important was his direct apprehension of God as the supreme object of love. Underhill quoted his poem to give evidence of his mystic understanding.

> O Servant, where dost thou seek Me?
> Lo! I am beside thee.
> I am neither in temple nor mosque: I am
> Neither in Kaaba nor in Kailash.

Neither am I in rites and ceremonies,
  nor yoga and reincarnation.
If Thou art a true seeker, thou shalt at
once see Me: Thou shalt meet me in a
moment of time.

Kabir says, O Sadhu! God is the breath
of all breath.[22]

Underhill compared Kabir to Ruysbroeck, Jacopone da Todi, and
Jacob Boehme. For them there were "no fences" between the natural
and the supernatural, and their vision of God was synthetic; in God,
perpetual opposites were reconciled. For Kabir, God was "the Root"
from which all proceeded, and the only need of man.[23] Like every
mystic, Kabir acted as a mediator between God, whom he adored,
and humanity to whom he conveyed the secrets of eternity.

Underhill's willingness to write an introduction to Rabindranath
Tagore's translation of his father's autobiography followed from her
indebtedness to the younger Tagore and her conviction that the autobiography was an authentic history of a soul. She found Devendranath Tagore's life marked by an abrupt experience of Reality, a
passion for poverty, and the achievement of "great fecundity," true
signs of mystic life.[24]

Of the English medieval mystics Underhill found the fourteenth-
century Julian of Norwich one of the safest guides. She was neither
excessively intellectual nor overly emotional, but drawing from both
the head and heart, was zestful, hopeful, and joyous. Like Angela de
Foligno, she had an ardent consciousness of God, a vision that was
both philosophic and practical.[25]

In an attempt to show that mysticism had modern expressions,
Underhill did articles on two little-known French mystics, Thérèse
Martin (Thérèse of Lisieux), the Carmelite nun, and Lucie-Christine,
a widow who died in 1908, both of whom found the transcendent in
ordinary life. Although Thérèse lived a sheltered and restricted life,
she committed her smallest acts to love and in so doing gave unity
to all her actions. Lucie-Christine lived in the world, but had an
inner life of great richness and originality. Like Angela de Foligno she
had an apprehension of the Divine as both personal and impersonal,
transcendent and immanent.[26]

In order to encourage others to reclaim the mystics, Underhill
often collaborated with friends. Her biographical introduction of
Richard Rolle was done for Frances Comper's edition of Rolle's *The*

Fire of Love or the Power of Love, and her piece on Jacob Boehme accompanied his *Confessions* edited by her friend W. Scott Palmer. She continued this work in later years, writing the biographical introduction for Emma Gurney Salter's translation of Nicholas of Cusa's *Vision of God*, Lucy Menzies' translation of François Malaval's *A Simple Method of Raising the Soul to Contemplation*, and John Watkins' edition of Walter Hilton's *The Scale of Perfection*.

Richard Rolle, "the father of English mysticism," was a particularly important subject. Underhill called him "the English Francis," because like that Italian romantic and natural artist, he believed poverty, simplicity, and self-stripping were the only routes to real freedom. Both believed contemplation and action went hand in hand and both committed themselves to God late in their lives. Rolle followed the life of intellect, only to "run away" to the only "great adventure of life," "total self-giving to God." His love images were of fire and heat, sweetness and song. His mystical passion set the pattern for all the great English mystics who followed him.[27]

One has the sense that it was friendship for Palmer rather than her inherent preference for the sixteenth-century Lutheran Boehme which prompted Evelyn to write her introduction to Palmer's edition of *The Confessions of Jacob Boehme*.[28] Although she acknowledged the great influence of Boehme in both philosophy and religious mysticism, and the importance of his intuitive perception of God, this biography did not have the vigor of her other pieces.

Her two most important biographical studies were those of Ruysbroeck, her favorite mystic,[29] and Jacopone da Todi. The Ruysbroeck biography appeared in 1915 as part of the Quest Series published by G. Bell & Sons, which included studies on Islam, Jewish mysticism, and Buddhist psychology. Her study of this fourteenth-century mystic was followed by a long bibliography, which gave evidence of her serious scholarship, and by translations from the Flemish of Ruysbroeck's writing done by Mrs. Theodore Beck. What makes this work so powerful is Underhill's interpretation of Ruysbroeck as an "ardent and industrious lover." His breadth and depth of vision and his personal integration she found particularly valuable. Her fluid use of language and her ability to capture the movement in his life were reminiscent of *Mysticism*, but here the attention was focused not on the process but on a life that incarnated it. For Underhill, Ruysbroeck's greatness was evident in the development of his consciousness. Every stage of his life built on a former one, and his vision of transcendence emerged from the widening, heightening, and enriching of his experience. It was through this process that reconciliation of opposites was carried out and integration achieved. In him she found not only the movement from the active to the interior, to what she called the superessential stage of the soul, but also the double movement of all mystic life, "the breathing in of God" and "the breathing out to man." Ruysbroeck's vision of God was synthetic. God was both intimate and infinite; personal and philosophic; near and far; transcendent and immanent; ethical and metaphysical.[30] It was his inclusivity and integration which drew her, not only because they were the marks of a great mystic but because at this point she saw them as essential to her own life.

The last of her biographies was a full-scale examination of the little-studied thirteenth-century Italian mystical poet Jacopone da Todi. Again, she proceeded to evaluate his life in terms of the mystic way. Unlike the balanced life of Ruysbroeck, Jacopone's was one of vehemence expressed first as a libertine, then as an ascetic, and finally as an ecstatic. Although his life was wild, passionate, and half-crazed at points, Underhill saw in it an attempt to reconcile the extremes of world denial with world renewal, the life of penitence with that of the troubadour, the ascetical ideal with that of the mystical. Reconciliation was achieved not through love as in Ruysbroeck, but through humility and poverty of spirit, the ideals of the Franciscan order with which Jacopone was associated. Never beatified by the church, he nonetheless captured in his ecstatic poetry the intensity of mystic life.[31] This work on Jacopone had significance for Underhill both in terms of gradually moving her toward a new vocation and in providing her with an intensive exposure to Franciscan spirituality, which she increasingly came to love.

These biographical studies were augmented by her editing of original texts. As early as 1910 she published extracts from a British Museum manuscript of "The Mirror of Simple Souls." In an article published the following year she explored the work of the fourteenth-century English translator of the manuscript, the prologue of the anonymous thirteenth-century French author, and the content of the writing.[32] In 1912 she prepared an edition of *The Cloud of Unknowing* and included a brief introduction to the text tracing its history from the sixth century through the fourteenth, when it was translated into vernacular English. She acknowledged the help of J. A. Herbert, a vivid reminder of his efforts years earlier when he had prodded her to work on the medieval legends of Our Lady of St. Mary. Underhill found the ancient mystic text of *The Cloud* to be one particularly suitable for the contemporary reader with activist tendencies. Prompting not a quietist spirituality but one of ardent and industrious will, it showed that at the heart of mysticism were charity and humility, not visionary experiences.[33]

Underhill's early edited texts were followed by an edition of three works by Ruysbroeck — *The Adornment of the Spiritual Marriage, The Sparkling Stone, The Book of Supreme Truth* — which had recently been translated from the Flemish. These works set out all of Ruysbroeck's major ideas and formed a companion piece to her biography that had been published the year before.

While biography and texts gave illustration to mystical consciousness, Underhill also worked to expand and clarify the implications of that consciousness. Through two books, *The Mystic Way* and *Practical Mysticism*, she established herself as both the exponent and the popularizer of mysticism. The former, subtitled *A Psychological Study in Christian Origins*, was a very difficult book to write. She had to consult many sources and traverse a new terrain, researching the lives of Jesus and Paul and the history of the Gospels and the early Christian church. Her intent was a daring one: to apply her understanding of the mystic way and the development of mystic consciousness to the origins of Christianity, to establish that Christianity was a mystical religion, and to show that the root of Christian mysticism was in Jesus and not the Neoplatonists. There was much at stake here. If her position was accepted, all her work would be vindicated. Christianity would be understood as essentially a mystical rather than a historical or institutional religion; and the "invisible" church, which existed independent of the "visible" church would be strengthened. Equally important was her claim that Christianity was an organic process, distinct from the Neoplatonic philosophy which had greatly influenced it. Christianity, with its emphasis on self-surrender, heroic love, and divine fecundity represented true mysticism, she maintained, whereas Neoplatonism, holding out ecstatic union with the Absolute as its goal, had no place for participation in the infinite love which "outflowed" in gifts to others. *The Mystic Way*, dedicated to Dominica (Ethel Barker), was an attempt to take the insights she had learned from medieval mystical literature and apply them elsewhere, so as to bring further credence to her case.[34] She knew her position was an iconoclastic one[35] but she was nonetheless unprepared for the attacks it engendered. Von Hügel was generally supportive of the book but gave her, as she wrote,

> a firm but gentle lecture on my own Quakerish leanings! His main point seems to be that such interior religion is all very well for our exalted moments, but will fail us in the ordinary

dull jog-trot of daily life, and is therefore not a "whole religion" for men who are not "pure spirit."[36]

Her old friend Arthur Machen wrote to say that he no longer considered her a Christian,[37] and she described J. A. Herbert's comments about the book as "very painful reading."[38] She said she was "not vexed" by his letter, but in fact she was decidedly vexed and found "it rather difficult to write coolly" about some of the issues Herbert raised.[39] "What seems to you to be blasphemy," she wrote him, "seems to me to make the things I love best more real."[40] Of course, what she loved was the mystic consciousness and she wanted to find that embedded in the origins of Christianity. In doing this, she ruffled orthodox readers. It was not, as she sternly told Herbert, that she had made Jesus inferior to the best mystics; "He represents the classic and perfect achievement all of the greatest saints have aimed at but never reached."[41] She wanted not only to establish Jesus as the greatest of the mystics, but she wanted to show how revelation took place within the context of human growth. Was it not more consistent with God's glory to have his revelation in Jesus emerge through the normal human processes of life and complete humanity than through some "conjuring trick"? She stated clearly that she was trying to repudiate Docetism, the belief that Jesus only appeared to be human; "and personally," she wrote, "I find my own heresy, horrible though it be, better to live with than that."[42]

Underhill was thrown on the defensive in these attacks on her orthodoxy, and she responded strongly. "Personally," she wrote to Herbert, "If I didn't think the whole of life was the work of the Holy Spirit, I should give everything up. It is the centre of my creed: so vivid that the things which seem to us disgusting, cruel, unjust — can do nothing against it."[43]

Her statement was both clear and clairvoyant. As opposed to a theocentric or Christocentric worldview, she announced a spirit-centered one. At the same time she made a claim that no evil could dim the vividness of her creed. It was in the years that followed that she would confront not only "the ordinary jog-trot of daily life," but the horror of war. Her creed would be challenged and she would be brought to the threshold of new decision.

Like *The Mystic Way* her next major effort, *Practical Mysticism*, elaborated the insights of *Mysticism*. It also broke new ground by focusing not on the insights of the "great pioneers of humanity," but on the potential of mystical consciousness for ordinary people. *Practical Mysticism* was then a link between her former work and what was to come — her vocation as a writer for ordinary people. The fact that the book was "practical" implied a utility and non-esoteric character. As its subtitle indicated, it was *A Little Book for Normal People*. It was "little" in that it was less than half the size of her "big" book on mysticism and was written in nontechnical language, assumed no prior knowledge of the subject, and presupposed, she claimed, no theological or metaphysical system. While the latter was not actually true, it was written in neither technically theological nor philosophical language; hence it was accessible, a book for everybody. The word "normal" clearly meant that it was for ordinary people, but it implied too that mysticism was normal and natural and not principally associated with the abnormal experiences of visions and voices. It was on this point that she began the book: mysticism was rooted in a natural tendency which every person possessed to a greater or lesser degree. "The essence of mystical contemplation," she wrote, "is summed up in these two experiences — union with the flux of life, and union with the whole in which all lesser realities are resumed — and these experiences are well within your reach."[44] She then went on to discuss the training of this mystic faculty, the self-discipline and attitude toward life it implied, the various forms of contemplation, and the active vocation it demanded.

She also raised these concerns in two articles, "The Place of Will, Intellect and Feeling in Prayer" and "The Education of the Spirit." These two articles, more than any of her other writings, portend her future direction. In the latter she discussed the atrophying of the human tendency toward the Divine and the need to awaken it through moral education, through devotional and aesthetic enrichment, and through contemplation.[45] The former article was the one piece that focused exclusively on prayer, what she defined as "that part of your active and conscious life which is deliberately oriented toward, and exclusively responds to, spiritual reality."[46] This responsiveness took various forms — adoration, petition, meditation, contemplation — and involved the thinking, feeling, and willing or acting faculties, each of which had a different role in this process. The intellect prepared consciousness, feeling inflamed the will, and the will, the most dynamic and important faculty, one of desire and intention, explored the Infinite.[47] One hears echoes in this article of her early advice to Margaret Robinson: "Never forget that the key of the situation lies in the will."[48]

If *Practical Mysticism* encouraged contemplation, it also encouraged active vocation in the world. She wrote, "It is your business," to actualize within the world of time and space — perhaps by great endeavours in the field of heroic action, perhaps only by small ones in field and market, tram and tube, office and drawing-room in the perpetual give-and-take of common life — that more real life, that holy creative energy, which this world manifests as a whole but indifferently. You shall work for mercy, order, beauty, significance: shall mend where you find things broken, make where you find the need.[49]

Like *Mysticism*, the thrust of *Practical Mysticism* was to promote a consciousness that was not quietistic. She reiterated this in her preface because many would suspect that such a book, published during the early months of the war, would be irrelevant to the national crisis. Although mysticism and war seemed inimical, she argued they were not. If practical mysticism meant anything, if it was not merely "a spiritual plaything," then its principles had to stand up to and be reconciled with "human history now being poured red-hot from the cauldron of war."[50] What this made clear was that she had accepted the challenge of von Hügel: to show that her mysticism was not for "pure spirit," that it could sustain one "in the ordinary dull jog-trot of daily life" and even in the brutality of war. As she saw it, the merit of mysticism was that it both "detached" one from the violence of the world, made one impenetrable to it, *and* engaged one in the world with renewed vitality. She wrote in the preface:

[T]he mystical consciousness has the power of lifting those who possess it to a plane of reality which no struggle, no cruelty, can disturb: or conferring a certitude which no catastrophe can wreck. Yet it does not wrap its initiates in a selfish and other-worldly calm, isolate them from the pain and effort of the common life. Rather, it gives them renewed vitality. . . . Stayed upon eternal realities, that Spirit will be far better able to endure and profit by the stern discipline which the race is now called to undergo, than those who are wholly at the mercy of events.[51]

It was in *Practical Mysticism* that Underhill first mentioned the cataclysmic event of war. While never a dominant theme in her writing of this period, the war had to be dealt with both in her life and in her writing on mysticism. Like everyone, Underhill was shocked by the war and inconvenienced by its demands. Although neither she nor Hubert was ever injured, a home on Campden Hill Square was hit by a bomb and Lincoln's Inn, Hubert's place of employment, was destroyed.[52] Hubert continued to work throughout the war, to serve on a number of hospital boards, and to put his considerable practical talents to work designing artificial limbs.[53] At the start of the war Evelyn did social work among the families of soldiers and sailors[54] and in 1916 she began to work in naval intelligence, the African section, at the Admiralty. There she prepared and translated guide books, but as in many bureaucracies, there was much idle time. On one occasion, apparently just for the fun of it, she invented an African country, complete with flora and fauna, and sent her guide book on through the various channels until it was finally recognized for what it was, a joke. Her immediate colleagues at the Admiralty were a lively group which included Emma Gurney Salter, with whom she would cooperate subsequently in a translation of Nicholas of Cusa's *Vision of God*, and Robin Collingwood, the future historian-philosopher, and his sister Barbara.[55]

Neither the war nor her efforts for it diminished her writing. Only a small portion of her works, however, touched on the event of war itself. In a short article on prayer published in 1915 she claimed that the cultivation of the spiritual life was a patriotic duty![56] In other articles she countered the conventional wisdom that mystics were antisocial, useless to the nation, and selfish in their intent. She called them, "atoners," "bridges," "lookout men upon the cross trees, assuring us from time to time that we are still on our course."[57] In her biographical piece on Charles Péguy, the French poet who was killed in the early weeks of the war, she took up the conflict between the spiritual and material realms. Péguy was an ardent missionary who, rejecting the intellectualism, materialism, and individualism of France, longed to restore the simple, childlike faith of the French peasant, a faith he believed drove the mystic-patriot Joan of Arc. A deeply religious Catholic, he was forced to live outside the official church. Unlike Underhill's favorite mystics who achieved a reconciliation of opposites in their lives, Péguy never resolved the war between his destructive and proud impulses and his mystical and poetic ones; he died on the battlefield of France without achieving inner peace. Underhill's piece was a eulogy to this patriot, whom she recognized as a mystic poet, a divided soul crushed by the war in its march.[58]

While most of her writing dealt only indirectly with war, in four articles published in 1915 and 1916 she discussed the subject directly as it related to mysticism.[59] On the one hand these articles were defensive; they tried to ward off those who attacked mysticism as unpatriotic. On the other, they were evangelical, arguing that now more than ever mysticism was needed. In any case, they were written within the cultural context of a nation at war, and Evelyn Underhill was not free from those cultural constraints. These articles are important because they reveal her assumptions about war, violence, suffering, and God. She began, not by discussion of these assumptions, but with questions raised by the war. Had not war arrested the mystical revival? Did not mysticism detract from the duty of the citizen? Was not the mystic by inclination a pacifist and hence a nonparticipant in the national war effort? Was not war incompatible with brotherhood and the notion of a loving God? In each case she answered negatively. Mystics did not detract from the war, they could in fact help and enliven the national effort. War, while temporarily distracting from things of the spirit could, nonetheless, help to transcend personal selfishness and build a national consciousness which would revitalize spiritual life. She believed that war and struggle were inevitable and as such could be used for positive ends. Although war brought suffering and seemed to destroy brotherhood, it actually offered the opportunity for heroism and great acts of kindness. As for God, he was not on the side of war or peace, but his mercy was never in question.

For Underhill, mysticism offered an alternative view of war, one allowing detachment from its violence and destruction. Of the mystic she wrote:

> Having won that true detachment which is the perfection of unselfishness, and harmonized his will with the movements of the spiritual world — achieving thus at least a measure of the "union with God" which is his goal — he knows that he may safely act as the pressure of the Spirit directs.[60]

Having accepted struggle, the mystic was detached; being detached, the mystic could act heroically in the world. Far from being pacifists, the history of mysticism revealed, so she contended, that the great mystics lived in times of strife and conflict and entered into it. Above all, mystics were not quietistic, she reiterated. They were active and their lives were, as she wrote in *Mysticism*, characterized by "divine fecundity." Hence the real question was not "Should one fight?" but "What should one fight for?" The answer was close at hand — "Fight for Right," a slogan that served as the name for a patriotic movement of noncombatants for which she worked. In the literature she wrote for this group she insisted that England had been given the honor and responsibility to fight on the side of "moral beauty" and that men willing to risk all for the nation were a "spectacle of great spiritual beauty." Germany's aim was selfish and aggressive; its national idea was that of a wild beast, and war against Germany was a war against a relapse to "bestial ways." Underhill called on all noncombatants to fight outwardly, to overcome selfishness, to sacrifice material pleasures, to endure restrictions patiently so as to deliver both their own souls and their country. Her war poems, especially "Non-Combatants," dealt with this theme of total participation.

> Never be said of us: we had no war to wage.
> Because our womanhood,
> Because the weight of age,
> Held us in servitude
> None sees us fight.
> Yet we in the long night
> Battle to give release
> To all whom we must
> Send to seek and die
> For Peace.[61]

Although these statements seem shrill, even bellicose, Evelyn Underhill was not a militarist. Rather she was a deeply religious woman whose principal insight about the love of God was tangled both in Neoplatonism and the cultural assumptions of her time. The "cauldron of war" in which she lived externally had by 1917 become an "internal cauldron" as well.

The year 1917 must have been a difficult one for her. Her writing fell off precipitously; she produced only one book review. This was the third year of a war that had been expected to last only a few months. It was the year of the revolution in Russia and the closing of the eastern war front. It was the year in which her two cousins, Guy and Harold Thorne, were both killed,[62] and the year that Ethel Barker, her most intimate friend, became terminally ill. Ethel endured several operations and her suffering was great; Evelyn visited her every day.[63] The greatest strain of these events was unmitigated by the solace she once experienced by attending Mass. During this time she developed, as she later wrote to von Hügel, "an increasingly anti-institutional bias" and drifted to what she called an "inwardness."[64] Her one extant letter from the war years reveals how she saw her own dilemma and that of her times:

What has happened to you is happening in a greater or less degree to everyone. The present abnormal conditions are as bad for the spiritual life as for every other kind of life. We are all finding it frightfully difficult and most of us are failing badly. The material world and its interests, uproars and perplexities are so insistent that detachment is almost impossible. Some are utterly overwhelmed: others, as you say of yourself, take refuge in interest in little things. Transcendence of the here and now demands at present a strength of will and a power of withdrawal which very few possess.[65]

Underhill's remark to von Hügel that during the war she "went to pieces" reflects her experience of 1917. Her dilemma was an intellectual and an emotional one. Its resolution would come slowly in the gradual turning in a new direction. Although the turning would take years to complete, it must have begun already in 1918.

In *Mysticism* she had written that suffering was "a grave and kindly teacher of immortal secrets . . . "; by 1918 she might have written that "life" was the teacher. In that year she was at work on her study of Jacopone da Todi, a book which would be important for her future development.[66] In Jacopone she saw the world-denying tendency of the Neoplatonic overcome by the world-affirming orientation of the Franciscan. The link between these two disparate positions was Jacopone's profound sense of poverty which led him from a life of asceticism to one of an ecstatic poet.[67] In the end, Underhill saw him as a mediator of the infinite to others.[68] In some indirect way the vocation of Jacopone da Todi presaged her own future vocation.

While working on the Jacopone da Todi biography, she published a short article on the future of mysticism in which she assessed whether interest in mysticism could be revived after the war. One prerequisite for such revival was a sympathetic public opinion that she believed existed. What was needed as well was the appearance of one or more great mystics who would serve as centers of spiritual vitality. The history of mysticism revealed, she contended, that it flourished best when allied with a high moral code, a strong sense of duty, and a definite religious faith; it was more likely to arise within the historic churches than outside them. Her recognition of the role of institutional religion vis-à-vis mysticism was something new. While she believed that "[t]rue mysticism is the soul of religion," that it brought "fresh life" to religion, she also believed that "like the soul of man, [mysticism] needs a body if it is to fulfil its mighty destiny."[69] The future of mysticism lay in religious institutions, for "divorced from all institutional expression it tends to become strange, vague, or merely sentimental."[70] As with so much of her writing, "The Future of Mysticism" was autobiographical. Underhill knew personally the peril of such "vague" mysticism, "inwardness," and "anti-institutional bias."

In 1919 the war was over and some normalcy began to return to life. *Jacopone da Todi* appeared in this year and Underhill continued to write reviews for *The Saturday Westminster Gazette.* In a review of G. G. Coulton's *Christ, St. Francis and Today* she again took up the question of institutional religion. She agreed with Coulton that institutional religion had "lost hold of the hearts and intellects of men" and that what was needed to restore it was a greater tolerance toward individual belief and greater devotion to historical truth. These could be achieved if there was a return to "a more intense and unfailing life and love for which men crave; and these, save in rare instances, can only be mediated to them by the more ardent faith and vision of their fellow-men."[71] In short, her view was that true mysticism could only flourish supported by institutional religion, and institutional religion could only be enlivened if persons of great "faith and vision" renewed it. The clear need was for those who could mediate, those who like Jacopone da Todi would take the "raw data" of the "great explorers" and make it accessible to ordinary people.

What is evident in these brief articles is a gradual shift toward a new vocation and a new attitude toward institutional religion. In both cases the prerequisite was a shift away from Neoplatonism and its argument for detachment from the world. Although in both *The Mystic Way* and *Practical Mysticism* she recognized some of the limits of Neoplatonism, subsequently in a review of Stephen MacKenna's new translation of Plotinus' *Ethical Treatises* she pointed up the importance of Plotinus, his great influence on Christianity and compatibility with its doctrines, and his counterweight to so much that was sentimental and occult. Plotinus was for her "the best corrective to that invertebrate mysticality which is so commonly mistaken for spiritual religion."[72]

In a review of Inge's book on Plotinus, however, she acknowledged the majesty and purity of Plotinus' vision, but was very critical of Neoplatonism. The Neoplatonists, she argued, put all the burden on man to do everything for himself. Christianity, she wrote, says, "God so loved the world." The Neoplatonists say, "So the world loves God."[73] As a religious philosophy, Neoplatonism had no place for the notion of self-giving on the part of the transcendent object. Neither did Plotinus do justice to the social side of religion but saw the spiritual life as "an exclusive system of self-culture" which had as its final aim a "flight of the alone to the Alone." Because it was directed solely toward the transcendent, Neoplatonism was incapable of dealing with the problem of evil, it offered no remedy for failure and grief and suggested only "lofty withdrawal" from conflict and violence. In the end, Neoplatonism produced "a self-sufficient sage," unmoved by suffering and ruin. The "detachment" and "transcendence" she urged previously were here rejected; and Christianity, while greatly influenced by Neoplatonic ideas, offered an alternative view.[74] In another article, "The Essentials of Mysticism," in which she summed up many years of thinking about mysticism, she clarified the particular contribution of Christianity vis-à-vis Neoplatonism. The universality of Christianity was most important; it was addressed to all people, and its concept of sin, of humility, and of charity filled in the gaps left by Neoplatonism. Christianity was founded not on

a lofty aloofness from human failings, but on a self-giving and disinterested love, the complete abolition of egoism. This alone, it declared, could get rid of the inward disharmony — one aspect of the universal conflict behind the instinctive and the rational life — which Boehme called the "powerful contrarium" warring with the soul.[75]

While Evelyn Underhill had considered herself a Christian from 1907 onward, her Christianity had been of a mystical type that was rooted in Neoplatonism. By 1920 she realized the great deficiency of that religious philosophy. It produced only a "self-sufficient sage" and urged flight from a "failed world." Not only were sagacity and self-sufficiency not the highest aim, she realized they ran counter to the drive toward inclusivity that was so deeply rooted in her. Neoplatonism could nurture adoration, but it could do little to insure an outflowing of love to the world. Tied to detachment and transcendence, it offered no creative way to deal with sin, with God's love for the soul, or with one's relationship with others. For her the future of mysticism lay not with Neoplatonism but with Christianity.

That future also lay within the historic churches, institutions from which Underhill had separated herself for most of her forty-six years. By late 1920 she was moving toward an institutional affiliation. The year before, she had learned of a secret fellowship, the Spiritual Entente, which had been founded by Sorella Maria, an Italian Franciscan nun. Its purpose was to work silently, like leaven, in the world. The Entente had no meetings, no rules; members were to be "seekers" after the presence of God, capable of prayer, and absolutely loyal to their own Church, "not only outward observers, but striving to live as to convince others that "verily Christ is known there."[76] Underhill had a sense that the Entente was already a "curiously strong little organization" whose members did seem to be in actual spiritual contact. Its emphasis on prayer, the "invisibility" of its work, and its ecumenicity certainly must have been important to Underhill; what was new in this commitment, however, was the expectation that one be loyal to a church. Such commitment it would seem presupposed participation in institutional religion. In 1907 Evelyn Underhill had claimed she could not accept Anglicanism, but by 1920 she knew she needed to belong to a church. Not only was the future of mysticism linked to the spiritual revival of the churches but her "inward" religion was now insufficient. If not before the end of 1920, then certainly by early 1921 Evelyn Underhill had made an intellectual decision to place herself in the Anglican church.[77] Here she encountered no obstacle; she had only to slip quietly back into the church in which she had been baptized and confirmed.

Underhill spent most of 1921 preparing for a series of eight lectures she would give at the Unitarian-affiliated Manchester College of Oxford University. The lectures, established by the late Professor Upton, began in October and carried over into 1922. Since they were to memorialize two women, Upton's sisters, it was thought appropriate to invite a woman to deliver them.[78] In giving them, Underhill became the first woman lecturer in religion to appear on the university list.[79] The lectures, which were "largely attended" and "deeply appreciated"[80] were published in 1922 as *The Life of the Spirit and the Life of Today* and dedicated to Ethel Ross Barker, who had died during the course of their preparation.[81] Ethel's death after four years of suffering was a great loss to Evelyn. She was the person who came as "near sanctity . . . as anyone I have known"[82] and it was fitting that the book was dedicated to her.

As *The Life of the Spirit and the Life of Today* marks an end, it also marks a beginning. As the title indicates, it is not about mysticism but about the spiritual life, a new way of framing the human response to the Divine. It was as well about contemporary life and its relationship to the deepest reality. In some ways the book linked back to *Practical Mysticism*, but it was a work that was wiser, more balanced, more compassionate, and more attuned to the great needs of her contemporaries. In its preface she thanks von Hügel, whose influence was almost exclusively through his writing, and her old friend William Scott Palmer, who read *Mysticism* in manuscript, collaborated on the editions of Jacob Boehme, and now had given "generous and valuable advice" on this book.[83] William Scott Palmer was the pen name of Mary Emily Dawson, who, although thirty years Evelyn's senior, was a cherished friend, having shared the same pilgrimage from agnosticism to mysticism to Anglicanism, being both a Modernist and lover of Bergson along the way.

The purpose of *The Life of the Spirit and the Life of Today* was to subject "the classical experiences of spiritual life to the conclusions of modern psychology."[84] It was not a book about mystic life, which she considered a more intense manifestation of the spiritual life, but one about the normal life of the spirit that manifested itself first in a vague but persistent apprehension of an enduring, transcendent reality, what she called the instinct for God. The characteristic marks of a fully developed life of the spirit were reminiscent, however, of those of the mystic life — integration of personality, the complimentary tendencies toward contemplation and action, and a new sense of power and vitality. Entrance into this natural process of the spiritual life usually began with an experience of dissatisfaction or disillusionment that forced a crisis and some sort of decisive break with the past. The first consequence of the life of the spirit was the sublimation of the instinctive life, the transfer of interest and energy to new objectives, in psychological terms, the redirection of the craving of the psyche so as to achieve more life and love. Underhill made it clear that the spiritual life was available to all and that education could pave the way for its development. Her chapter on "The Life of the Spirit and Education" was reminiscent of her article, "The Education of the Spirit" which had appeared in 1916. What was needed was unconditional self-surrender to the Divine, a little silence and leisure, and a great deal of faithfulness, kindness, and courage. This life expressed itself in work, prayer, self-discipline, and social service. Its distinctive mark was not "happiness but vocation; work demanded and power given, but given only on condition that we spend it and ourselves on others without stint."[85]

Underhill believed that a regenerate life of the spirit often appeared associated with institutional religious life. What institutional religion could not give, however, was direct spiritual experience or any fresh insight into the spiritual life. It exalted the corporate and stable; its instincts were conservative, authoritarian, and dogmatic. And it distrusted individual intuition and encouraged dependence and obedience. Nonetheless, institutional religion could make a positive contribution to the spiritual life. It gave a group consciousness, provided unity with contemporaries and predecessors, offered a discipline that was particularly helpful in times of slackness, and passed on a culture, particularly that of the saints. Although it carried special dangers with it, "in the last resort," she wrote,

> criticism of the church, of Christian institutionalism, is really criticism of ourselves. Were we more spiritually alive, our spiritual homes would be the real nesting places of new life. That which the church is to us is the result of all that we bring to, and ask from, history: the impact of our present and its past.[86]

Above all *The Life of the Spirit and the Life of Today* was a defense of the spiritual life and an attempt to counter the prevalent trend in contemporary religion to reduce everything to the social gospel. Such a trend was detrimental, atrophying this natural tendency and promoting an unbalanced life. Needed were prayer and the direction of desire toward God who was at the center of life. Her imagery, borrowed from Ruysbroeck, was that of a widespread love directed to all things. The priority of God and the inclusivity of love became the twin bases on which she constructed all of her future work. "Thus," she wrote, the spiritual life

> means an immense widening of the arc of human sympathy; and this is not possible to do properly unless we have found the centre of the circle first. The glaring defect of current religion — I mean the vigorous kind, not the kind that is responsible for empty churches — is that it spends so much time in running round the arc and rather takes the centre for granted.... And it is at the centre that the real life of the spirit aims first; thence flowing out to the circumference — even to its most harsh, dark, difficult and rugged limits.[87]

The Life of the Spirit and the Life of Today was a synthesis of her past work and a prolegomenon. It outlined her future work, which was not to reclaim the mystics, but to prompt the life of the spirit in her contemporaries. As such, it was a dedicatory work, and she must have felt happy at its completion. But she must have known that she had neither the courage nor the vision to undertake this new vocation. In the face of this she made two decisions which were to have important consequences for the rest of her life: she accepted the invitation of her friend Annie Harvey to attend a retreat at an Anglican retreat house,[88] and she wrote to Friedrich von Hügel for help.

4

SEEKING
"REAL, PERMANENT LIFE"

<hr>

EVELYN UNDERHILL WAS FORTY-SIX YEARS OLD when she entered what would prove to be a transition in her life, one which brought with it personal suffering and new direction. By her own description she was at this point "professionally very prosperous and petted."[1] The Upton lectures brought prestige, and the publication of *The Life of the Spirit and the Life of Today* with its emphasis on psychology, spirituality, and contemporary life positioned her as a leader in the hoped-for religious revival that had been delayed by war. The fact that she was now a member of the Church of England meant she could operate as an insider within that institution. She had every reason to believe that the coming years would bring continuing success.

The war had caused inner turmoil which she dealt with at least in part by her decision to become a practicing Anglican. Although she made it reluctantly, it was a decision she would gradually come to appreciate. But there was in her as well an awareness of some "thinness" in her emotional life, some blockage that impeded growth. "The art of life," she had written in 1911, "is learned only in the living — lookers-on know nothing of the game."[2] Ardent and intense by nature, she did not want to be a "looker-on"; she turned to von Hügel to help her live again.

The choice of von Hügel, a married Roman Catholic theologian, was an appropriate one. The fact that von Hügel was a Modernist and the author of *The Mystical Element of Religion*, a study of Catherine of Genoa, made him a kindred spirit. Underhill had met him a decade earlier. Although he had agreed to read her manuscript of

Mysticism and give suggestions, he disagreed with her on some matters. Nevertheless he respected her unique talents. As early as 1916 he wrote: "I have long felt how many souls will be led right or wrong by yourself, with your rare charm of style, large knowledge of literature, and delicate interestingness of character.... You can and do reach more people than I can ever expect to reach myself."[3]

What attracted Underhill most was von Hügel's person. She called him a "scholar," a "saint," "a lovable old man" with a "massive passion for God." She described him as having "rock-like faith," "a lofty intellect," and "an intense interior life."[4] He was a man who had suffered not only from deafness and years of mental breakdown, but from ecclesiastical suspicion during the Modernist crisis. This suffering brought with it a profound sense of the love of God. It was this quality that was most evident to her, that kept her coming to him, that gave hope that her spiritual life might deepen under his direction. Evelyn Underhill trusted von Hügel, and in that trusting she learned to trust the painful process that she would undergo.

Von Hügel served as Underhill's spiritual director between late 1921 and early 1925 when he died. Although they lived near each other in Kensington and Underhill saw von Hügel in his home, they corresponded as well. Perhaps it was the Baron's deafness which led to this correspondence between them. The letters and a private notebook which Evelyn kept during this period provide an inside view of the particular problems she confronted. From the very beginning she knew the peril of what she had undertaken. "In my lucid moments," she wrote in her diary,

> I see only too clearly that the possible end of this road is complete, unconditional self-consecration, and for this I have not the nerve, the character or the depth. There has been some sort of mistake. My soul is too small for it and yet it is at bottom the only thing that I really want. It feels sometimes as if, whilst still a jumble of conflicting impulses and violent faults, I were being pushed from behind towards an edge *I dare not* jump over.[5]

When Evelyn Underhill came to von Hügel for direction she was a well-known religious writer, a published author for nineteen years, and an acknowledged authority on mysticism. What von Hügel, the carer of souls, saw before him in her was one who needed nurture, who had grown in inappropriate ways and who needed to be directed toward new life. His diagnosis was that she was afflicted with "exclusive" or "pure" mysticism, that she misunderstood the spiritual life as some sort of self-cultivation, and that she was emotionally starved. In fact, these three maladies were interconnected, and their healing would come not through their direct purging but through a gentle turning toward God.

The relationship between von Hügel and Underhill was not one of equals. He admired her, but she adored him. Affectionate and caring toward her, he was nonetheless sometimes bracing and patriarchal. During their sessions she reported that he always made her sit on an uncomfortable chair facing the light.[6] When someone complained about her severity in dealing with her own directees, she said: "You should see *my* old man dusting me down! You are all very lightly dealt with."[7]

Von Hügel had a profound appreciation for diversity among people, what he called one's *attrait;* yet his method of dealing with those who came to him for help was generally consistent. He was schooled in the writings of the seventeenth-century French spiritual directors, especially François Fénelon, and his own director had been Abbé Huvelin. Grounded in that tradition, he consistently argued for balance in the spiritual life and a curb on vehemence and excess of any kind. What he hoped for were "solid, simple, sober souls." In her younger years, the adventurous, intense, and ardent Evelyn Underhill had called his a "hard and dreary doctrine."[8] She was now at a point to endure it.

Von Hügel's balanced spirituality was based on a simple discipline that was evident in his direction of both Underhill and his niece Gwendolyn Plunkett-Greene. In both cases he advocated a minimal devotional program which was always to be adhered to; a requirement to visit the poor (a suggestion Underhill had urged on Margaret Robinson years earlier); the reading of Fénelon; and the development of nonreligious interests. Greene played the violin, and Underhill took up scriptwriting and did gardening. Von Hügel's method was never didactic. His ideas were not so much "taught" as "caught." It was this method of "contagion," or teaching by example, which had great power to influence. Yet Underhill was not always docile in particulars. "The Baron dosed me with Fénelon at one time," she wrote Lucy Menzies, "till I told him that a Perfect Gentleman giving Judicious spiritual advice to Perfect Ladies was no good to me — since then his name has not been mentioned between us."[9]

In an anonymous article written after his death, Underhill spoke of von Hügel's contribution as a spiritual director and the "unmeasured gratitude of those whom he rescued from outer darkness, delivered by his own unique method from intellectual entanglements and set firmly

on their feet."[10] The intellectual framework von Hügel provided was
what he called "critical realism," a philosophy opposed to the subjective idealism he saw everywhere. At the heart of this philosophy was
the notion that reality was twofold, temporal and eternal, a graded
world of sense and spirit, nature and grace. In this reality, humans
were "amphibious," conditioned by the sense world yet craving the
supersensual or God. This latter tendency had atrophied but could be
developed not by denying the temporal, but by immersing oneself in
it. The finite was the sacramental, the way to the infinite and eternal.
A philosophy that understood the interpenetration of the transcendent and the immanent was needed, and a religion which valued the
mystical, the intellectual, and the institutional. This "critical realism" was at the heart of von Hügel's contribution to modern religious
thought, but it was, as Evelyn wrote, his "power of holding, and practicing together in all their fullness and variety, the pastoral and the
philosophic sides of the spiritual life which made him,... without exception, the most influential religious personality of our own time."[11]
He was certainly the most important religious personality in her life
and for the same reason. Evelyn was no mere disciple of von Hügel,
but she could and did say, "...I owe him my whole spiritual life."[12]

Underhill was a newly practicing Anglican when she went to von
Hügel for counsel. Early in their relationship the Baron brought up
the question of her ecclesiastical affiliation. Having recently committed herself to Anglicanism, she was unwilling to confront again the
issue of membership in the Roman church. Her decision had been
made. Von Hügel pressed her on this and she offered the excuse that
she would not go over to Rome because, among other things, it would
hurt her husband too much. Von Hügel tried to show her the falsity
of such an answer and argued that if her conscience urged her to be
received, she should do so. Since his own Modernist tendencies had
brought him harsh treatment by Rome, he was reluctant to encourage others to join. What he wanted her to see was that she must be
open to God, wherever that might lead.[13] In addressing this question,
von Hügel gave her the criterion she must use to make decisions. He
wrote to her:

> To my mind, the only quite satisfactory, just and balanced, defi-
> nitely supernatural position, is to hold most firmly that all who
> in any way depend upon you — hence above all your husband —
> possess an inalienable right to be as much sustained and con-
> soled by you, and as little pained by you, as is ever possible;
> that no mere preference or greater helps and consolations, reli-

gious or otherwise, can justify your inflicting grave pain upon your husband; but that if and when your conscience came to make you, after waiting and testing, to feel *bound* to move, you ought to do so, trusting to the same God, who is determining you, to make it less of a pain, and in some way a spiritual gain for your husband also, whilst you would yourself, of course, do everything possible to minimize that pain for him.[14]

But the real question was not about denominational affiliation, but whether she had a "Catholic" or "sacramental" understanding of reality. What von Hügel meant was the ability to appreciate the fact that the finite was the way to the infinite, that history and matter were in fact the way to God. This was a direct counter to her "exclusive" or "pure" mysticism. He was aware that her problem was not merely intellectual but psychological as well. "You badly want de-intellectualizing," he wrote, "or at least developing homely, human sense-and-spirit dispositions and activities."[15] For this he recommended work with the poor. This work "if properly entered into, and persevered with," he wrote, will "discipline, mortify, soften, deepen, widen, quiet you; it will, as it were distribute your blood — some of your blood — away from the brain where too much of it is lodged at present."[16] These must have been painful and almost incomprehensible words for a woman who through dint of enormous effort had achieved remarkable intellectual success.

In order to counter her "intellectualism," he urged her in addition to working with the poor and developing nonreligious interests to accept the historical nature of Christianity and to practice Christocentric devotion.

I'm *not* asking you to accept the Church's position. All I ask is that you accept that some *historical* happenings are necessary, that belief in them is necessary for all powerful religion or that historical happenings can flourish after every single supposed historical fact has been demonstrated non-historical. I'm sure that some historical happenings are essential for every and all powerful and perfect religion and I'm sure that the reduction of religion to a system of mere ideas, principles, etc. is profoundly false.[17]

Von Hügel's argument for accepting some historical happenings was an argument to ally her to the temporal, to the finite; so was his argument that she become more Christocentric. Underhill worried to him that she was totally theocentric. "God seems to me the centre and the only inevitable Object of adoration and all that I know at first hand."[18] Christocentric devotion seemed impossible. "I can't do it," she wrote. "Yet I really am a Christian — at least I believe so — though in the Modernist rather than strict orthodox sense."[19] To counter her tendency toward theocentrism he suggested "the less of an Individualist, the less of a judge of the worth of Christocentric devotion you become, the less also will be the danger and the starving which will accompany and follow sheer theocentrism as practiced by yourself."[20] He gently urged: "If you can't pray to Jesus, the Christ, then pray to God unincarnate with thoughts and affections as to Nazareth, the lake of Galilee or Calvary."[21] He suggested rather than "slip in" Christocentric devotion that she " 'slip away from' " one who says " 'I could not do this' " and " 'I could not do that.' "[22]

Von Hügel saw that Underhill was a divided woman: "There are two interhostile currents which exist in your mind...."[23] The "tremendous logicality of mind[,] of unbending principle which you give — ... is, I am confident, very largely the result of oscillations, the doubleness in you which I have tried to lay bare."[24] What he suggested was a "gradual interworking of both currents" that is, the mystical and philosophical and the catholic and sacramental with special emphasis on the latter. What she needed was more of "[t]he sensible, contingent, historical, incarnational current, since this current has been especially starved."[25] While her problem was an intellectual one, its remedy was devotional and emotional. On all three issues — the historical basis of Christianity, the importance of Jesus Christ, and emotional enlivenment through working with the poor — Underhill was won over within the year.

Under von Hügel's direction Underhill experienced a gradual opening to a new understanding of Christian faith. This was deepened when in early 1922 she agreed to attend a retreat at the Anglican retreat house at Pleshey[26] in the Diocese of Chelmsford. Her friend Annie Harvey, warden at Pleshey, had invited her previously; in May of 1922 she accepted the invitation and attended a retreat for elementary school teachers led by Father Henry Monks.

The Retreat House, built on an ancient religious site and surrounded by the beautiful Essex countryside, was to become a place of great importance for her.[27] The program of the place, its daily Offices and Holy Communion, its silence, created an environment which she found "unstrained" and "natural." "The whole house" she wrote "seemed soaked in love and prayer." This experience, she reported to von Hügel,

cured solitude and gave me at last really the feeling of belonging
to the Christian family and not counting except as that. I lost
there my last bit of separateness and wish for anything of my
own and gained a wholly new sense of the realness and almost
unbearable beauty of Christian life. I came away quite tranquil
and determined on entire surrender.[28]

This was Evelyn's first experience of connectedness and belonging
to a community of belief, and since it occurred within an Anglican
context it probably contributed to her acceptance of an ongoing life in
that tradition. A few months after the retreat she wrote to von Hügel:
"In fact I feel now quite satisfied as an Anglican; having discovered
a corner I can fit into, and people with whom I can sympathize and
work."[29]

The retreat also helped her progress with the historical basis of
Christianity. She could write to von Hügel at the end of 1922:

You forced me thoroughly to reconsider my own foundations
and realize that a mere philosophy of value, however sublime,
has no power to redeem unless these values have been incarnated in human life. The main historical happenings... especially the passion are absolutely necessary to Christianity... I
never doubted their occurrence but they now mean a great deal
more to me.[30]

On Christocentric devotion she reported:

I take back, with shame, every word I said against this. This
does not, however, mean a devotional *volte-face*. I am still
mainly theocentric; but the two attitudes are no longer in opposition in my mind — they are two aspects of one thing. Something
you said showed me how to bridge the gap between theism and
Christian devotion, which had worried me for years and lately
had been driving me steadily in a direction not *much* removed
from Unitarianism, as you perceived (though I did not at all like
it when you said so!). Now I have got my universe all in one
piece again.[31]

By 1923 she wrote:

The Christocentric side has become so much deeper and stronger
— it nearly predominates. I never dreamed it was like this. It

is just beginning now to dawn on me what the Sacramental Life really does involve: but it is only in flashes of a miraculous penetration I can realize this. . . . I have never known before such deep and real happiness, such a sense of at last having got *my real permanent life* and being able to love without stint where I am meant to love. It is as if one were suddenly liberated and able to expand all round. . . . All this, humanly speaking, I owe entirely to you.[32]

Irrespective of what she said here, she remained principally theocentric in her orientation, although years later she reiterated her indebtedness to von Hügel for bringing her to an appreciation of the Christocentric way. "Somehow by his prayers," she wrote,

he compelled me to experience Christ. He never said anything more about it, but I know that humanly speaking he did it. It took about four months. It was like watching the sun rising very slowly. And then suddenly one knew what it was.[33]

The guidance of von Hügel and the experience of the Pleshey retreat brought her to a deeper emotional understanding of incarnation. This is evident in her response to visiting the poor which von Hügel had suggested she undertake. This experience of two visits a week to eight poor families in North Kensington not only confronted her with the material security of her own life, but also had "a tranquilizing effect" on her. She wrote von Hügel that she had been "starving for something of the kind," and that the visiting was "a source of real happiness."[34] "I can't tell you what a sense of expansion and liberation I have got from this."[35] Being with the children meant much to Evelyn too, she admitted.

You see, when you have none of your own, it does rather freeze you up; and I am too shy and awkward to get on with educated kids. But these are such nice and friendly appealing little creatures, like tiny flowers in those grimy places; and one can enjoy them without self-consciousness or anyone knowing.[36]

Visiting the poor was an activity carried out by other women of Evelyn's station, but breaching the gap between the social classes was a unique achievement for that time. At least in one case she was able to do that. She developed a close relationship with Laura Rose, a sickly young widow, and her three children. Even Hubert got involved with the Roses by providing for their needs. Laura Rose was a woman of quite different economic background from Evelyn, yet she became a real intimate. She was interested in the spiritual life and was fond of John of the Cross.

While Underhill had gained a certain stability and balance on some issues by 1922, others were yet to be resolved. Again, the problems were both intellectual and emotional. One of the first questions Underhill brought to von Hügel was her inability to trust her experience. "The chief point is," she wrote,

> am I simply living on illusion? It seems impossible but all the same, I feel I must be sure. I don't mean by any unwillingness to make a venture or any demand for impossible clearness of faith, but simply to be *certain* my own experiences are not simply imaginary?[37]

She was preoccupied with the question of certitude. In late 1922 she claimed to have heard a voice and that afterwards she felt "called out and settled once and for all."[38] Increasingly, however, she became aware that what was important was not sense experience but something deeper. "More and more,"

> I should like to get away from sensible consolations or at least their dominance. They are entrancing and overwhelming; but they don't really lead anywhere. It's the deep, quiet, mysterious love one wants to keep and gradually transfer focus to the *will*.[39]

She went on a few days later to write that she had been through a "black bit," that she feared her invisible experience might be subjective, that she had no way to evaluate it, and that she would ask the Baron about it and accept his judgment.[40] She wrote to him of

> [a] terrible overwhelming suspicion that after all my whole "invisible experience" may only be subjective.... I may have deceived myself right through, and, always studying these things, self-suggestion would be horribly easy. These doubts are absolute torture, after what has happened [her experience of being settled]. They paralyse one's life at the roots, once they lodge in the mind.... *how* am I to know for certain this is not just some psychic mechanism? There are times when I wish I had never heard of psychology. Sometimes an even more terrifying visitation, when not *only* my own inner experience, but the whole

spiritual scheme seems cast iron and the deterministic view
the obvious one.... I have no guarantee of genuineness.... these
mental conflicts are just pure horror.[41]

Underhill always looked to experience as the test of truth; now
suspicious of its validity, she was thrown back to skepticism; but she
continued to long for certitude. Von Hügel rebuked her for this. "I
don't like this craving for absolute certainty," he wrote,

God and Christ and our need for death to self are certain. At
times you're tempted to scepticism (who is not?) so you want
direct personal experience which is beyond all reasonable doubt
but such an escape is not possible and even if it were it would
be dangerous for you. Don't build your faith on these lights.[42]

Only gradually would von Hügel's admonition to focus on what
was sure — God and Christ and the need for diminishment of self —
be absorbed by Underhill. While she understood intellectually that
this might be the way to gain certitude, she was unable to free herself
from the notion that spiritual experience was acquired through self-
effort. She reported to von Hügel that after a number of years of
"inwardness" all she had known previously was "given back" to her
without self-effort.

Now I have got back, but what seems to me so strange and
makes me nervous is that I should have expected to have to
fight my way back inch by inch. Instead of that everything has
been given back to me that I ever had, and more.[43]

She questioned von Hügel: Was such "completely undeserved
restitution" "normal" and "all right"?[44] Obviously the experience
of unearned acceptance was startling to her. Her focus on self-
achievement was connected to her sense of personal imperfection and
sinfulness. As an adolescent Evelyn already showed a great sensitivity to her imperfections; unfortunately this did not diminish with
age. Her Neoplatonic tendencies not only oriented her toward self-
preoccupation, but they provided no escape from this imperfection,
except through greater self-effort. Since she had no sense that she
was forgiven, her imperfections increasingly horrified her. After an
experience of "self-loathing" when she "felt vile through and through,
body and soul, just rubbed in the mud," she wrote to von Hügel of
what was apparently a new realization.

[I] realized that only Christianity can meet the need of coming right down to one in the dust.... Plotinus can never have had to face his own beastliness. Neo-Platonism goes to bits when one gets really to the bottom and knows oneself unmendably displeasing to God.[45]

Underhill's letters to von Hügel and her notebook entries are filled with self-recriminations. She is a "rebellious and hardened beast," "a cur," "a coward about... religion." She speaks of a "hateful and unconquerable habit of introspection," "an unescapable sense of sin and utter loneliness," "the blackest depression." She accuses herself of anger, jealousy, rigidity, hypocrisy, envy, hostility, pridefulness, hardness, and criticalness, all of which she dealt with vehemently.[46] Her horror at her own sinfulness was compounded by the fact that she saw it as "the greatest argument against genuineness [in the spiritual life]."[47]

If there was any area which perplexed and tortured her it was her "claimfulness" in friendship. While von Hügel assisted her in dealing with this, it was a problem that persisted long after his death. His diagnosis and proposed cure were instructive. He claimed that her attachments resulted in part from

the ardour of [your] natural temperament, but... largely from the too intellectual character of your religion.... [I]f you get a greater variety of homey emotions and activities into your religion, you very possibly will lose the hunger for *ardour* of human affection.[48]

He urged her not to check her affections directly or be vehement in fighting them but to turn gently to God. "In this way," he wrote, "you will practice detachment with attachment."[49]

Another problem was her attachment to her professional status. "It is a struggle to leave *all* one's professional vanity at the foot of the Cross — but unless I can do this, I may as well give up altogether."[50] Von Hügel's response to this was that this was "excessive." "For to the very end of your life," he wrote, "you will be more or less tempted to and you will fall into such faults;..."[51]

Von Hügel's diagnosis, remedy, and goal for her are all of one piece. He saw that her hunger for human affection resulted from starvation in that area and that this deprivation had to be dealt with gently and through indirection. Years before, she had told Margaret Robinson that "detachment" was "the whole secret."[52] Von Hügel reconfigured this and proposed not the goal of detachment, but "detachment *within* attachment."

It was detachment that now dominated her life, and in countering this von Hügel consistently urged, as he did succinctly in his last letter to her, that she turn "to God and Christ and the poor, and you will grow in peace and power."[53] Very slowly his advice began to restructure her life. In 1923 she wrote to him that there were still many religious practices she could not do. Self-examination and confession fanned her scrupulosity; she found instead that it was more humbling and beneficial "to keep on trying to look at Christ."[54] She wrote in her notebook of a "steady getting smaller and smaller,"[55] and of a "deep and clear sense of the all penetrating Presence of God."[56] It was not that all sense of sinfulness was removed, but that gradually it became subordinated to the desire for God. "I *am* fundamentally a beast," she wrote, "but a beast that can't get over the ceaseless thirst for God."[57] She recorded a movement away from emotional fervor to a quiet deepening of adoration and self-abandonment. "One is *so* tiny and so much nothing — that the question of one's own awful imperfections doesn't come in."[58] Finally she came to see that what was important was not her goodness, but whether she was focused on God. "I don't think God will ever make me *good*," she wrote, "[W]hat he wants is to use me as a tool, to reach others and do His work in them. But in the end, probably my sort is for the dust heap. If his purposes are advanced and one does what He calls for, one ought not really to mind this."[59]

While preoccupation with her faults would never be entirely eliminated, what emerged from this gradual focusing on God was a new consideration of vocation. "More and more I realize," she wrote in her notebook,

> the union with Christ one craves for can and must be only through union with his redemptive work always going on in the world. If I ever hesitate before this,... then I draw back from Him and break the link. So the "life of supremely happy men" is *not* "alone with the alone" — it's the redeeming life,... union with the spirit of Jesus ceaselessly at *work* in the world. Only one must have the quiet times, too, to consolidate that union and stretch-out the house of one's soul, and feed on Him.[60]

The Neoplatonic goal of "alone with the alone" was replaced with that of dedication to God's purposes. In late 1924 she wrote:

This morning in prayer suddenly I was compelled to say: take all my powers from me rather than ever let me use them again for my own advantage. When I'd said it, some strange and quite unseizable movement happened in my soul — I knew I had made a real vow, a more crucial act of dedication than ever before and shall be taken at my word.[61]

This act of dedication was accompanied by a new connected self-image. She had a "clear sense," she wrote, "of being as it were a *cell* in a boundless living web through which redeeming work can be done and so closely linked with others — ... "[62] This sense of a community of connectedness and of cooperation with God now provided the framework in which she could interpret reality and her place in it.

Under the guidance of von Hügel Underhill had come to a deeper sense of her vocation as a spiritual guide, a work she had begun as early as 1904 with Margaret Robinson. She was now giving spiritual guidance to a number of persons, including Lucy Menzies, a Presbyterian and author of religious books, who became an Anglican in 1923 and served as warden of the Retreat House at Pleshey for a decade. As with Margaret Robinson, Underhill recommended to Menzies a balanced spiritual life free of stress and strain, a fixed devotional rule, and nonreligious activity, in her case singing in the Choral Arts Society. Although she offered the same framework to Menzies as she had to Robinson, her advice now had different nuances. Most notable was Underhill's new commitment to the importance of the sacramental life. "After being myself both a nonsacramentalist and a sacramentalist," she wrote Menzies, "there is no doubt at all left in my own mind as to what is the simplest and most direct channel through which grace comes to the soul."[63] By sacramentalism she meant a corrective to "loftiness," and "pure mysticism," "the humble acceptance of grace through the medium of things — God coming into our souls by means of humblest accidents — the intermingling of spirit and sense."[64]

With Menzies and others she now also stressed the importance of participation in some kind of corporate religious life. "I don't mean by this that I admire churchiness," she wrote a young student, but a linking of the self to corporate religious life was essential.[65]

Nothing can save you from narrow intensity and "verticalness" if you reject all the corporate and institutional side — always rather repugnant to people of our temperament. I do not mean that perpetual church-going and sermons are necessary, but *some* participation in the common religious life and some sacramental practise.[66]

In all her counsel she was eminently balanced. "Hot milk and a thoroughly foolish novel are better things for you to go to bed on just now than St. Teresa.... Remember as a general rule running right through the spiritual life, that the more any particular aspect or exercise attracts you, the more ordered, regular, moderate should be your use of it."[67]

In a case where the personality was ardent, vehement, and obsessed with sin, Underhill was able to speak out of her own experience. She wrote to Menzies in 1923, "You've got to get rid of that obsession of sin, you know":

it's a crudeness, an inferior sort of humility at best — and really rooted in a disguised self-occupation! I've had it badly so I know all about it. Look at Christ and not at yourself. Regard the inclination to remorse as a temptation. There is not much to choose between the best and the worst in us, seen in the spiritual light, is there? Just let the love of God wash over the whole thing. It's the only Christian attitude.[68]

Much as the Baron had counseled her, Underhill urged Lucy Menzies to avoid holding on to consolations and preoccupation with fluctuations, and to focus on God. She gave advice which she herself would need to remember at the very end of her life. "As to God's absence," she wrote, "it is of course illusion; it is He who casts the shadow that distresses you so."[69]

In a self-revelatory letter she counseled a preoccupied Lucy Menzies:

Get out of your head the idea that the love of Christ is "withdrawn" from you and that you have "no spiritual life." You are far more truly living the spiritual life holding on through this darkness than when you were enjoying yourself in consolations. And one proof of this is that people came to you for help and you are able to deal with them. Why be vexed about that? It is extremely good for you to do it, as well as a blessed privilege. Certainly do not tell them "You have no spiritual life" or indeed unless inevitable anything at all about yourself! There's no occasion to feel hypocritical, and even when, as so often happens, those who come to us for advice are so immeasurably better than we are ourselves, keep it all on impersonal levels.[70]

She ended that letter with the reminder that "God sends such work and will help you to do it." Underhill continued to do the work of spiritual direction even when she herself was in turmoil. Many came to her, young and old, men, but especially women. She must have been aware of her unique role as a Anglican woman carrying on a work which historically had been the purview of ordained men done within the confessional. Yet for her, "care of souls" was a natural outgrowth of her life. It was a "redeeming work" that connected her to a "boundless living web."

Underhill's increasing self-dedication expressed itself not only in spiritual direction but in public activity in which as never before she shared ideas directly with others. In 1922 she gave an address to the Health Guild at Girton College, to a meeting of Girls' Club Leaders, and to the International Summer School of Social Services at Swanwick. In each case these addresses were published and reached a larger audience than those who actually heard them. In "Degrees of Prayer," her Girton address, she attempted to demythologize prayer and explain it in terms of both psychology and grace. Prayer, she said, was not willed struggle but humble surrender. From a psychological point of view it was a "widening arc of consciousness." It took a variety of forms, each of which was valid and contributed to the suppleness of the soul. While she borrowed phrases from von Hügel to describe prayer, the accessibility of her language and the clarity and immediacy of her presentation were uniquely her own.[71]

The Swanwick conference in the summer of 1922 offered her the first opportunity to speak about Christianity and the social order. This was new terrain for her. While her address, "Some Implicits of Christian Social Reform," was not her best work, it was ground-breaking. In it she claimed that Christian regeneration was not only a supernatural but a psychological fact that initiated a series of changes in the individual, enhanced efficiency, fed power, and gave life. As the supernatural and psychological or natural are linked, so must be the response to God and to others — one prays to God and helps others. The result of this was that spiritual values would replace material ones, the desire for justice would replace the desire for luxury, respect for beauty would replace respect for wealth, and love between people would replace the tyranny and hatred between races and classes.[72] The Christian, she argued, would be the mediator of God's reality to others.

In the midst of activity her writing did not abate. In 1922 she produced several reviews on religious and psychological topics for *The Weekly Westminster Gazette* and *The Daily News*. *The Life of the Spirit and the Life of Today* was published as well as "Suggestion and Religious Experience," a chapter from the book that appeared independently. This article was important because it dealt with Underhill's long-standing interest in the psychological phenomenon of suggestion which dated at least from her participation in the Golden Dawn. In the article she maintained that the unconscious operated principally through suggestion and that religion used it extensively. Since the plastic psyche could be molded either in a positive or negative way by suggestion, she urged that it could be used to encourage real holiness rather than religious sentimentality.[73]

In the summer of 1923 Underhill went to a philosophy conference in Durham and then on to the Alps with Hubert. When she returned to London she became very ill and was diagnosed as having bronchial asthma, resulting at least in part from being chronically run-down. Her convalescence in Hastings brought temporary relief, but her asthma would recur, weakening her and slowing her work. During this year she had published what would be the last of her editions of mystic texts, Walter Hilton's *The Scale of Perfection*.

The choice of Hilton is instructive. The *Scale*, like *The Cloud of Unknowing*, was a guide book addressed to a specific person.[74] It had, she claimed, more enduring influence than any other English devotional work. Its author, the fourteenth-century "God-intoxicated" Hilton, was the patron of all those who worked in obscurity to bring the life of God to others. Neither an ecstatic nor a contemplative, Hilton was above all a "devoted father of souls" who in his practical and homey guidance led one on the unbroken ladder between the natural and supernatural life. In his life Underhill found confirmed the original method for the spread of Christianity. "It oozes out — drop by drop from hearts that have been transformed in love: and is generally found, when tracked to its source, to arise from the hidden, sober life of consecration and prayer led by one devoted soul."[75] The hidden life of prayer that transformed one and allowed one to give to others became the model for her work. Hilton epitomized this vocation.

Under von Hügel's care Underhill became clearer about the general nature of her future work. But the events of 1924 gave her vocation specificity. The year began with intense activity. By February of 1924 she was well enough to go to St. Andrews to deliver two lectures which Lucy Menzies had arranged for her. Then in the spring, in response to an invitation from Dorothy Swayne, warden of the interdenominational group, Time and Talents Settlement, she lead a retreat at Pleshey for Settlement members.[76] Conducting this first retreat confirmed for her a new vocation, and recognition of her ability gradually prompted many invitations to give retreats throughout England. In 1925 this lay married woman would be invited to address the clergy conference at Liverpool, and in 1927 her competence was acknowledged by an invitation by Dean Bell of Chichester to be the first woman to lead a retreat in Canterbury Cathedral.

Retreat work was not only new for her, it was a relatively new activity within the Church of England. Encouraged by the Oxford Movement, the first retreats were given in the 1850s at both Oxford and Cowley. By 1913 the Association for Promoting Retreats was formed and in the following year a retreat house was opened; by 1932 there were fifty-five of them.[77]

Evelyn was pleased by Dorothy Swayne's invitation to conduct a retreat at Pleshey. She worked diligently to prepare the addresses and enlisted her friends to pray for her efforts.[78] She prepared the retreat during months of hectic activity while writing her book *The Mystics of the Church* and working on lectures to be given at St. Andrews and others to be given at York, Leeds, and Darlington.[79]

Even though her spiritual life was more settled now, she recorded that she felt completely lost when she started the Pleshey retreat. She gave five addresses on love, joy, peace, prayer, and the communion of saints, each of which was written out in her black leather retreat notebook. Afterwards she recorded that in retreat her manner was "dry, thin and impersonal," but that "something" carried her through it all; that it had "self-giving to it." What encouraged her was not her success, but that the experience "enlarged" and "clarified" her horizon.[80] As a result of this first experience as a retreat director she saw that the

> [o]bject of my life towards God is not, I'm now convinced, any personal achievement or ecstasy at all but just to make one able to do this kind of work, self-dedication to His purposes for others — this is destructive of self-occupation and gives a most lovely free sense.[81]

Right before Underhill left to give the retreat at Pleshey she was asked to be a speaker at the Conference on Politics, Economics and Christianity (COPEC) in April. The busyness of this time was broken by the death of Evelyn's mother, Lucy Underhill. Although she experienced sadness at her death, she felt ambivalence toward her. On the one hand, Evelyn was caring and dutiful toward her mother, spending time with her each day; on the other hand, there seemed to be no great intimacy between them. Neither Lucy Underhill nor Sir Arthur shared their daughter's religious interests. Apparently they were annoyed that her work, most of which was unpaid, deprived them of her attention.[82] Friends acknowledged that Evelyn and her mother were very different personalities, made of "different material."[83] Von Hügel alluded to this difference as well. "Your mother's going," he wrote, "the very difference of outlook between you must be adding to the trial, must indeed be giving a special discomfort to it."[84] The sadness at her mother's death was compounded by Evelyn's concern about her father and how he would manage alone. There was some discussion of the Stuart Moores' moving into No. 3 Campden Hill Place to care for him, but this never came about.[85] Evelyn's cousin Miss Corisande Thorne moved in instead.[86] Evelyn served as his hostess-companion on formal occasions, and she and Hubert continued to vacation with him on his yacht.

In addition to her lectures, retreats, writing, spiritual direction, and visiting the poor, Underhill led an active social life during these years. She attended concerts of the Kensington Music Club, the Bach Cantata, and the Oriana Madrigal Society. She and Hubert hosted regular Sunday tea parties at their home and made frequent trips to the countryside first in their motorbicycle and sidecar and later in their automobile. In summer they usually sailed on the *Wulfruna*, Sir Arthur's yacht, and some years they traveled to Italy.

In January of 1925 Underhill's beloved von Hügel died. It was a great loss. A few days after his death Underhill wrote to Lucy Menzies: "I'm trying, with my heart in my mouth, to write a bit about the side of him I knew."[87] That side was not principally the intellectual or even the pastoral, but the personal, the integrating aspect that made God accessible to her. For Underhill von Hügel was an icon, a way through to the reality she had sought for years. She could say that she owed her whole spiritual life to him, not because she was his disciple but because he reignited her love and gave her the means to steady it for the long haul. Now he was gone.

In the spring and fall of 1925 she was ill again, but she continued her work. She gave three retreats at Pleshey, a retreat for clergy at Liverpool, a lecture on the philosophy of religion at King's College, a lecture on prayer at High Leigh and the Student Christian meeting, and one on social action at the Anglo-Catholic Summer School. One of her great joys in that year was a meeting in September in

Italy with Sorella Maria, the foundress of the Spiritual Entente.[88] Since Underhill had first joined the Entente in 1920, this meeting had been eagerly anticipated; it was to have a moving impact on her.

Since the nature of her work had changed, so too had her writing. Unlike her early writing on mysticism, almost all of her work published in 1924 and 1925 was on the relationship between prayer and ordinary life. It was first presented in lecture form and subsequently published. Two lectures from this period, "The Will of the Voice" and "The Christian Basis for Social Action," were explicitly directed toward service. "The Will of the Voice," the address she was to have given at the first COPEC session in Birmingham, was read in her absence since her mother's illness prevented her from attending. In it she critiqued contemporary Christianity which she found wanting because it divorced prayer from action.[89] In the other lecture, the influence of von Hügel is evident. She argued that the "sacramental" or "catholic" understanding of reality is that all is sacred because it has been loved by God. This implied that one could not accept human conditions that made it impossible for others to lead a moral life. When the concept of God became a living, all-penetrating reality and not merely a theological principle, one was required to spend oneself in love and service. Very concretely that meant that the Christian must work against everything that checked healthy life — bad housing, prostitution, drink, tyranny, embittered class and race relations. These were all matters with which religion must deal.[90] Although she insisted that the sacramental view of reality implied effort to change the world, she also insisted that the social objective was never the adequate basis for Christian community.

In "Christian Fellowship" she examined the history of religious groups and argued that those that endured based their identity on a shared transcendent aim and not principally on a common social objective.[91] This conclusion, drawn from the history of Benedictine, Franciscan, and Quaker fellowships, was confirmed by the findings of modern psychology which proposed that organic and lasting groups were characterized by a common tradition, some sort of acknowledged authority, a shared belief or enthusiasm, and the existence of external antagonistic conditions. "Christian Fellowship" was not an attempt to prove these points through historical examination but one that stated what she already believed to be true.

She was on more secure ground when speaking about religious experience, a subject which she had thought about extensively. Her address to the conference of the Anglican Fellowship at Oxford, "The

Authority of Personal Religious Experience," dealt with the knotty problem of how to evaluate personal religious experience, that is, how to discriminate between the hysteric and the saint. The authority of the saint, she argued, was self-evident. It emerged from a super-abundance of Being and prompted certitude in others. Its validity was beyond argument. It always was linked to creative vocation and an enlivening of the dormant spiritual sense in others. This insight about the relationship between the experience of God and vocation was implicit in *Mysticism* and became dominant in her later writing about the spiritual life. Although she developed other criteria to evaluate personal religious experience, none was as convincing as the claim that it resulted in life-giving work in the world. She suggested that such experience was always nurtured by corporate experience and that while the great saints and mystics might rebel against religious formalism, they were not hostile to the great outlines of religious doctrine.

Although her 1924 lecture at St. Andrews, published as "Our Two-Fold Relation to Reality," carried the clear influence of von Hügel, it might well have begun with one of Underhill's favorite quotes from Augustine: "God is the only Reality, and we are only real in so far as we are in His order, and He in us." In it she is concerned with how one becomes more real, that is, more like God. She concluded that "only in and through a definite relation to a Real other will men ever develop a Real self."[92] It was here again that Underhill tied together the search for God and the search for self; the two were inextricably linked. She suggested that there were essentially two ways in which one became more real — through prayer and through the life of the church. These themes were considered again in two pieces she produced in 1925, a lecture on prayer, which was published subsequently in booklet form by the Y.W.C.A., and her one major book of this period, *The Mystics of the Church.*

The piece on prayer (like "Degrees of Prayer" which she had published three years earlier), was one of the earliest examples of the homey, simple, and compelling writing she would do for the rest of her life. In it she wrote that the soul, like the mind and body, needs proper food, fresh air, and exercise. Its food was reading and meditation; its air, an environment of wonder and splendor; and its exercise, prayer. Prayer she defined as above all adoration, the consequence of which was adherence, the desire to be useful to God. The central power of prayer was that it transformed the person and allowed for everything to be loved with new intensity, for pain and suffering to be dealt with, and the drudgery of life to be transformed. Prayer, she wrote, was not just saying prayers, it was an art form that represented one's whole life toward God.[93]

The publication of *The Mystics of the Church* brought to an end one phase in Underhill's life. It was her last book on the mystics and placed their contribution squarely within the history of the church. Whereas in *Mysticism* they were portrayed as largely independent of religious institutions, in this book they were seen as "life-giving" members of the church who helped create its mystical character. *The Mystics of the Church* was "the story of personal religion in relation to corporate Christian life."[94] It was a book of compensation, a collection of short biographic studies of over a hundred mystics. She had written about many of them previously, but here she treated them in a different way. Unlike *The Mystic Way*, in which she subordinated the lives of her subjects to the stages of mystic consciousness, here she focused on their individual contribution and the importance of history and national tradition in shaping them. In short, she emphasized their diversity. She treated mystics in the Bible, in the early church, and in the medieval period, and then according to national groups — English, French, German, Spanish — and added two final chapters, one on Protestant and the other on modern mystics. While her vignettes are interesting and memorable, the book, like so much of what she wrote, was born of her personal need to integrate a new idea, in this case the importance of the church in nurturing and protecting personal religious experience. The vehicle she used to achieve this integration and make sense of the personal decisions in her own life was writing. She wrote for herself and to fulfill her youthful desire to influence others. *The Mystics of the Church* brought her beloved mystics within her own new home and announced the great mystical wealth within the Christian church.

The transitional stage of Evelyn Underhill's life was over. She was fifty years old, an Anglican, and a religious writer with a new vocation, that of retreat director. Von Hügel was dead, but his great gift to her was not diminished. Through him she had gained a deeper intellectual and emotional understanding of the "catholic" mind. She had by 1925 new strength and balance, and a whole new work lay ahead. "[A] true contemplative vocation," she wrote to Lucy Menzies, "involves...the development of a spiritual force by which you exercise not only adoration, but mediatorship — a sort of redemptive and clarifying power working on other souls."[95] The events of her life prepared her now to stand as mediator between the seen and unseen, to work to bring others to a clearer vision of what an infinite life might involve.

5

"CALLED OUT AND SETTLED"

In 1925 EVELYN UNDERHILL WROTE: "Now the experience of God...
is, I believe, in the long run always a vocational experience. It always
impels to some sort of service: always awakens an energetic love. It
never leaves the self where it found it."[1] This was an autobiographical
statement and it reflected that at mid-life, after three years of work
with von Hügel, Evelyn Underhill was at a new point of departure.
She had been "called out and settled"; the next decade would be one
of new vocation.

The years 1926 through 1934 were dominated by Underhill's
single-minded effort to explain the spiritual life to her contemporaries. With few exceptions, all of her writing of this period was
first presented orally either as a lecture or a retreat.[2] Her retreats
were given chiefly to Anglicans, either to clergy or to women,[3] some
of whom continued under her "after care" as spiritual directees. To
them she was known as "Mrs. S. M." She lectured to a wider audience,
including Methodists, Baptists, and Quakers, as well as Anglicans.[4] In
all her work she cut across denominations, encouraging each person
of whatever affiliation to deepen the spiritual life, "a life in which all
that we do comes from the centre where we are anchored in God."[5]

By 1926 her lecture on Jacopone da Todi gives hints of how she
understood her new vocation. She said that Jacopone's was "not the
uncompromising work of the convinced contemplative, awe-struck,
dazzled and unable to find adequate language for that which he beheld" but the work of a mediating poet, "who takes the raw materials
provided by the great explorers of the spiritual world and makes it
accessible to other men."[6] As an artist and mediator Jacopone ap-

preciated the material presented to him, entered into it by dramatic sympathy, and described it and made it "splendid" for others.[7] His "[t]rue function," she wrote, "was not to discover but to express."[8] Like Jacopone, Underhill turned now from discovery of the mystic vision to expressing it for others. Through lecturing and the conducting of retreats she became a public explicator of Christian life as lived out by ordinary people.

In addition to all her professional activities, Underhill's domestic responsibilities continued unabated. When she was a home with Hubert, he was the center of her attention.[9] He was an easily contented man who was "quiet and happy fixing things"[10] or "messing about in a boat"[11] or "going to luncheon with old ladies."[12] The Stuart Moores' social life was a busy one which included hosting friends and colleagues. Sunday tea at their Campden Hill Square home might include the likes of E. I. Watkin, the lay Catholic philosopher; Maisie Spens, writer on spirituality; Margaret Smith, the Islamic mystical scholar; Friedrich Heiler, the German thinker who wrote on prayer; or T. S. Eliot, who during this period was editor of *The Criterion*, a periodical for which Underhill sometimes wrote.[13] There the illustrious mixed with the ordinary; students and directees were included, as well as friends of both Evelyn and Hubert.

Hubert's work as a specialist in marine law allowed him to take long vacations. He and Evelyn often took holidays together to the English countryside, and until 1930 they went sailing every year with Sir Arthur. They also traveled abroad: to Spain in 1928, to Northern France in 1929, to Norway each year from 1931 through 1935. In Spain Evelyn particularly liked Avila and Toledo; in France she visited the tomb of Saint Martin at Tours, and in Norway it was the pristine beauty, the wild flowers, and the mountains that charmed her. Sometimes a friend would accompany them. Clara Smith, Evelyn's secretary, went with them to Spain in 1928; and Lucy Menzies joined them in Norway in 1933.

It was not this busy private life, but her public life which made Underhill exceptional in her time. She must have been aware of her own uniqueness. After all, she was a married woman who moved all about England giving lectures and retreats on subjects that were the preserve of men. Most years she gave seven or eight three-day retreats; three were usually at Pleshey, and the others at Moreton, Leiston Abbey, Glastonbury, Little Compton, Water Millock, St. Leonard's, or St. Michael's Home.[14] In the autumn of 1927 she gave a retreat for fifty women in Canterbury Cathedral. In addition to retreats, she also conducted Quiet Days for theological students in

Cambridge, Lincoln, and London, gave a few radio broadcasts, and kept religious books and issues before the public as a book reviewer and religious editor for the *Spectator*.[15] Her public visibility meant that she was sometimes appointed to Anglican church commissions, often as the only woman among ecclesiastics and laymen.[16] In 1927 her own King's College formally received her as a Fellow.[17] But it was her retreat work and the writing which emanated from it — books on spiritual direction and books on the spiritual life — which were her principal contribution during this period and the basis for Michael Ramsey's claim that she did more than anyone else to keep the spiritual life alive in the Anglican church during the period between the wars.[18]

Evelyn Underhill was now a public personage; her appearance reflected the change. The somewhat out-of-fashion clothes and the little lace cap, worn presumably as a sign of detachment, were gone.[19] Lucy Menzies made her some new clothes, mostly of the blue, gray, and silver variety, and her gray hair was cut. Since many expected her to look pious, she tried to defeat that stereotype.[20] Since they expected her to be intellectual, she kept her competence and learning subordinated. Although physically fragile, she had a strength about her. She was not handsome, but her face was open and inviting; her manner was totally attentive. When with her one had the sense of being in the presence of an unusual person. While the pompous may have annoyed her, she expressed her criticism of them only in private.[21]

As a public personage Underhill worked within the confines of the Anglican church. She tried to restore peace on the controversial issue of the revision of the Prayer Book, worked with the Association for Promoting Retreats, gave papers and attended meetings of the Anglican Fellowship, served on a commission for deepening the spiritual life of clergy and laity, and lectured at the Central Council for Women's Church Work. Although her attitude was never denominational, her personal allegiance was to Anglo-Catholicism, that group within the Church of England rooted in nineteenth-century Tractarianism. It was the Tractarians, she believed, who had restored to the Church of England a sense of its Catholic connection, revived sacramental and liturgical worship, and supported a disciplined life which led to sanctity.[22] She opposed anything that weakened the influence of this tradition. At the Central Council for Women's Church Work in 1932, for example, she publicly opposed the ordination of women to the priesthood because it would weaken the link between Anglicanism and the Catholic tradition.[23] She wanted expansion of opportunities for women, but believed these must emerge from love of God and service to others; at least in part, she was suspicious of the motivations of those who sought the ordination of women.

While her new work was intimately tied up with her affiliation with the Anglican church, some people continued to urge her to join the Roman Catholic church. She insisted that Anglicanism was "a respectable suburb of the city of God — but all the same, part of "greater London."[24] Her own position was clear:

> [T]he *whole* point to me is in the fact that our Lord has put me *here*, keeps on giving me more and more jobs to do for souls here, and has never given me orders to move. In fact, when I have been inclined to think of this, something has always stopped me: and if I did it, it would be purely an act of spiritual self-interest and self-will.[25]

What was clear to her now was that the important question was not about denominational affiliation but vocation. Extending her city versus suburb metaphor, she wrote, "[a]fter all He has lots of terribly hungry sheep in Wimbledon and if it is my job to try and help with them a bit it is no use saying I should rather fancy a flat in Mayfair."[26] While attracted to the Roman church with its great spiritual treasures, she nonetheless believed that the question was not what attracts "but 'Where can I serve God best?' and usually the answer to that is, 'Where He has put me.' "

> It is obvious that people who can pray and help others too are desperately needed in the Church of England. And to leave that job because the devotional atmosphere of Rome is attractive, is simply to abandon the trenches to go back to Barracks. If all the Tractarians had imitated Newman's spiritual selfishness English religion to-day ... would be as dead as mutton! There is a great deal still to be done and a great deal to put up with, and the diet is often one not good, but we are here to feed His sheep where we find them, not to look for comfy quarters![27]

The vocational issue was central to her remaining in the Anglican church; she was not there by default. She admired certain aspects of Roman Catholicism, but she believed that Anglicanism reflected the English mind[28] and that it was her duty to make it Catholic. "I feel a great call to help on the renewal of sane Catholicism in England and am sure it is a work of God."[29]

As she grew more deeply convinced of her place in the Anglican church, she began to find sources of support there. She made her own retreats at Anglican retreat houses, especially at Moreton, and she contacted persons within the Anglican communion who could give her counsel.

The death of her beloved director von Hügel in January 1925 left her without direction. During this time she began to write *Man and the Supernatural,* an attempt to summarize what she had learned from him.[30] It was her most philosophical book and not at all typical of her writing during this period. Writing it must have been a way of closing one part of her life. She dedicated it to von Hügel and said that when writing: "I felt almost as if he were leaning over my shoulder."[31]

Man and the Supernatural is about the fundamentals of religion and offers an explanation of how human life is transformed by spiritual reality. The point of departure is the persistent fact of the human attempt to appropriate supernatural reality. Religion, as well as the mystics, "those who insist that they know for certain the presence and activity of that which they call the Love of God,"[32] witnesses to this fact. The book is a discussion of the four ways through which men and women experience supernatural reality: in history and the great acts of humanity; in human personality through incarnation, that is, in Jesus Christ; in sacrament and symbols that serve as bridges to the unseen; and finally in prayer, which transforms and sanctifies human life.

What *Man and the Supernatural* makes abundantly clear is how thoroughly Underhill avoided discussion of Christology. Under von Hügel's influence she managed to curb her one-sided theocentrism, but no matter what she said, she never did become Christocentric. As late as 1932 she wrote "I came to Christ through God, whereas quite obviously lots of people came to God through Christ. But I can't show them how to do that — all I know about is the reverse route."[33] If "left to myself," she wrote, I "would just go off on God alone."[34] Although in this book she moved closer to orthodoxy than she had been in *The Mystic Way,* her portrayal of Jesus is not as the atoner but as the most important means of revelation of supernatural reality, a revelation which continues in time.[35]

At about the same time as the publication of this book she made her clearest statement of the uniqueness of Christianity as a world religion. In *Essays Catholic and Missionary* she claims that Christianity, relative to other theistic religions, is distinct in kind and superior in effect."[36] Its richer, deeper, and more inclusive concept of God and its more adequate life-giving means of communion with him are both linked to the incarnation, which insured not mere access to the Numinous but the ability to bring the Numinous into relationship with human life. An incarnate God is both infinite and personal, transcendent and immanent, Wholly Other yet in history and in each soul. Unlike other forms of theism, Christianity's goal is not the attainment of an individual mystical experience, but the perfection of charity lived out in life. At its heart is not ritual obligation or creedal statement, but a life transformed by love. Both this essay on Christianity and *Man and the Supernatural* illustrate her understanding of Christianity, one born of her long association with the mystics.

Von Hügel's philosophical ideas appropriated by her and expressed in *Man and the Supernatural*, provided the intellectual framework for all her subsequent writing. With von Hügel's death she was now without personal spiritual counsel. At this point, help would come from within the Anglican church. Walter Frere, Bishop of Truro, became her spiritual director in mid-1926.[37]

Frere had been an Anglican bishop since 1923, but his ecclesiastical position belied his monkish nature. Underhill referred to him as "My Bishop," but it was his simplicity and humility which attracted her. He was, she said, a man with an "intense feeling for perfection," a "great aesthetic sensitivity" and a "hidden personal austerity." Although devout and intellectual like von Hügel, Frere never would have defined religion as "a metaphysical thirst," as the Baron had.[38]

Frere "lived in the presence of God" and his "love of beauty order and tradition" and his "profound incarnationalism" were expressed in his sensitivity toward worship and the Russian Orthodox tradition. These interests must have nurtured Underhill's own growing appreciation for these subjects. As early as 1929 she gave a lecture on worship which contained the seeds of the book on that topic that she would write seven years later.[39] Frere's interest in Russian Orthodoxy also ignited her latent attraction for the Orthodox tradition, which she had first encountered in its Greek expression in 1910 on her trip to Rome.[40] The genius of Orthodoxy, as she wrote in 1926, was its unique ability to see the inward in the outward, the world of sense and spirit woven together. Its spirituality, much like that of the Franciscans, linked a "profound supernaturalism" to a "lovely naturalism."[41] This interest in Orthodoxy continued until her death. She joined the Fellowship of St. Alban and St. Sergius in early 1935[42] and wrote eloquently on the Orthodox liturgical expression in *Worship*. In this her last major work she acknowledged the help of her "dear and kind friend" Walter Frere. Implicitly she acknowledged his nurture of her interest in Russian Orthodoxy as well.[43]

Frere continued to direct Underhill for six years. Sometimes she would visit him in Cornwall, and he would stop at Campden Hill Square when he was in London. Frere was a theoretician and practitioner of the contemplative life, and his letters to Evelyn reflect his great simplicity and trust. But he was not a prompt respondent and his letters were brief and the advice tentative. Evelyn's preference was for strong guidance from a director, and Frere's was not substantial enough for her. Still in emotional turmoil, she needed a different kind of help.

Von Hügel had made it clear to Underhill that while under his care she should not take advice from other directors.[44] Apparently Frere did not impose a similar restriction. In 1929 on a pilgrimage to the grave of von Hügel at Downside, near Bath, she met Dom John Chapman, convert to Roman Catholicism, abbot of the Benedictine Abbey, and the person she later said knew more about prayer than anyone she had ever met.[45] He became for her "My Abbot," a "contemplative saint" who carried on the tradition of the great spiritual teachers of the past.[46] Although their contact was intermittent and lasted only a few years, Chapman gave her a solace and assurance that Frere was unable to give. When he wrote to her: "We are in God's hands, so there is nothing to be afraid of,"[47] it was possible for her to believe him.[48]

Chapman, the Roman Catholic abbot, supplemented the advice of Frere, the Anglican bishop; but in 1932, thanks to her friend Margaret Cropper, Underhill met Reginald Somerset Ward, a remarkable Anglican "soul specialist" who would serve as her principal director and confessor until her death.[49] Ward, in his own unique way, was finally a replacement for von Hügel. In point of view and method of direction, she found him much like the Baron.[50] At last she had found someone who was "fatherly" and with whom "[o]ne felt absolutely in the presence of a specialist working for the Love of God and brimming over with common sense."[51] It is curious that Underhill never sought out women directors. While Ethel Barker, Sorella Maria, Laura Rose, and later Sister Mary of St. John were all revered by her, she did seem to want a firm "fatherly" mentor, one who was both intelligent and saintly.

Ward was both extraordinarily competent as a spiritual director and impressive as a person. A married Anglican priest with children, he gave up the security of a pastorate to become a full-time spiritual director who traveled throughout England to various centers to meet and hear the confessions of some two hundred directees who were sustained after his visits through letters. Underhill joined in with others visiting him in Oxford, London, and at his home in the south of England.[52] A pacifist, Ward must have influenced Underhill in this regard, although her later pacifism was not explicable merely in terms of his influence.

It was within the context of Anglicanism and with the help of Anglican directors that Underhill was sustained in her demanding work and helped to confront the inner turmoil which afflicted her for years. Her external serenity, obvious in her person and her writing, was not matched in her inner life. This disparity can only be understood in terms of the vision she knew and explicated for others and her preoccupation with her own infidelity to that vision. Her earlier concerns with doubt and her fears of self-deception and suggestion had now abated. What remained, however, was a fixation on her own faults which blocked her growth. The result was "psychic storms," "vehemence," "depression." She was "incurably self-occupied"[53] and, one must add, relentlessly unforgiving of herself. Her desire to be "indifferent" and "detached" led her to want to "punish" herself for her failure, to "crush" and "mortify" her worst passions, which she lists as "impatience, pride, self-will, uncharitableness, egotism and claimfulness."[54]

It was her domestic and social life that were most problematic. She should be gentler with the servants, more gracious with an elderly aunt, more genial and companionable to Hubert, more grateful to friends, more understanding of her father.[55] By 1928 she wrote that she was "self-occupied, claimful and irritable";[56] and a year later she castigated herself for her tremendous dislike of the psychic dependence of Lucy Menzies and for her own excessive longing for the total affection of Clara Smith, whom she claims she could not give up.[57] She characterized herself as "a spoilt child" who now needed to "grasp the cross."[58] Her need to deal with her possessiveness and desire for the affection of another was particularly difficult.

Although she was under the care of Frere she sought out the advice of Father Edward Talbot and Bede Frost, O.S.B., on this matter as well. Talbot suggested she put the past behind her and accept the suffering, offering all to God; and Frost urged her to see her turmoil as a means of purification from her excessive affection toward creatures.[59] This advice played into her deepest emotional weakness, her lingering Neoplatonic desire for detachment that had been overcome as an intellectual position but not as an emotional one.

Whatever her emotional needs, it is clear that she had no sense, other than through self-recrimination and punishment, of how to extricate herself from the psychic turmoil. The period of greatest "spiritual blackness" occurred in the summer of 1929[60] and seems to have focused on what she called her claimfulness and possessiveness of others. There was some problem with her relationship with Clara Smith, whom she had known for some time, beginning even before 1921.[61] Clara was the sister of Margaret Smith, professor of Girton College and scholar of Islamic mysticism. In 1916 Clara published a novel with Theodora Bosanquet and later in the 1930s served as assistant to Bosanquet at *Time and Tide*. She was not a particularly outgoing personality, but "mousey" and somewhat intimidated intellectually by those around her.[62] For many years she worked as Evelyn's personal secretary.

Clara was devoted to Evelyn and deeply religious. She attended almost all of Underhill's retreats at Pleshey where she was listed as "wayfarer" or assistant helper."[63] After 1929, however, she abruptly stopped attending retreats at Pleshey. This occurred at the same time that Evelyn records her fears of losing the affection of Clara, something she finds unbearable.[64] This fear might well be connected to the fact that at some point, presumably at about this time, Clara became a Roman Catholic.[65] As such she could no longer attend retreats or receive the spiritual direction of an Anglican. Lucy Menzies, who may well have seen Clara as a rival for Evelyn's affection, claimed that after this conversion Clara and Evelyn became less intimate.[66] In her notebook Evelyn documents what she claims is Clara's coolness and indifference.[67] Whatever the failure of friendship between them, it would take a number of years to be resolved. As late as 1933, Evelyn discussed with Ward this preoccupation with possessiveness.[68] Their difficulties did not result in a loss of friendship, however. Clara was very much in evidence in Evelyn's life right up through her death. It was Clara who worked to prepare one of Evelyn's last manuscripts for publication; it was Clara who was awarded a large sum of money in Evelyn's will; it was Clara who wrote Evelyn's obituary for *Time and Tide*. Evelyn believed in loyalty; whatever the problem between her and Clara, they remained friends.

Some relief from her depression of 1929 came during the winter of 1930 when she experienced a bout of physical illness and then a new sense of peace. It was not that her faults had diminished, but rather she had "experienced the power and help of God as never before in delivering me from psychic and emotional storms, giving me strength when ill and giving me interior knowledge of when I must accept helplessness."[69] By 1930 she saw that her cure needed to be based on an active confidence in God and a continuing effort to "reduce self-love and increase charity."[70] But the problem persisted. In 1933 she recorded "intolerant judgment and secret explosions of suppressed fury" and "a horrible streak of hardness and bitterness" in addition to irritation and resentfulness, acquisitiveness for comfort and money, and claimfulness and the desire to possess the affection of others.[71] It was Ward, with his deep understanding of human psychology and his single-minded commitment to bringing persons to God, who would help her.

Ward's approach to Underhill can be reconstructed based on his general principles of spiritual direction laid out in his anonymous *Guide for Spiritual Directors*[72] and the specific advice from him recorded by Underhill. In his attempt to "diagnose" and "cure" the maladies of the soul, Ward pointed to fear in its various forms as the principal culprit in blocking a closer contact with God. Fear, be it of blame, of guilt, of sickness, of sex, of insecurity, of inability to reach a standard, weakened love and trust in God and was the source of many temptations that led to sin. Fear, usually rooted in one's early life, was generally repressed during youth and adolescence and emerged again as one matured. As he saw it, the goal of the spiritual director was to help a person discover the fear which dominated in his or her life. Ward must have used this diagnostic approach with Underhill, attempting to help her uncover the source of her turmoil and hence free her for growth. In her case, his diagnosis probably included the disease of scruples, a malady characterized by a fixation on personal defects and an inordinate stress on the negative. Scrupulosity was a form of "spiritual hypochondria," a self-centered state which stifled prayer and interfered with the experience of God's love. Ward believed that scrupulosity sometimes had its origins in too great a "severity in a sensitive childhood." Its treatment was in the diminishing of "the inflamed conscience" by stressing God's love.[73]

What Evelyn Underhill shared with Ward of her early life is unknown. Among those who knew her it was commonly acknowledged that she did not speak about her childhood.[74] She was lonely in her youth, and her father did not take much interest in her until she was older.[75] The few documents from her adolescence show her as an intense and intelligent young woman, preoccupied already with her faults and inadequacies. This preoccupation with her limitations does not emerge again until later in her life. What dominates in her twenties and thirties is a desire for intimacy that she found neither with her parents nor with Hubert. In the mystic's relationship with God, however, she saw both intimacy and freedom from self; this became the paradigmatic relationship not only for herself but for all humanity. She spent the first part of her adult life explicating and describing that relationship. What characterizes her last years is her growing recognition of her personal failure to internalize that intimate relationship in her own life. Her final obstacle to freedom was her self-preoccupation.

Ward helped her deal with self-preoccupation and its consequences. In his advice to her he urged gentleness toward self and others as the best way of driving out hardness and lack of charity. She was to cultivate a gentle spirit and to put that gentleness into action. Such gentleness would defeat pride as well as irritability and anger. Additionally, she must rid herself of a "depressed attitude" toward her nature in general and focus on God's grace and love. Only within that context of God's love should she "make war" on specific sinful dispositions, especially her possessiveness of persons. He warned her to discriminate between temptation and her consent to temptation, the actual willing of evil. It was only the latter which should concern her. She recorded his diagnosis in her own words.

> Root trouble is intense possessiveness deeply and suddenly injured and unable to adapt itself. The result is the formation of a severe neurosis having a deep scar right across the soul. Condition is aggravated by chronic overstrain but the Godward life is still active and still strongest treatment; avoid touching or rousing the wound still too tender to bear it. Leave that, accepting the fact that the bouts of suffering do arise from the above cause.[76]

Ward diagnosed her as having a "delicately balanced psychophysical nature,"[77] one which needed moderation, variety, and the avoidance of self-preoccupation, a remedy similar to the one recommended by von Hügel. Under Ward's regime of gentleness and balance the vehemence and harshness of the previous years began to abate. In mid-1934 she wrote: "My way should be that of dependence and abandonment. No more struggle to be what I think I'd like to be but a total yielding of myself to God. Not standing about on the brink saying I'm not good enough, but a plunge into the sea without retour sur soi-meme."[78]

During the period 1926 through 1934 her inner turmoil was not directly evident in her work and writing. Although she berated herself for her faults, she somehow knew that her work was useful. In the summer of 1929, in the midst of what was the worst of her depression, she wrote: "And as to advising people, if it is put into one's hands, one just has to do it in simple trust that if one keeps as quiet as possible, God will do it through one and that one's own insufficiency does not matter much."[79] The same theme of trust in the midst of uproar and turmoil is taken up again a few years later.

Yes! I think too it is possible to be used as a channel without feeling peace, indeed, while often feeling on the surface in a tornado! Nevertheless, the essential ground of the soul *is* held in tranqillity, even through the uproar and every now and then the soul perceives this. The real equation is not Peace = satisfied feeling, but Peace = willed abandonment.[80]

In giving spiritual direction to others, she continued to focus on the needs of those who came to her. Her advice to her spiritual directees during this period deals with the usual questions of prayer and the merits and limitations of institutional religion and theological systems. In all of this she spoke in homey, accessible language. Of institutional religion she wrote: "The Church is an 'essential service' like the Post Office, but there will always be some narrow, irritating and inadequate officials behind the counter and you will always be tempted to exasperation by them."[81] As regards theology, her preference was for von Hügel. Of the current interest in Karl Barth she said:

Barth is rather like a bottle of champagne...too intoxicating to be taken neat but excellent with a few dry biscuits! He is not "the only real religion" [but]...a neglected and splendid *part* of the whole rich complex of religion. Consider what Barthian religion *alone* would have to give to the poor, the miserable, the lonely, the childlike, and all in fact to whom Christianity is specially addressed. You must have the gentle and penetrating intimacy to balance the over-againstness surely, to get the total need and experience of the soul expressed?...Barth and Eckhart are interesting, stimulating excessives — too exclusively transcendent and abstract, carrying the revolt from naturalism too far. But splendid if kept in their place.[82]

On possessive friendship, a problem she herself would deal with, she wrote to one directee:

But the fact remains that a competing emotional interest though technically "innocent" can't be kept in one's life once one has given oneself to God. This very friendship may, later, return to you in the tranquil and purified form in which all one's human loves can be woven into the substance of the spiritual life. But as things are now I am sure you are right in feeling that a clean cut is the only way. The fruit of all you experienced at Pleshey really hangs on your willingness to make the first definite sacrifice asked: and that you *have* made it, is the best guarantee for your future steadiness.[83]

What is important here is the remedy Evelyn recommends — a "clean cut." This is not an unusual response for one who admitted that she had been "a white-hot Neoplatonist"[84] and one who had believed that the secret of perfection lay in "detachment."[85] By 1927, however, she is aware that "detachment" is not an end in itself. She wrote consoling this same directee: "As Huvelin said: 'We are detached in order to be attached to something better, not to fall into a hole!' "[86] Although she intellectually knew the perils of "detachment," she continued to revert to it.[87] In spite of her conflicting views on this subject and her ongoing preoccupation with her own faults, she was able to continue on "in simple trust" with her work of spiritual direction.

As her inner turmoil did not negatively influence her work as a spiritual director, neither did it diminish her writing. During this nine-year period Underhill wrote six books, twenty-six articles, and more than one hundred seventy reviews for the *Spectator*[88] of works on prayer, philosophy, psychology, the church, poetry, the mystics and saints, and of books written by friends.

Her book reviews are especially revealing of her preference for spirituality over theology. Her most ancient source of inspiration remained Augustine, but during these years her early preference for Ruysbroeck seems to have diminished[89] and was replaced by the Italian Franciscans, beginning with Saint Francis of Assisi. The English mystics had an obvious historical value for her, and the French writers — de Sales, Huvelin, de Caussade, Tourville, and Poulain — were influential in her thinking on the spiritual life. But Angela de Foligno, Jacopone da Todi, and her own contemporary Sorella Maria held a special place. All of them were imbued with the spirit of Saint Francis, the artist and mystic saint, who was set off from others by his "metaphysical craving for God." She saw in Francis as she did in the Orthodox tradition a sense of the sacred in the natural world and a love and delight in the senses. Francis's "creaturely simplicity" and "awe-struck sense of God" were also the same characteristics that she found so dominant in her beloved von Hügel.[90] But, "[t]he real greatness of St. Francis," she wrote,

> is the same as the greatness of the Christian religion, when fully understood. For it is one thing to be a believer in Christianity, or even a courageous practitioner of its hard demands, another thing to be sensitized to all its mysterious implications: and it is just these mysterious implications which the poetic intuition and intrepid love of Francis seized and expressed in terms of human life.[91]

Her most immediate example of Franciscan spirituality was Sorella Maria, "[m]y darling Italian Saint,"[92] whom she commemorated in an article in the *Spectator*, "Franciscan Hermitage."[93] It was in Italy again that Evelyn found compensation and balance for her own spiritual life which always tended to veer off toward the abstract, "to God alone." In Maria's small family of women living the Primitive Rule in the Umbrian countryside Underhill found a simplicity, hospitality, and powerful spirituality. There is no doubt that in their "awestruck" and "surrendered" lives she saw a vital link to Saint Francis.[94]

While the great bulk of Underhill's writing — reviews, articles, and books — focused on the spiritual life, she occasionally wrote on some aspect of mysticism. She did introductions to E. M. Salter's translation of Nicholas of Cusa's *Vision of God* and Lucy Menzies' translation of François Malaval's *A Simple Method of Raising the Soul to Contemplation*, wrote essays on Richard the Hermit, Jacopone da Todi, Walter Hilton, and Saint Francis, and published a long article on medieval mysticism that appeared in the *Cambridge Medieval History*. But her most important effort was her revision of *Mysticism* for its twelfth edition. Through deletion of certain sources, additions of others, and deft change of language, she brought this book into line with recent scholarship and with Christian orthodoxy.[95] In the new preface she acknowledged recent developments in philosophy, theology, historical studies, and psychology, all of which contributed to a better understanding of the phenomenon of mysticism. She specifically mentioned the work of John Chapman, Cuthbert Butler, Karl Barth, Rudolph Otto, the Neo-Thomists, and, of course, Baron von Hügel, who she said did more than anyone else to recover the concept of the supernatural.[96] The influence of von Hügel is evident not only in her new emphasis on the supernatural and its implications for an "inclusive" and incarnational mysticism, but in her stress on grace and the importance of God as the first cause of mystic experience. While she did tinker with the edition and state where changes might be made, she did not rewrite it. *Mysticism*, with all its limitations, still expressed her most basic insights.

By 1930 she also had other interests. At this point in her life she was dedicated to showing her contemporaries how they too might lead lives of contemplation. Prayer, holiness, love, vocation, purification, the spiritual life, become the themes she explored. It was in the retreat format that she was most successful, winning over a small group of less than twenty people.[97] Many of her retreatants came back year after year and became her personal friends and ardent followers. Regular attendees at Pleshey included Agatha Norman, a theological student; Olive Wyon, writer and advocate of world peace; Marjorie Vernon, translator; René Haymes, writer; Daphne Martin-Hurst, medical social worker and subsequently an Anglican nun; Margaret Cropper, dramatist; Dorothy Swayne, leader of Time and Talents Settlement; Lucy Menzies, writer and warden of Pleshey; Margaret Smith, Islamic scholar and teacher at Girton; Maude Hance, Evelyn's maid; Laura Rose; and Clara Smith.[98]

For Underhill, the retreat was "a spot of rebirth" in which one steeped oneself in silence in the mystery of God. "*Shut* the door," she urged retreatants.

> It is an extraordinarily difficult thing to do. . . . It is no use at all to enter . . . that inner sanctuary, clutching the daily paper, . . . your engagement book and a large bundle of personal correspondence. All these must be left outside. The motto for your retreat is GOD ONLY.[99]

Unlike the Ignatian retreat, which she thought demanding and bracing, she envisioned the retreat as a dedicated time, but one which was a part of the normal spiritual routine. Its purpose was the same as all Christian life, to promote and sustain holiness.[100] Underhill's zest, humor, and caring brought a lightness to the retreat which otherwise might have been a long-faced affair.

At Pleshey the retreat house itself fostered solitude. Nestled at the edge of a village of thatched cottages, it shared common ground with an eighteenth-century stone church. Further along were fields on both sides of the narrow road. In the house, Evelyn went to great lengths to create an environment of tranquillity for participants. She named each bedroom and made room assignments herself. She posted Scripture quotes and pictures, chose the hymns for Lucy to play during worship services, served as sacristan, and enlisted her friends to pray for the retreatants.[101] The daily schedule followed a standard pattern including meals, Holy Communion, Evensong, Compline, usually three addresses, and free time during which individuals might talk with the conductor. Retreats offered Underhill the chance to lead corporate worship, give spiritual direction, and present addresses. For each retreat she would usually prepare five to seven addresses on one topic organized around some image or metaphor that would be sustained throughout. This unified set of addresses was then repeated on several different occasions and at several different locations throughout the year. These addresses were subsequently published in book form and the books were dedicated to friends or retreat participants.[102]

In one sense all of Underhill's retreats focus on the spiritual life, although each pursues it from a different angle. Prayer and vocation, purification and holiness, love and the church, all intertwine, producing an interlocking web of ideas. The retreats used metaphor, analogy, and visual imagery and were discursive and descriptive, not analytical. *The Golden Sequence,* "a personal little book" contains her most basic premise about the spiritual life, namely, that there is a personal holy presence and energy in which all things live and have their being; it prompts in those who recognize it not only acknowledgment but adoration.[103] This holy presence has its most profound revelation in Jesus, is witnessed to by the lives of the saints, and is available to each person. Participation in the holy presence is the spiritual life. It is not separate from life itself but is a particular way of apprehending it. The spiritual life is the "commerce" between a person and the holy presence — God — an exchange which can suffuse and take over all of life, radically transforming it as it gains control.

Because Underhill premises an all-penetrating holy presence, she can claim that to be fully human is to be oriented to both the world of sense and the world of that presence, the spirit, to live in two directions, not in one, to be part of both the finite and the infinite order.[104] It is in the realm between the natural and supernatural that all great human saints live; there human personality takes up the characteristics of the realms beyond; there religion operates to nurture the incipient supernatural life which is in each person.

For Underhill the function of religion was to nurture the spiritual life and to bring the natural into relationship with the supernatural. It often failed to do this, however, and for that failure she called religion to task:

A shallow religiousness, the tendency to be content with a bright, ethical piety wrongly called practical Christianity, a nice brightly varnished this-worldly faith, seems to me to be one of the ruling defects of institutional religion at the present time. We are drifting toward a religion which consciously or unconsciously keeps its eye on humanity rather than on Deity, which lays all the stress on service, and hardly any of the stress on awe and that is the type of religion, which in practice does not wear well.... It does not lead to sanctity: and sanctity after all is the religious goal.[105]

If the purpose of religion is to foster sanctity or holiness, how is this achieved? Prayer, she says, does this work of transformation. It is not an action or a duty, or even an experience, but a vital relationship between the whole individual and the being of God.[106] Initiated by God, it is nonetheless a mutual act, dependent both on grace and the will of the individual.[107] More than a specific act, prayer is a state, a condition of soul at the heart of which is not intercession but adoration, the "awe-struck" love which brings with it a sense of humility and gratitude,[108] a communion with God, and a self-offering.[109] In short, prayer is the organic life, having adoration as its root, communion as its flower, and loving action as its fruit.[110]

The goal of prayer is to ignite that which is already present, a "latent capacity for God."[111] Once ignited, the individual becomes a "live wire," a "link between God's Grace and the world that needed healing," a "distributing center" for God's creative power. A person of prayer is one who has "a more wide-spreading, energetic, self-giving and redeeming type of love,"[112] one who senses that "he is a child of God, who is and knows himself to be in the deeps of his soul attached to God."[113]

Attachment to God, the result of prayer, is the clearest mark of the spiritual life, a "life in which God and His eternal order have more and more their individual sway; which is wholly turned to Him, devoted to Him, dependent on Him, and which at its term and commonly at the price of a long and costly struggle, makes the human creature a pure capacity for God."[114]

Conceived in another way, the spiritual life is principally the life of holiness. This theme is woven throughout all of Underhill's retreats but figures importantly in *Concerning the Inner Life*, her 1926 retreat for Anglican clergy from the Liverpool Diocese, and in *The School of Charity*, her 1933 retreat address which was published a year later. As the mystic life was available to "normal people," the life of holiness could be participated in by them as well. "The difference between [the saints] and us," Underhill wrote, "is a difference in degree, not in kind."[115] "A saint is simply a human being whose soul has thus grown up to its full stature, by full and generous response to its environment, God."[116] The saints "are the great experimental Christians who have made the great discoveries about God."[117] They "do not represent a special triumph of human evolution...[but] the capture and transformation of the creature by an otherworldly love and energy, which becomes absolute in its demands on life."[118] Although sanctity takes many forms, all saints are characterized by a complete abandonment to God; it is this which marks them off from others.[119] "Sanctity...is childhood in God"[120] which impels deep immersion in the world. The saints

> do not stand aside wrapped in delightful prayers and feeling pure and agreeable to God. They go right down into the mess; and there, right down in the mess, they are able to radiate God because they possess Him. And that, above all else, is...that priestly work that wins and heals souls.[121]

Like the mystics, the saints' work in the world is to create. "The final test of holiness is not seeming very different from other people, but being used to make other people very different; becoming the parent of new life."[122]

Holiness results from prayer and from the redirection of personal energy, the process Underhill called mortification or purification. "[T]he very essence of the spiritual life is gathered and presented in a point":

> first the Vision of the Perfect, and the sense of imperfection and unworthiness over against the Perfect, and then because of the Vision, and in spite of the imperfection, action in the interests of the Perfect — co-operation with God.[123]

The "Vision of the Perfect" makes saints but not before it prompts a "sense of imperfection and unworthiness." In fact prayer, holiness, and purification all proceed together. Prayer attends to God and mortification concentrates on bending the individual will toward God, filling one with God and in the process making a saint.[124] Yet for Underhill, emphasis on mortification is always subordinate to the responses of awe and adoration. This subordination is one of her most important legacies.

Only in her retreats of 1931 and 1932, both years of personal struggle, does the theme of mortification emerge with any prominence. *The Mount of Purification* was based on Dante's *Purgatorio* and is a discussion of the "cleansing of the soul." Although given in 1931, it was not published until after her death. Unpolished and unrevised, it nonetheless provides a rich and immediate description of the process of purification.

In it, sin is defined principally as a negation. "What is called a sense of sin," she writes "only has meaning because of the beauty and splendour and glory of Holiness."[125] Sin is a lack, an absence of what could be. It is "the self-regarding, irresponsible use of instinct which cripples the will, the real driving force of the soul, which is always, when pure, tending to move toward God — the supreme attraction, the supreme life."[126] Sin is a blockage against the action of God. Although various in its forms, it expresses itself in three ways: in energy set toward the self, for example in pride and avarice; in loving too much, as in lust and gluttony; and in loving too little as in sloth and envy. As for treatment of these sins, Underhill, concurring with the "old moralists," argues that they can only be eliminated by developing an opposite quality. Humility drives out pride; tranquillity eliminates anger; charity overcomes envy, and generosity defeats avarice. Her emphasis is not on "crushing" but on reorienting energy. "We are asked not to kill but to transform, reorder, discipline our ardour of life and love."[127] These words, written precisely at the time she was attempting to reorder her own love, carried this warning:

> But the passion of personal love and desire must not be killed or we cease to be human. It has got to be transmuted into its immanent energies, cleansed of the poison of claimfulness and taught the difficult paradox of detachment in attachment. The purity of heart which God asks is not the chilly safety of something that is killed in the refrigerator; but the serene and ardent love of Christ and His saints.[128]

The "white-hot Neoplatonist" had gradually become the incarnationalist. "It is not a harsh dualism," she wrote, "but a profound incarnationalism which requires us to set in order our physical and emotional life and subordinate all vagrant longings to the single passion of God."[129]

Although slow to learn this in her own life, her teaching and writing give God's love much more prominence than the need for mortification. In her retreat *Abba* (given in 1934), she wrote that it is God's Charity which compels self-knowledge, braces the will, mortifies desire, heals, redeems, transforms, and purifies.[130] God who is love compels all, but in the compelling the individual assents and is transformed to love. As prayer is the way to God, so love is what is sought and what is given; having been loved and transformed by God's love, one can "stand alongside the generous Creative Love, maker of all things visible and invisible (including those we do not like) and see them with the eyes of the Artist-Lover."[131]

Cooperation with God meant work for God's purpose, or vocation. In fact, vocation is one of the themes implicit in much of her teaching. She specifically addressed herself to the vocation of religious workers and teachers. The vocation of the religious worker, ordained or lay, was important because through it many were either attracted to or repelled by the spiritual life. This vocation, however, placed great demands on one's spiritual energy and sympathy. For these reasons religious workers must give special attention to prayer which would both rejuvenate their sense of wonder and awe and steady them against great demands.[132] Likewise teachers needed rich inner lives to sustain both their vision and their ability to see the unique value of each of their students.[133] Whatever one's particular vocation, prayer linked one to another reality, sustained one, and gave new and more expansive meaning to work.

Although persons of prayer were impelled outward in service to the world, their work was not so much to improve the world or even the church as it was to witness to God's love. "What we look for then," she wrote in *Abba*,

> is not Utopia, but something which is given from beyond: ... this means something far more drastic than the triumph of international justice and good social conditions. It means the transfiguration of the natural order by the supernatural: by the Eternal Charity. Though we achieve social justice, liberty, peace itself, though we give our bodies to be burned for the admirable causes, if we lack this we are nothing. For the Kingdom is the Holy not the moral; the beautiful not the correct; the perfect not the adequate; Charity not law.[134]

The real miracle was not social change, but personal transformation:

> Yet the coming of the Kingdom does not necessarily mean the triumph of this visible Church; nor ... the Christian social or-

der.... It means the re-ordering, the quieting, the perfecting of our turbulent interior life, the conquest of our rampant individualism by God's supernatural action.[135]

It was this commitment to personal transformation that dominated Underhill's approach and explains her reluctance to be associated with specific political or religious causes. She wrote to Father Conrad Noel in 1933:

You see I do feel that my particular call, such as it is, concerns the interior problems of individuals of all sorts and all opinions: and therefore any deliberate labelling of myself, beyond the general label of the Church, reduces the area within which I can operate and my help is likely to be accepted: but telling *you* what I think is quite another matter![136]

She went on to explain what she saw as the saints' relationship with the world, one that she tried to emulate:

The deep love and sympathy with mankind, and often with all life, which one finds in them seems to be the direct result of their sense of union with the Divine Charity. They aim at that first, and thence flow out, as Ruysbroeck said, in a "wide-spreading love to all in common." The saints whom I have known in the flesh have often been quite unable to keep anything for themselves, and have agonized deeply for the world's suffering; but I don't think they felt any mystical absorption in life in general. They just loved all things with God's love. *That is why I always feel that the best way to teach the Second Commandment is to concentrate on the First!*[137]

Underhill was clear, however, that the spiritual life did not imply retreat from the world, in fact, it had broad implications for the way one lived one's life. The spiritual life

will be decisive for the way we behave as to our personal, social and national obligations. It will decide the papers we read, the movements we support, the kinds of administrators we vote for, our attitude to social and international justice. For though we may renounce the world for ourselves, refuse the attempt to get anything out of it, we have to accept it as the sphere in which we are to cooperate with the spirit, and try to do the Will. Therefore the prevalent notion that spirituality and politics have nothing to do with one another is the exact opposite of the truth. Once it is accepted in a realistic sense, the spiritual life has everything to do with politics. It means that certain convictions about God and the world become the moral and spiritual imperatives of our life; and this must be decisive for the way we choose to behave about that bit of the world over which we have been given a limited control.[138]

Although the moral and the just must be supported, the spiritual life drove one beyond that to "spendthrift generosity," toward those who need restoration and healing, even though it disturb one's "spiritual comfort."

When we neglect the needs of the sinful and helpless because they conflict with our religious or moral ideas, when we elude the intimate companionship of the Magdalen and the leper, the nerve-ridden clutch of the possessed and all the variety of psychological wrecks which strew the modern scene in their restless loneliness — then we neglect the interest of God.[139]

What Underhill communicated in all her writing was the idea of the spiritual life as a life of prayer, of love, of holiness, "simply a life in which all that we do comes from the centre where we are anchored in God: a life soaked through and through by a sense of His reality and claim, and self-given to the great movement of His will."[140]

In 1934, after years of active public life, she decided to scale back her work and devote herself to writing a major book. This "fierce decision" to take a year off was supported by those who knew her best — Somerset Ward, Lucy Menzies, and Marjorie Vernon. Her only hope was that "everyone won't think I've become an R. C. [Roman Catholic] or had a mental breakdown!!!"[141]

In fact 1935 would prove to be an important year for her. She neither became a Roman Catholic nor had a mental breakdown; rather she dedicated herself to the writing of *Worship*, her last major book and her definitive statement on humanity's adoring response to God.

6

NOT THY GIFTS BUT THYSELF

IT TOOK CONVINCING to bring Evelyn Underhill to agree to write
Worship. It was Dr. W. R. Matthews, Dean of St. Paul's, who finally
won her over. At that point she did not know that her book would
be received as a pioneering work, that it would be named Religious
Book of the Month in America, or that it would remain continuously
in print. All she knew was that writing it would be a formidable task,
one which would demand mastery both of a new subject matter and
an extensive body of literature. She was also tired, worn out from
a long decade of retreats and writing and dealing with allergies and
periodic bouts of asthma. After consulting Reginald Ward she finally
decided to undertake the writing; she would cut back on all activities
and devote herself to this one task. As a consequence, 1935 was a lean
year in terms of literary production. She wrote a few book reviews
for the *Spectator* and *Criterion* and gave one retreat at Pleshey. The
topic of the retreat, the mystery of sacrifice, grew out of her research
on worship.[1]

Although other interests were curtailed, her embryonic interest in
Russian Orthodoxy was expanded. She joined the Anglo-Russian con-
fraternity and attended Russian Orthodox services. Those liturgies,
she claimed, left her with an "overwhelming supernatural impression."[2] In all, 1935 was a year of greater leisure and more focused
writing. She spent most of her time in London, although she made
visits to Frere and probably to Reginald Ward as well, and she and
Hubert took their annual long vacation in Norway. Lucy Menzies
tried to persuade Evelyn to travel with her to Palestine, but she de-
clined, claiming that she was unwilling to leave Hubert who would

soon be sixty-seven.[3] The fact was that she also had an enormous amount of work to complete.

She began work on her manuscript in late 1934, and by February 1935 she had finished seven of the fifteen chapters. In pieces, it was sent off to be scrutinized by her friends Marjorie Vernon and Lucy Menzies and various authorities in the field. While a formal study of worship was something new to her, her appreciation of worship was old, dating from her early travels in Italy where the power of ritual and its link to art and architecture ignited a deep attraction for this form of human expression. Certainly her relationship with Frere nurtured this attraction, and by 1929 she began to speak formally on the topic.[4] But worship was not so much a new topic as a new angle from which to pursue her long-standing interest in the relationship between the human and the divine. As mysticism was the intense personal relationship between the individual and the Absolute, and the spiritual life the integration of all of life through prayer and cooperation with God, worship was the whole human response to the "Eternal."

Her book was part of a new series, the Library of Constructive Theology, which was directed to the contemporary spiritual crisis. The editors sought out authors who were willing to think creatively about Christianity and reconstruct theology based on religious experience. It is no wonder that they solicited a volume from Underhill, the most popular exponent of the power and authority of individual religious experience. For her part, the opportunity to present a lucid and powerful description and analysis of the human response to God must have had great appeal.

What is immediately striking about *Worship* is its similarities to her earlier book *Mysticism*. In both, the phenomenon is defined as a creative human response and developed in relationship to the Absolute or the Eternal. The books are structured similarly: first, the phenomenon is analyzed; second, its expressions are examined. In both, her ecumenicity and inclusivity are evident; she casts her net very broadly, examining the widest variety of examples to be used to support a simple yet powerful idea. In *Mysticism* she studied one hundred thirty-three mystics, all of whom she claimed gave evidence of the fact of transforming lives born of the love of God.[5] In *Worship* she examined eleven different historical forms of worship, each expressing the impulse of adoration; each she said was like "a chapel in the Cathedral of the Spirit." Both books were characterized by "an at-oneness" with the subject, "a loving sight" which lead to a discovery of the real secret of the thing.[6] In both she saw her subjects as similar to artists. She defined the mystic as a creative artist, and claimed that the adoring worshiper, like the artist, was not utilitarian in motive, but was filled with disinterested delight in what was beheld. Both were willing to be open to the new. The mystics were the great pioneers of humanity, those who went ahead of the race; the spirit of worship, she claimed, was a spirit of exploration.[7]

Although *Mysticism* and *Worship* were written almost thirty years apart, the continuity between them is striking; their differences are those of nuance and emphasis. The vigor and movement of *Mysticism* are that of a young author's. It is a passionate statement but one that is ahistoric, anti-institutional, abstract, and highly individualistic. *Worship*, on the other hand, shows a deep appreciation of the corporate nature of human response, its rootedness in time and space, its dependence on the material world, and the influence of history in shaping its expressions. As with so much of Underhill's writing, *Mysticism* and *Worship* are reflective of her own preoccupation and understanding at a particular time. *Mysticism* is the work of a highly intense, ardent young woman, driven to defend the claims of personal religion. *Worship* stresses not the creative achievement of extraordinary individuals but the universal impulse toward the transcendent and its historical and institutional expressions. It is a work born of a longer life, a deeper experience, and a fuller appreciation of human needs, limitations, and corporate potentiality.

Worship begins with definition and delineation of common elements: ritual, symbol, sacrament, and sacrifice. This last, sacrifice, summarizes all worship; it is an action which expresses the deepest relationship between God and humanity. Adoration demands sacrifice, not merely of one's gifts but of oneself. She quotes Thomas à Kempis to explain the nature of the worshiper's sacrifice: "What ask I of thee more...but that thou study to resign thyself to me entirely. What thing soever thou givest me else I care not for. For I demand *not thy gifts but only thyself.*"[8]

The sacrifice demanded of worship was not destructive but transformative and sanctifying; it aimed to increased the glory of God through the creation of saints, those who through worship were made instruments of God. "A saint," she wrote,

> is a human being who has become a pure capacity for God and therefore a tool of Divine action: and it is consistent with the doctrine of incarnation that God should be adored, not only in His pure Being, but also as present in these His instruments.[9]

In Christian worship, sacrifice was particularly expressed in the

Eucharist, the living presence of God. Although Underhill maintained that the liturgical life of Christianity was built on both this living presence and the Bible, the uttered word of God, her own sense of the importance of the Eucharist is evident throughout the book. For her it was the important act of worship — sacrifice, feast, source of spiritual strength, and communal act of fellowship.

Whereas in *Mysticism* she spoke about the transformation of human life and the outpouring of that life in "divine fecundity," in *Worship* she speaks of self-offering in the worship of God, which in turn transforms the worshiper and hence remakes life itself. Her premise and her conclusion are that worship is not an expression of religious life, it is religious life, and therefore coterminous with life itself. Worship is creation's response to its origin and creator.

In the second part of *Worship* she examines various corporate responses to the "Eternal" — Judaism, Western and Eastern Catholicism, the Reformed and Free churches, and Anglicanism. In each she finds a particular genius, a particular ability to nurture a life of devotion and adoration. She values Judaism's intensely theocentric worship, the Western Catholic mass, and the Orthodox sense of mystery and symbolism. What is striking, given her own preference, is her appreciation of the Protestant expressions of worship. The Reformed churches, Lutheranism, Calvinism, and Scottish Presbyterian, are understood as forms which stress the priority of God, the importance of his Word, the helplessness of humanity in the face of a holy God, and the intimate connection between faith and works. For them, the moral life is the ultimate act of worship. She sees the genius of the Free churches — Baptist, Congregational, Methodist, and Quaker — in their prophetic and ethical elements, in their stress on the priesthood of all believers, and their universal call to sanctity.

She defines Anglicanism not merely as a variant of continental Protestantism but as a special development of traditional Christian worship. Its peculiar character resulted not only from the conflict between Puritan and Catholic ideals but from certain paradoxes in the English mind, namely, its reverence for custom and institutions and its individualism and passion for freedom. As the *via media*, it escapes the extremes — the heights and the depths — of both Catholic and Protestant cultus. Modern Anglicanism is indebted to both the Evangelical and the Tractarian movements. As expected, she gives Tractarianism the greater weight, crediting it with a revival in Eucharistic expression, the rediscovery of the interior life, and the exploration of devotional paths of prayer and self-discipline. She ends the section on Anglicanism with a discussion of the retreat movement and the expansion of devotional literature. By merely pointing out these developments, she places herself and her contribution in the center of the contemporary rejuvenation of "English Catholicism."

The focused attention of 1935 continued into the following year until the manuscript was completed. Although finishing it must have brought a sense of relief, she was not yet done with the theme of worship; it continued to be prominent in her work for the next several years. Underhill needed time to integrate the learning from this big book. The great insight of *Worship*, that adoration demanded not one's gifts but oneself, had yet to be appropriated by her on the deepest level. The next few years provided time for such appropriation and for preparation to meet that demand.

The reprieve from regular commitments was now over. Six retreats were scheduled for 1936, but attacks of asthma forced half of them to be cancelled.[10] Increasingly as illness incapacitated her, it was Marjorie Vernon who cared for Evelyn. Much of the spring and summer of 1936 were spent with Marjorie and her husband Roland at Lawn House in Hampstead. The Vernons were a bit younger than the Stuart Moores, and quite wealthy. It was not uncommon for them to open their beautifully appointed home to visitors. Both the Vernons had great facility for languages. Marjorie was a professional translator and Roland, because of his linguistic competence, was able to help Evelyn with translations of Gothic, Gallican, Mozarabic, and Roman prayers for a small book she published in 1939. The Vernons were very companionable and generous people, and the Stuart Moores were grateful to them. Evelyn dedicated *The Mystery of Sacrifice* to Marjorie and thanked Roland for his help in her preface to *Eucharistic Prayers*.

The Fruits of the Spirit was Underhill's retreat for 1936.[11] Like much of the work of that year, it was the mature summary of what she had done previously. In fact, the theme of the retreat, love, joy, and peace, was identical to that of her very first retreat given at Pleshey in 1924, the one she neatly recorded in her black leather notebook. Marked by clarity and simplicity, *The Fruits of the Spirit* summarized the outcome of the spiritual life. First, there was an increase in love; joy and peace followed from it. These three fruits did not exist in isolation, however, but were found in conjunction with goodness, faithfulness, meekness, and temperance. When they were present, apathy, bitterness, anxiousness, suspiciousness, hurry, and impatience were not to be found.

Like a mirror, this retreat reflects earlier work now integrated on a deeper level. So too do her lectures, "The Parish Priest and the

Life of Prayer" and "The Life of Prayer in the Parish," given to the Worcester diocesan clergy in Oxford in September.[12] As in *Concerning the Inner Life*, her first retreat for clergy a decade before, Underhill spoke to the importance of the priest in the lives of ordinary people. By his own prayer life, the priest could make his church a house of prayer and through his own adoration, self-offering, and dependence on God, could inspire his congregation. Although Underhill was the greatest exponent of the spiritual life for ordinary people, she retained an exalted view of priestly vocation.

The tendency to summarize and hence finish with previous themes is nowhere more obvious than in her radio broadcasts of that year. The first, "What is Mysticism?" prompted "the most insane collection of letters from every kind of crank";[13] it was followed later in the year by a four-part series entitled "The Spiritual Life." With simplicity and clarity these talks summarized and brought to completion thirty years of work.

"What is Mysticism?" was her final attempt to explain this ambiguous phenomenon and its relationship to Christianity. The ideas were not new; what was new was the succinctness with which she presented them. The mystic was one with "a metaphysical thirst" for God. Like the artist, the mystic by giving full attention to one object learns its secrets. The mystic life is not an easy one because love and suffering are both involved. While the mystic way is difficult and rare, it is important because of what it discloses of the landscape beyond the borderland where humanity lives. Mysticism is important for Christianity too, for although Christianity is not reducible to mysticism, mysticism is at its heart. The particular character of Christian mysticism is its incarnational orientation, its turning toward rather than away from creation.[14]

Underhill's four broadcast talks on the spiritual life were a simple summary of her thought over the last decade. Her main point was that the spiritual life was not some narrow, disembodied life, but the apex of a full humanity. Borrowing from Cardinal de Bérulle, she defined the three relationships of the human with the divine — adoration, adherence, and cooperation; together they made up the spiritual life. The mystic stages of development which she delineated so thoroughly in her early work were replaced here by this simple conceptualization of human responsiveness. The measure of this spiritual life was in its fruits — tranquillity, gentleness, courage, and its commitment to service. It was a life which responds, "Here I am. Send me."[15]

What is new in these broadcasts is the brief allusions to evil and injustice, themes which by 1936 had already begun to preoccupy the

European mind. Although Underhill does not explain evil, she claims that in the face of it one must work for good. Discernment as to what is good comes from the great truths of Christianity and from a quieting of the mind and waiting for clarity. It was precisely such clarity that Underhill sought as the violence and hatred of the late 1930s engulfed the European world. She was aware that, much like the late medieval period, her own time presented a great challenge to all those who lead the spiritual life.

It was in this context of increasing world violence that Underhill read Aldous Huxley's 1936 peace pamphlet *What Are You Going to Do About It?* Although she supported European disarmament as early as 1932, Huxley's pamphlet raised the question of pacifism.[16] She was not yet ready to speak of it publicly, but as her health deteriorated and war became inevitable, the seed of pacifism grew, ready to bear fruit.

The following year, 1937, was dominated by bad health. She had flu, asthma, and bronchitis. Hubert's health was also precarious. She gave no retreats that year and cancelled a weekend with the Girls' Diocesan Association. By the fall she wrote that she "was leaving off active work."[17] Most of the summer had been spent with the Vernons in Hampstead, but in September she and Hubert went off to Northumberland for a vacation. With the help of Clara Smith she finished up the manuscript of *The Mystery of Sacrifice* and sent it to the publisher in the autumn. For the moment, at least, she had only "odd jobs" to do, although she had made a commitment to give the Mercier Memorial lecture at Whiteland College in November; she hoped she would have voice enough to carry it off. Illness had made her wary of making commitments she might not be able to fulfill.[18]

As it turned out, she was well enough to go to Whiteland College. Her lecture, "Education and the Spirit of Worship," was dedicated to the memory of Winifred Mercier, who had done so much to train primary school teachers. The lecture was one of Underhill's last bits of sustained writing, one in which she linked together the work of education and the cultivation of the spirit of worship. In it she took up again the theme of her big book. Worship, she said, was

> a total and selfless devotion to the great purposes of creation, believing in those purposes, trusting them, caring for them, more than we care for our own interests. It means not lovely feelings — which always fail us at a pinch — but an austere dedication of the will which, because it is so utterly disinterested, kills the self-centered fears and anxieties of our generation at their root.[19]

With almost prophetic insight she claimed that in the days to come, Christianity would have to spread beyond a mere devotional focus to become a complete philosophy of existence. It was only those who had the disinterested loving gaze of worship who would be able to point the way out of humanity's confusion, miseries, and sins.[20] Ironic as it might seem, it was the spirit of worship which was most needed in the contemporary world.

Her lectures on mysticism, the spiritual life, and now worship finished up a lifetime of work. As she turned away from that work, recognition of her contribution was announced. She learned in February of 1938 that the University of Aberdeen would award her a Doctor of Divinity degree. Hubert was proud and wildly excited, and Evelyn herself was pleased by the thought that she and Maude Royden would be honored together. She wondered if D. D. robes could be rented for small ladies and warned that she did not want any of the "Frau Doctor stuff"; "Dr. EU," she thought was "swanky and revolting and quite against Matthew 23:8."[21] As it turned out she was too ill to go to Aberdeen. The university postponed the ceremony for a year but she was never able to claim the award in person.

There was other wrapping up to do as well. She participated with Father Sprott in giving one last retreat; she did the interviews and led meditations, but gave no addresses. She knew it would probably be her last one, so she urged her former retreatants to come. She also made it to the Anglo-Russian Conference at High Leigh where she found the "Orthodox services quite unimaginably lovely."[22] Frere, who was to die later in the year, was there; it must have been a wonderful moment for her, even though illness forced her to leave before the conference was over.

Her asthma continued to sap her energy and she was forced to spend some time in Brompton Hospital. Her physician, Dr. Livingstone, ordered that her book-lined study be stripped of everything that might gather dust. Her workplace of almost forty years was denuded; only her embroidered Eternity plaque and her crucifix remained. This cleansing made sense in terms of her health and symbolized what was happening in her life. There were, of course, bits and pieces of work yet to do. She continued to write a few book reviews for *Time and Tide*, and during the summer and fall she worked to finish up the manuscript of *Eucharistic Prayers from the Ancient Liturgies*.[23] But relative to former years she was able to accomplish very little. In August she and Hubert went to Highden, the Vernons' home in Sussex. The house, enclosed by downs and beechwoods, was a light and airy place with big windows. Since it was only six miles from the sea, Hubert was able to spend time on the naval training ship, *The Implacable.* Evelyn mostly took it easy, and if she went to mass at the nearby Storrington church, she had to be put to bed when she returned. While Evelyn rested, Roland Vernon worked on the translations of the eucharistic prayers, helping her ready the manuscript for publication. The Stuart Moores returned to London in the fall and spent their last Christmas in their Campden Hill Square home.

It was the end in many ways: there would be no more large writing projects; no more retreats and lectures; no more beautiful home in which to entertain friends. She comforted her friend Lucy Menzies who, after a decade as warden of Pleshey, was also giving up her work. "You and I have both been allowed a good run of active work," she wrote, "but the real test is giving it up, and passively accepting God's action and work, and the suffering that usually goes with it."[24] "These losses of liberty I think are among the hardest demands of the Lord. At least I feel them so, but perhaps they are meant to drive us bit by bit into the solitude with Him, which He requires of us."[25]

Evelyn Underhill understood that the loss of health, of energy, of work, of home, of friends, was all part of the process of simplification. It was more painful because it came at a time when the whole European world moved inexorably toward war. There was no consolation from her long years of work; in fact such work seemed strangely incongruous and irrelevant in a world driven forward by hatred, fear, and violence. In the face of this incongruity and irrelevance, she became a pacifist. This was her way of meeting the final demand of worship. She gave not merely the gift of her work but of herself, a giving that had been in preparation for forty years.

7

PRECURSOR OF A WORLD
TO COME

THE FIRST YEARS OF THE WAR and the last of Evelyn Underhill's life
were difficult ones. During most of the 1930s there was still hope
that war might be averted, but by late 1939 the Nazis conquered
to both the east and the west. France fell in 1940 and the Battle
of Britain began. For months London endured the blitz, the nightly
bombing that killed and maimed many, disrupted all normal life, and
fed a growing fear and hatred of the enemy. Although there were
miraculous moments like the evacuation at Dunkirk in May 1940, the
hour was a dark one. By the middle of June 1941 there was little hope
and less sense of how to survive. It was, as Churchill would say, a time
which tried men's souls. In that darkness, Evelyn Underhill died. In
the few years before her death her illness and relative unproductivity
both prepared her for the end and gave her a stark clarity about what
needed to be done in that apocalyptic time. The illness made the
clarity possible and gave an urgency to her speaking out.

Her body was wracked by frequent asthma attacks; the elasticity
of her lungs deteriorated; her energy decreased and she found herself dependent on others for the most ordinary help. In the end she
was confined to one room, oxygen by her bed. It was difficult for
a woman who was used to working at express speed to accept these
infirmities and the necessary "laying down of tools" they required.
This incapacity was doubly burdensome because of the great need to
comfort and strengthen those physically hurt or emotionally strained
by the war. Although she "steadied" all who came to her, there was
need to do more — to speak about the war, the aggression, the hatred

that slowly eroded one's humanity. There were no clear answers. The suffering was immense; and while it had to be alleviated, its causes also had to be addressed. Although she reworked one retreat for publication and prepared an introduction for a book of letters, almost all her other writing was connected to the war. These were all short pieces on what appears to be a new subject, pacifism. But like worship, pacifism was merely a different angle on the same subject — the human relationship with the divine — a subject she had written about for forty years.

The pacifist response to the war seemed a curious one: to some it was ridiculous, even outrageous. To most people it was certainly an unintelligible response. Only approximately 15,000 Britons were pacifists, and most of them were members of the historic peace churches.[1] But for Evelyn Underhill, pacifism followed naturally from everything she believed. The fact that pacifism was in direct opposition to her position on World War I speaks not so much to a change in circumstance as to a change in her. She no longer defined herself as an advocate of mysticism, defending it against charges of quietism, but as a proponent of the spiritual life, which included everything in its purview. More importantly, she had learned that the love of God meant self-giving to God's purposes. If any of God's purposes was evident, universal charity was. Given this, war, either as a manifestation of self- or national interest or as violence against one's neighbor, was insupportable.

The year 1939 began with both illness and death in the family. She and Hubert were sick, and her father died at the end of January.[2] Sir Arthur Underhill's death at age eighty-eight was not unexpected, but must nonetheless have prompted a sadness in her. Their relationship had always been a limited one, and toward its end she experienced it as increasingly cool. It was not merely that he did not participate in or appreciate her passion for religion, but that there was little intimacy between them. He admired her intellectual competency, but although she tried to win his affection — first by her cleverness and then through duty — it never worked. *A Bar Lamb's Ballad*, her first literary attempt, was a clever little book about his world; her poetry, one book of which was dedicated to him, was another attempt to reach out, show affection, and prove herself. In the end her response to him was dutiful. There were the lunches, the visits, the yachting vacations. For his last fifteen years it was not she but cousin Corisande who cared for him around the corner at 3 Campden Hill Place. And it was Corisande who won the dedication of his autobiography. At his death Evelyn must have confronted the barrenness of what was and the loss of what might have been.

In the aftermath of his death she had the added burden of dealing with his affairs. Fortunately from February on she had an unexpected run of good health that lasted for about six months and made work more possible. *Eucharistic Prayers* came out in the spring, and her introduction to Lucy Menzies' English translation of the Abbé de Tourville's *Letters of Direction* appeared also.[3] Her commitment to Lucy, who was assisted by Marjorie Vernon, must have led her to do this piece, although it also offered an opportunity to salute the French school of spirituality she loved so much. Although she was put off by the founder of the school, Francis de Sales, because of his exclusive ministering to the French upper class, the "best set,"[4] she acknowledged that the school owed its inspiration to him and that it had produced Abbé Huvelin, who was mentor to both Charles de Foucauld and von Hügel. Abbé de Tourville, a contemporary of Huvelin, shared many of the characteristics of the school, particularly its tolerance, balance, vivid sense of the presence and transcendence of God, and generous acceptance of human nature as it was. Her reiteration of support for this forgiving spirituality remained in stark contrast to the spirituality she applied to herself.

While her vehemence and self-exacting attitude toward herself had abated somewhat, it had not disappeared. Sister Mary of St. John, a Carmelite prioress in Exmouth who corresponded with Evelyn for six years and who in many ways acted like her spiritual director in her last years, urged her, much as von Hügel and Ward had, to stop dwelling on her own defects and to trust in God. Apparently the prioress found the same preoccupation with personal faults in Marjorie Vernon, who also corresponded with her. "I think," the nun wrote to Evelyn, her "step-daughter," "both you and Mrs. Vernon are far too occupied in making 'self' such a presentable person."[5] The desire for the perfection of self was not yet dead in Evelyn Underhill.

Because of her renewed health, Evelyn was able to take up a small measure of group work, which she had put aside when she gave up conducting retreats. It was an innovative work, one which continued even during the difficult circumstances of war. The group of young women, who had been formed into a theological reading group by Agatha Norman after the 1936 Girls' Diocesan Association meeting, now in 1939 requested Mrs. S. M., as she was known to them, to supplement their intellectual work with prayer and meditation. The first meeting of what came to be known as the Prayer Group met with her in July. She discussed its purposes and its simple rule, which was to include prayer, Bible reading, weekly communion, devotional reading, and self-discipline.[6] At its first two meetings she conducted the meditations. The procedure was to read a biblical passage or prayer very slowly, drawing participants into the words which lead to prayer. This converse with God, she was sure, brought one to a self-offering to God as well.[7]

The war soon scattered the twelve members of the Prayer Group, but Evelyn kept in touch with them through a series of letters keyed to the liturgical year. She wrote ten letters in all; each carried specific suggestions for shared reading and disciplines, and was characterized by both a tenderness toward the recipients and an urgency to "steady" them during a time that threatened to destroy every vestige of the spiritual life.[8] Acknowledging that "the wilderness confronts this generation in a very harsh and concrete form,"[9] that overstrain and lack of leisure destroy a sense of peace and trust in God, and that institutional religion offered little help, she urged her "little flock" to resist the temptation to neglect worship and adoration of God. It is only those who stay faithful and close to God, she warned, who can hope to discern how to respond in these difficult times. Faithfulness expressed itself in waiting and listening for God, as well as in discipline, abstinence, and almsgiving. The point was to simplify oneself, to clear the ground for God, to make oneself supple, so as to put oneself at God's disposal and hence to lift up the suffering of the world.

She consistently maintained that love of God entailed self-giving to God, for the good of the world. One of the consequences of self-giving was intercession for others, a theme increasingly obvious in her last writings. Taking her lead from Ruysbroeck, she urged the prayer of intercession first for those who needed it most — the wicked, those most alienated from God. She repeatedly requested prayer for the so-called enemy, Hitler and Mussolini, so that their hearts might be changed. God's healing and power flowed to them along a "path" created by prayer as it did to the victims of war and all good persons who worked for love and justice. One must pray for the enemy, for the victims, for the good, and only finally for oneself. This last prayer was one for protection from a spirit of hatred and bitterness.

When Evelyn Underhill spoke of intercession she meant a general offering of one's will and love to God, through Christ, so that the one who offered might become a means through which God's mercy, healing, and power might reach someone and achieve, not a particular purpose, but God's purpose for them. She acknowledged that the operations of prayer were unknown, and that there was no direct causal connection between prayer and specific occurrences. Help given at a particular time might come from the prayer of some unknown person, and prayer made in one place might be fulfilled elsewhere. What she was sure about was that all self-offering, all movements of love on one's part, were responded to by a living and personal energy. The prayer of intercession was open to all those who loved God, desired the realization of God's will, and cared deeply for the needs of all humanity.[10]

The letters to the Prayer Group were general letters, but communicate nonetheless a tenderness and deep personal concern for the recipients, who in her last years became like daughters to the childless Evelyn Underhill.[11] The quality of these letters, as well as their content, needs only be compared to her early letters to Margaret Robinson to see the distance she had come. Whereas she urged Robinson to be detached in order to hold on to the "vision splendid," she now counseled members of the Prayer Group to accept the imperfect as the vehicle through which God works. The point was not to be disappointed by the imperfect, but to see it as God sees it — with eyes of love.[12] As for detachment, she now wrote,

> [W]hat has to be cured is desiring and hanging on to things for their own sake and because you want them, instead of offering them with a light hand and using them as part of God's apparatus; people seem to tie themselves into knots over this and keep on asking themselves anxious questions on the subject — but again, the cure is more simplicity! They *must* shake themselves out of their scruples. The whole teaching of St. John of the Cross is directed to perfecting the soul in Charity, so that all it does, has, says, is, is transfused by its love for God.
>
> This is not a straining doctrine though a stern one, as of course it does mean keeping all other interests in their place and aimed at God all the time.[13]

Evelyn's work with the little Prayer Group lasted until two months before her death, when she sent out her last letter. In it she asked the members to pray for the renewal of the power of the Holy Spirit in themselves and the church. "It is this power and only this...which can bring in the new Christian society of which we hear so much. We ought to pray for it; expect it and trust it; and as we do this, we shall gradually become more and more sure of it."[14] In this final letter she gave the summary of all her teaching: it was to the power of the Spirit that she looked for both individual and societal transformation.

The spurt of good health that allowed her to work with the Prayer Group in the summer of 1939 also allowed her to revise her 1934 retreat address on the Lord's Prayer for publication as *Abba*, and to participate again in a social life. She attended a cocktail party at the Hampstead flat of *Time and Tide*'s Lady Rhondda. "I loved that party. I felt as though I'd really come alive again," she wrote.[15]

By July she and Hubert had finally closed their home, sent away their two servants Maude Hance and Margaret McLoughlin, parceled out the cats, and moved to Sussex with the Vernons. Hubert went off to *The Implacable* for a short time and Evelyn rested at Highden. By the end of September war had been declared. Since neither Hubert nor Roland Vernon had work in London, the two families decided to remain in the country for the winter.

During the autumn, the reality of war slowly gripped Evelyn. She wrote of the terrible sense of universal suffering and ruin which pervaded everything, the confusion about what one should do, and her sense of guilt in enjoying anything while others suffered so much.[16] Since she was still feeling relatively robust, she offered to develop a weekly intercession service at the local parish church. The original service was modified and was published as "A Service for Use in War-Time."[17] Although the "Service" came to be used in many churches, Underhill believed its tone was more patriotic than Christian — a lot about victory and little about penitence and love.[18] Because the local vicar was ill, she also agreed to take on the education of thirty-three eleven-to-fourteen-year-olds. She was supposed to teach them about prayer, but never having taught children or adolescents before, she was "terrified" by the prospect.

Underhill's pacifist sympathies had been developing for years, and the outbreak of war only confirmed them. Although it is unclear when she actually became a pacifist, the reading of Aldous Huxley's pamphlet *What Are You Going to Do About It?* in 1936 made a marked impression on her.[19] She became a member of the Peace Pledge Union, and in 1937 she lamented the death of its leader Dick Sheppard as a great blow to pacifism.[20] By 1939 she was a member of the Anglican Pacifist Fellowship,[21] and her "A Meditation on Peace" was published that year in a magazine of the Fellowship of Reconciliation, another pacifist organization.[22] "Prayer in Our Times," "The Spiritual Life in War-Time,"[23] and "The Church and War" also appeared.[24]

These publications and her public avowal of pacifism came at a time when many of her friends were repudiating this position. "Most of my quasi-pacifist friends," she wrote in December 1939, "are becoming more warlike, apparently feeling that provocation is more important than principles and that the only way to combat sin in others is to commit sin ourselves."[25]

Not only was she disappointed by the response of friends but she was disillusioned with the church as well. To her friend Maisie Spens she wrote:

> At present the whole attitude of the Church strikes me as getting steadily more sub-Christian, more and more forgetful of absolute standards.... And as the earthly situation deteriorates — as it must — all this will get worse, unless some vigorous movement is made in the opposite direction. However it has generally been in times when the temporal outlook was darkest, that the great swings back of the human spirit toward the Eternal have taken place.[26]

"Christendom," she wrote to E. I. Watkin, "has never had the nerve to apply this [pacifist] teaching without qualification, right up to the point of national martyrdom. When it does, perhaps the Kingdom of God will come."[27]

The attitude of the church was particularly painful for her, because she believed that pacifism could only ultimately be sustained by faith. "In fact it [pacifism] *can* only be held for supernatural reasons and by a supernatural faith that love *is* the ultimate reality and must prevail."[28] She blamed present Christianity for much of the inability to respond creatively to the times:

> It is because our Christianity is so impoverished, so second-hand and non-organic, that we now feel we are incapable of the transformation of life which is needed to get humanity out of the present mess.... It all comes back of course (a) to the lack of concrete realistic faith; (b) to the failure to realize what Unity really involves.[29]

Underhill's final writing was addressed both to Christians who were not pacifists and to those who were. In her short "Meditation on Peace" she anticipates the problems of the pacifist and clarifies the meaning of that position. Aware that the violence and hatred of the times pushed one toward a gloomy and embittered view of the world, she reminded the pacifist that the fruits of the spirit — love, joy, and peace — must even govern one's relationship with those who cause war and contribute to it. The real test was not whether one could be peaceful in a warlike time, but whether one could be peaceful with warlike people. If they were seen with "God's eyes" then anger and bitterness toward them would be replaced by a pity and generosity. This new way of seeing was possible because the pacifist was first given over in self-offering, without condition, to God. Like a redeemer, the pacifist bore the world's suffering and sin not with indifference, but at great personal cost.

In *The Church and War*, a pamphlet written for the Anglican Pacifist Fellowship, Underhill explained the connection between Christianity and pacifism. Although the church had a duty to promote social order and could sanction legitimate police action, it could not support war because war, originating in either sin or fear, inflicted destruction and death and worked against love. The church, which should be the rallying point for all those who believed in the creative and redeeming power of love, was being presented with a great opportunity to advance its work in the world. It was incapable of seizing this opportunity, however, because its supernatural life was so weak and ineffective. Afraid to risk and to suffer, it agreed to "please men," not God, to accept the world's standard, not God's. While she acknowledged that there was only a small minority within the church which recognized this opportunity, Underhill was assured that the Spirit worked through them. Through the small nucleus of the Anglican Pacifist Fellowship, a group pledged both to repudiate war and to build up international, economic, and personal peace, the church could be moved to do the work of the Spirit — the work of love and peace in the world. She pleaded for every Anglican who believed that Christianity implied a commitment to peace to join so that the work of the Spirit could be accomplished.

As the war began, she was hopeful that more and more Christians would join the pacifist cause. For those who were not pacifist, she felt a need to try to steady them in the life of prayer, which was being overwhelmed by duty on the one hand and oppressed by the suffering of the world on the other. Recognizing that many believed that prayer was a selfish activity, Underhill argued that it was more necessary than ever, that staying "spiritually alert" was the best thing that could be done.[30] In fact, lack of prayer made one less able to serve the suffering because one's own sense of hope was diminished.

Prayer was first adoration and worship that also demanded self-offering to the will of God. Those who prayed were a "Sixth Column" through whom God's work was done in the world. Through them the force of goodness was released and support was given to those who suffered. Through them the situation of hatred could be transformed.

Although the question of suffering did not have a large place in Underhill's thought, the war forced her to address it. Her final position was one she borrowed from von Hügel. "I cannot get much beyond von Hügel's conclusion," she wrote to C. S. Lewis, "that Christianity does not explain suffering but does show us what to do with it."[31] What must be done was to bear the suffering with others, alleviating it as one could.

In addition to steadying Christians in their prayer, she also worked to increase their consciousness of their complicity with war. The war, she argued, was not the work of a few people, but the complete crash of law and order, truth, mercy, and justice, for which all bore some responsibility. Since everyone was in some sense complicit with the war, everyone was responsible for alleviating its ravages and none could condemn the opponent as an unrighteous enemy.

This writing about war was made possible because the last months of 1939 were relatively good ones for Evelyn; but soon her health was to give out. *Abba* was published in January 1940. By the end of February she was seriously ill. It was, she said, "a fierce time"; the asthma attacks were ferocious and she was given maximum doses of morphine to ease the pain. The elasticity of her lungs was now gone. Oxygen was kept by her bed all the time, and her activity was restricted. She just had to "stay put" and have everything done for her. It was only after Easter that she was able to be moved from Sussex to Hampstead, where she stayed until her death.

Ill and physically dependent, she made a will after the winter siege.[32] It was a telling document which spoke of her sense of obligation and her emotional attachments. Her sentimental items were to be parceled out. Lucy should get her personal books, the Eternity plaque, and the Russian crucifix she wore on retreats; she wanted Clara to have the painted crucifix that hung in her room; and Agatha Norman, her Bibles. Marjorie Vernon was to be given other select items; and Gillian Wilkinson, her goddaughter, awarded some of her jewelry. Fifty volumes from her library were to go to the Dr. Williams Library. Her servants Maude Hance and Margaret McLoughlin each were to be awarded a small sum of money, and Clara would get two hundred pounds. From the wife's fund[33] a scholarship was to be endowed at King's College for a candidate seeking Holy Orders; Clara and Maude were to be given yearly and monthly allotments respectively for life, and the remainder was for relatives, including Corisande.

By spring, the worst of the illness was over, and she began to complain that slowing down and dependence were difficult for "one who prefers to do everything for herself at express speed."[34] She was supposed to be writing a book on Christianity and the spiritual life for the Christian Challenge Series, but her illness and the fact that she was in someone else's home without books or space made the task largely impossible. She continued to write reviews for *Time and Tide;* thirteen were published in 1939 and seven in 1940. In late May, she, along with every Briton, was thrilled by the evacuation at Dunkirk. The "unselfishness" of the soldiers and their "patient endurance" gave her a small hint that goodness could show through in the midst of war.[35] In addition to these glimmerings of human goodness, Underhill believed that one of the few "consoling elements" of the war was that it produced real growth in unity among churches.[36] These beginnings of religious unity were counterbalanced, however, by increased hatred, especially of aliens, refugees, and the enemy.[37] What really alarmed her was the use of religion to support the war. She wrote to her old friend Dorothy Swayne:

> People are so anxious at present to have the support of religious faith while performing irreligious acts, and to claim God as an ally who must be on their side, instead of abandoning themselves to His Will. The immense awakening to the need of prayer is of course one of the good results of the war, but if it is to remain at the natural level and be concerned mainly with our military success or defeat, it will not do a great deal for us. We all, as you say, manage to ignore the "hard sayings" of the New Testament but now they are coming true under our eyes.[38]

This fear of an alliance between religion and the war was one she voiced privately and in the pages of *Time and Tide.* In response to a letter that called for religion to provide the ecstatic enthusiasm for war, Underhill pointed out that Christians were unable to do this because they could not draw a self-righteous contrast between themselves and the enemy. Furthermore, Christianity took as its model a God whose chief attribute was universal charity. While she appreciated that many Christians supported the use of force in the present situation, she felt they should not use religion to bless military acts. Spiritual victories were not won on the battlefields, and she queried: "And in view of our past record, can any of us dare to say that a victory for our arms would be a victory for the Spirit of God?"[39]

Although she always expected and hoped that the church would respond more creatively, she believed then, as she always had, that the real religious work was that of the individual, not the institution.

It was "the God-intoxicated man" who pointed to a God of universal charity whose purposes would be worked out in the midst of the disasters of history. In this case this was the pacifist, one who could speak prophetically in these difficult times.

Her devastating illness which ushered in 1940 was paralleled by another horror that ushered out the year. The blitz of London began in the late summer and by autumn had disastrous consequences for the city. The Hampstead area was on one of the air attack routes and took a battering. Life was rendered primitive; regular water, gas, light, and telephone could never be counted on.[40] The nightly raids forced the Vernons and the Stuart Moores to move to the basement and ground floor where they slept with packed suitcases by their beds. They were stripped down to a few possessions, and Evelyn admitted that this pooling of possessions was far harder than she had thought.[41] The bad conditions and the homelessness and misery of others pressed on her, but the bleakness of life was alleviated by the kindness and companionship of the Vernons and the visits from Lucy and Maude, from former retreatants and members of the Prayer Group, from Somerset Ward and T. S. Eliot.

It was during this very difficult winter of 1940–41 that she wrote "Postscript," her final and most extensive pacifist piece.[42] In it she carried to conclusion her thought of forty years and pointed, much as she had done in *Mysticism*, to the future. Using the words of the Abbé de Tourville she calls the pacifist a "forerunner," a "precursor" of a world yet unseen.

"Postscript" stands in marked contrast to "The Problem of Conflict" and "Mysticism and War," her writings on World War I. Not only did she now repudiate war, her writing reflects a new understanding of reality. In *Mysticism* she claimed that mystic knowledge was that born of love, a knowledge which transformed the individual and resulted in creative activity in the world. What she learned from subsequent years of experiencing Christianity from within was that the love of God demanded not merely one's gifts but a personal response of self-offering and that this sacrifice of self opened up the possibility of God, the universal charity, working in the world. While mysticism taught her that God was love, Christianity taught what to do with that knowledge. Pacifism was merely the logical and specific application of what she called "the universal law of Charity." If one were self-given to Love, then one could not engage in war against another of God's creatures. Pacifism was not, however, merely a repudiation of war or a practical expedient for ending disputes; it was a whole orientation of life which followed from faith and hope in God.

Pacifism was therefore the response of the faithful creature, whose eyes, "cleansed by prayer," were given the gift of opening to the purposes of God who was Love. In short, pacifism was a vocation given by God, for God's ends.

Although she saw pacifism as rooted in trust in God and war as caused by possessiveness that orients all of life toward self-satisfaction, either national or personal, her tack was not so much to condemn war as to explain peace. Sin and war were seen not so much as opposites of charity and peace, but as that which is overcome by them. Pacifism was the unlimited practice in life of the doctrine of charity; it was the conquest of sin through the "costly application of sacrificial love."

"Postscript" ends with a brief admonition about what must be done. Begin where you are, she urged the pacifist, not with large denunciations of war, but in the quiet acceptance of one's own place in a sinful order and with the commitment to create a "cell of tranquility" in a world at war. It was through the personal witness of love and peace that sin, violence, and hatred would be conquered. As regards others who did not share the truth of pacifism, one must remember that although closed to that truth, they may be open to other truths which were also essential.

"Postscript" might well have been retitled "Pacifism as the Extension of the Love of God," because that was its conclusion. Pacifism was an integral part of Underhill's thought, a particular angle on the relationship between the human and the divine. It is unlikely that she would have taken up this theme if the question of war had not been forced on her. But it was and it became the principal subject of the last years of her life. Unlike mysticism and the spiritual life to which she devoted many years, pacifism was barely explored. Yet she was fully aware that it was a subject with prophetic implications. Pacifists are those who have known "the vision splendid" and who as persons of prayer are able to proclaim in the midst of violence and hopelessness a message of peace. They were in fact planted in this "inhospitable soil" by God. "God," she quotes from de Tourville,

> sows in the world, at every epoch, precursors who assume or know, at least inwardly, things that are to come. We should bless God if we happen to be forerunners: even though, living a century or two too soon, we may find ourselves strangers in a foreign land.... Rejoice then in the light that you have been given, and do not be surprised that it is so difficult to pass it on to others.[43]

In "Postscript" and her other pacifist writings, she was aware that pacifists were part of "a tiny minority," that they were "stranger[s] in a foreign land." At the end of her life, as in the beginning of her career, she had a clear sense of the marginality of her subject and hence of herself, an experience of living on a borderland, looking out to a yet unknown world. Although she had been acclaimed and claimed by the literary and ecclesiastical establishments, she was now nobody's darling. For the first time she publicly allied herself with a political position. Difficult as that position was, its burden was compounded by the awareness of human suffering created by those she could not call enemy. In the face of violence and immense suffering she steadfastly maintained her pacifism. Yet it was precisely in this "minority" position that she found a sense of integration she had not known previously. It was not that pacifism made sense according to logic or survival instinct, but it was congruent with — in fact, implicit in — the notion of God as universal charity.

Pacifism, then, brought her back to the fundamental insight of *Mysticism*, admittedly from a different vantage point. What she had seen as central in the lives of the mystics, she now came to live in her own life. Her friend T. S. Eliot, writing at precisely this time, described in general the experience of integration and simplicity which came at life's end. "And the end of all our exploring," he wrote, "will be to arrive where we started: And know the place for the first time.... A condition of complete simplicity (costing not less than everything)."[44] Although not written for Evelyn Underhill, this nonetheless describes her place: she was back to her beginning, knowing it in a new way. The cost for such knowing was everything, complete self-offering.

As the war dragged on into 1941, Underhill continued as a pacifist, acknowledging that the "future seems very dark and uncertain." She wrote to Mildred Bosanquet:

Yes — I am still a pacifist though I agree with you about the increasing difficulty of it. But I feel more and more sure that Christianity and war are incompatible, and that nothing worth having can be achieved by "casting out Satan by Satan." All the same, I don't think pacifists at the moment should be controversial, or go in for propaganda. The nation as a whole obviously feels it right to fight this war out and must, I think, do it. I think Hitler is a real "scourge of God," the permitted judgment on our civilization; and there are only two ways of meeting him — war, or the Cross. And only a very small number are ready for the

Cross, in the full sense of loving and unresisting abandonment to the worst that may come. So those who see that this alone is *full* Christianity should be careful not to increase the disharmony of life by trying to force this difficult truth on the minds that are closed against it and will only be exasperated by it. At present I think one can do little but try to live in Charity, and do what one can for the suffering and bewildered. We are caught up in events far too great for us to grasp, and which have their origin in the "demonic powers" of the spiritual world. Let us hope that the end of all the horror and destruction may be a purification of life![45]

Three months before her death she wrote to her friend E. I. Watkin:

I've never felt an inclination to change my views about the war. One cannot fight evil by the use of evil. Of course, none of us has an idea what the real and spiritual events are. We are witnessing Armageddon. But to adhere to the Eternal God, and help others to steady their lives in the same way, must always be right.... Our future seems very dark and uncertain as so much we thought permanent has fallen away.[46]

Days before her death she wrote:

I feel more and more to be living through the Apocalypse. I remain pacifist but I quite see that at present the Christian world is not "there" and attempts to preach it at the moment can only rouse resistance and reduce charity. Like you I think the final synthesis must reconcile the lion and the lamb — but meanwhile the crescendo of horror and evil and wholesale destruction of beauty is hard to accept.[47]

Given the destruction of war and the failure of Christianity to respond, Underhill could have retreated from pacifism. She did not; neither did she retreat from the suffering of the world, even though the Carmelite prioress recommended that she do so in order to gain a greater sense of peace.[48]

The winter of 1941 brought neither an improvement in the war nor in her health. She spent it enclosed in one room at Lawn House, reluctant to go out lest another asthma attack be provoked. She wrote little — three reviews for *Time and Tide*, an entry in the Hampstead Church Bulletin entitled "Keeping Lent," and the usual letters to those who sought her help. One of her last *Time and Tide* pieces was written for the five hundredth anniversary of the publication of *The Imitation of Christ*, what she called "the great textbook of interiority." In many ways her own writing followed in the tradition of the *Imitation* and its prayer — to "[d]efend and keep... thy servant... and... direct him by the way of peace to the country of everlasting clearness" — was her plea for her own life.[49]

If she prayed to be directed "to the country of everlasting clearness" on the one hand, she also resonated with the prayer of Søren Kierkegaard, whose work she also reviewed for *Time and Tide*. From his *Christian Discourses* she quoted this:

As the bird sings without ceasing to the glory of the Creator, such also is the Christian life, or at least he understands and admits that it should be such.... For this properly is the hymn of praise, the paean, the song of songs; by joyful and unconditional obedience to praise God when one cannot understand Him.[50]

This was, in short, her certain position in these uncertain times: to sing the praise of God even when one could not understand.

The long winter of 1941 ended with renewed attacks of asthma and bronchitis. Her letters during the last few months include one to Lucy about how hard it was to give up activity, freedom, and doing work. She suggested that "praying for people" might be an exchange for instructing them.[51] Another letter records bombing damage to the Campden Hill Square house and Hubert's worry that his appointment at the ministry of Labor, a position which produced most of his income, would soon end. There was as well her lament over the general "slipping into animalism" resulting from insecurity, overwork, and wretchedness in the society[52] and her confiding that after Hitler, "probably very little of what we know as the ordinary framework of life will survive.... "[T]he new life when it comes... will well up from the deepest sources of prayer."[53]

She did not live to see life after Hitler or what might well up from a war-ravaged Europe. By early June she was sick again and in considerable pain. On Sunday the 15th, she died of a cerebral hemorrhage.[54] Her funeral was held at nearby Christ Church, and, in keeping with her wishes, there were no flowers or "lugubrious hymns."[55] It was not to be an occasion for mourning, but a celebration of a life that she believed endured forever. The one hundred thirty-fourth Psalm was read.

Come, bless God
All you who serve God
Serving in the house of God
in the courts of the house of our God!

Stretch out your hands toward
the sanctuary
Bless God night after night!
May God bless you from Zion
He who made heaven and earth!

It was a fitting ending for one who sought and stretched out her hands to God, who was for her the infinite life. Her body was buried a few blocks away in the cemetery of St. John's Church, the grave marked subsequently by a large upright gray stone.

With Hubert's help, Clara and Marjorie returned to Campden Hill Square to sort through her letters and papers; her personal items were distributed and the house closed up again.

Few signs of Evelyn Underhill's life remain. The elegant house, now remodeled, still faces on the quiet wooded square; her beloved Pleshey keeps the Eternity plaque, and her Donatello frieze of the Virgin and Child adorns its chapel; her crucifix graces the altar of the small All Saints' chapel in Canterbury Cathedral, and sixteen of her books remain in print. There are a few women still living who knew her in person. But Evelyn Underhill is gone; what remains is the "myth" Yeats spoke of, which lured her on and wove a thread of continuity in her life and work. Although variegated at different stages, the myth is nonetheless recognizable throughout her sixty-five years. It was for the myth, the belief in the possibility of the infinite life, that she gave her own life. She was its artist, one who knew its forms and colors, who described its expressions over thousands of pages.

"In my beginning is my end," wrote Eliot, a seeming description of how the myth weaves throughout a life, giving it integrity and continuity. From Evelyn Underhill's beginning, the desire for the infinite life is evident. It led her to architecture and painting in Italy, to nature and poetry, through the eddies of magic and the occult, to the allure of Roman Catholicism. It burst forth in her exploration of mystic knowledge that revealed itself as born of love. It found expression in the editing of ancient texts, in biographies, and in the translation of religious experience into the language of ordinary life.

It appeared quietly in the continuous "care of souls" and in their nurturing in retreats, and emerged again in her pursuit of worship, the most primitive response of awe and adoration. In the dark hour of war and death, the infinite life was hidden from her, yet she clung tenaciously to its power and intimacy. It is her myth, the desire for the infinite life, that endures. Substantiated by her life, revealed in her work it draws one to her unkempt grave, to clear hard dirt, to chop away grass, to offer a gift of wild flowers.

AFTERWORD

ONE OF THE MOST PROVOCATIVE ASPECTS of writing this life has been the discovery of how others respond to Evelyn Underhill. These responses, communicated both in writing and in person, have prodded, encouraged, and forced me to think more deeply about her complex person and times.

Evelyn Underhill's corpus is a very large one, written over a forty-year period. Although there is great continuity in her thought, her writing — depending on when it was produced — carries different nuances. Because she is known best and sometimes exclusively as the author of *Mysticism*, she is associated with Neoplatonism. This highly spiritualized worldview, emphasizing transcendence and other-worldliness, has particular appeal to those with developed aesthetic sensibilities. It prompts deep affection for her in some readers. In others it stirs suspicion. For the latter, Evelyn Underhill represents sentimentalized, cozy spirituality. This reaction takes various expressions. She is seen as a typical Edwardian, a mentor to the well-heeled Kensington set, the "Agatha Christie" of spirituality.[1] Others suspect that she has only a second-hand knowledge of the spiritual life[2] or that she is intellectually unsound, having drawn faulty conclusions from her research.[3] There are those who try to make sense of her huge corpus by categorizing her. For some she represents the last gasp of the dying Oxford Movement; for others she follows in the French school of spirituality founded by de Sales; for still others she is a disciple of von Hügel and hence not an original thinker.[4] While each of these criticisms has some truth in it, each is false precisely because of its narrowness. None is a comment on the totality of her work.

The uniqueness of Evelyn Underhill's work rests both on the kinds of questions she asked and the eloquence, power, and authenticity with which she answered them. There are those who recognize her contribution. T. S. Eliot, Thomas Merton, Alan Watts, and Charles

147

Williams all acknowledge her influence.[5] Scholars of religion credit her with describing mysticism as democratic, futuristic, and creative;[6] with her, mysticism becomes a way of life[7] linked to social concern.[8] Her work is seen as a bridge not merely between believer and unbeliever but between religion and the behavioral and natural sciences.[9] While this recognition is important, what convinced me that Evelyn Underhill was a woman who had real meaning for our time were the diverse and sometimes inarticulate claims by so many that her writing confirmed their own experience of the holy as it expressed itself in ordinary life. While there were men who spoke to me of Underhill's impact on them, it is clear to me that her influence is greater among women.

Evelyn Underhill's broadest contribution is in redefining religion and what it means to be a religious person. Although religion may be connected to dogma, doctrine, institution, and moral code, she believed its essential element was the mystical, that is, the personal experience of the love of God that gives authenticity and authority to religion. This love was, she claimed, a gift from God to which the response was awe and adoration. This mystical element of religion is paradigmatic; it provides the standard by which one relates to others. Having been loved by God, one is free to love others as one has been loved. Even the unlovable and the enemy can be embraced. It is as well the basis for the transformation of all of life; it causes what she called "divine fecundity," the birthing of new life in the world. While this is the work of the great mystics, it is also participated in by ordinary persons.

Because Underhill had such a keen sense of both the transcendent and the immanent aspects of the holy, she has been called incarnational. Yet her incarnationalism is not Christocentric. While she claimed she was theocentric, in fact she was more Spirit-centric than anything else; she saw all of life as infused with the Spirit. When one probes for the sources of this spirit-centered view, they are found not in Scripture or in doctrine but in art and in the lives of those "God-intoxicated" individuals, the mystics. Yet one finds in Evelyn Underhill a prior awareness and orientation that makes her alert to the mystical. This awareness, while not determined by her gender, was influenced by it.

The fact that Evelyn Underhill was a woman is important to understanding her contribution and her limitations. The abundant literature on gender and its impact on the individual suggests that the process of identity formation in females is achieved principally through attachment to rather than detachment from those outside of self.[10] As a young woman, Underhill was clear about her need for inclusivity and the development of a sense of oneness with all things. Later she spoke of a sense of being part of a cell, a boundless living web. Her way of knowing was through attachment; it was relational. Her emphasis on mysticism as participation in the love of God, on the spiritual life and pacifism as outpourings of that love, and on ecumenicity as a form of inclusivity are all congruent and reflect her early emphasis on attachment to and participation with the other.

If Underhill reflects a way of knowing through attachment and relationship, in her religious life she reflects what appears to be a typical female pattern as well. Some recent historical studies of piety in the medieval period show that the single most important factor in determining the shape of piety was gender. For medieval women, religious life had greater continuity than it did for men. Conversion was earlier for women than for men, and it was more gradual than abrupt. Women far less frequently than men made heroic acts of casting off wealth, power, or things. For women, ordinary experience was seen to be full of meaning; mysticism was more evident in their religious expression, and their devotional life was more penitential and ascetical than that of their male counterparts.[11] In many ways, Underhill's life reflects these same characteristics.

As gender may have implications for the way one understands self and reality and the way one both embraces religion and expresses it, so gender has sociological implications that are both advantageous and disadvantageous. Historically, women have been more marginalized than men; that is, they have lived at a distance from the loci of power. Although some implications of this have been pernicious, it has given women a unique vantage point from which to understand reality. In Underhill's case this worked to her advantage. Living outside the hierarchies of both the university and the institutional church, she had a certain freedom to examine unorthodox subjects and to give counsel on the fringes of these institutions. In her case marginality produced innovation and allowed for a certain protection.

If gender worked as an asset in her life, it was not an unmitigated one. In some sense she was uncomfortable with what she saw as the limitations of women, their sentimentality, and their self-serving attitudes. She had women friends, but those she admired most were men.

The negative implications of gender on self-identification are also obvious in her life. As a public person she had a strong self-image, but in her inner life she was dominated by a sense of her unworthiness and her failure to lead what she believed was a transformed life. While she saw this as a religious failure, it was a psychological failure as well. Underhill epitomizes what has been called the greatest female sin — the devaluation of self and the inability to love oneself.[12] For most of her life, Underhill was unable to experience for herself what she saw so clearly in the lives of the mystics — unearned love that makes one lovable. It was her greatest failure.

It is precisely at this juncture that the interpretation of her life and work is most difficult. There is a doubleness about Evelyn Underhill that results from her inability to push through and carry to conclusion the implications of her own positive worldview. It can be argued that it was precisely the desire for love, for intimacy, which drove her to enormous productivity and eloquent testimony of the great love she saw in the lives of others. Seeing that life, she interpreted it and made it available to ordinary people. It is an integrated life, rooted in the source of all being, transformed and transforming in its activity. She proclaimed the way of affirmation, yet it was that way that she was not fully able to accept for herself. Her inner life was guided by detachment, by intellectual doubts, by suspicion of experience, by a great inability to acknowledge love and forgiveness. It is, I think, only in her very last years that she came to trust the love she so easily identified for others.

Evelyn Underhill's work points to the new while at the same time drawing from the very old. In the medieval world she found healing for the modern malaise. But as a person born and formed in the late nineteenth century she carried the limitations of that time with her; she was unable personally to accept her healing discovery. Caught between the "no longer" and the "not yet," she is a transitional figure. But most importantly she is one who with the greatest eloquence and passion revealed what she saw in the long history of religion — lives which were transformed and as such lives which offered hope and direction to her contemporaries.

I have called Evelyn Underhill an artist of the infinite life; I think she would like that designation. Like Jacopone da Todi, she saw herself as an interpreter who stood between the great mystics and ordinary people, portraying "the vision splendid," and inviting all to embrace it. She would have denied for herself any special claim of being a mystic, as she would have denied any claim of being a saint.[13] What she could not have denied is that she was an artist in the service of humanity, painting the infinite life, luring each one on to its beauty.

NOTES

Introduction

1. T. S. Eliot, MS A. ff. 90, 91. Cited in H. Gardner, *The Composition of the Four Quartets* (London: Faber and Faber, 1978), pp. 69–70.

2. "E. Stuart Moore — Obituary," *The Times*, London, 18 June 1941, p. 7, col. 4.

3. H. Bergson, *Two Sources of Morality and Religion*, trans. R. Ashley Audra and Cloudesley Brereton (Garden City, N.Y.: 1935), p. 216.

4. M. Ramsey, "Foreword," in C. Armstrong, *Evelyn Underhill* (Grand Rapids, Mich.: Eerdmans, 1975), p. x.

5. M. Pachter, ed., *Telling Lives: The Biographer's Art* (Philadelphia: University of Pennsylvania Press, 1985), p. 3.

6. Nicholas of Cusa, *The Vision of God* (New York: G. P. Putnam's Sons, 1951), chapter 9.

7. E. Underhill, "Sources of Power in Human Life," *The Hibbert Journal* 19, no. 3 (April 1921):397.

8. L. Menzies, Underhill's first literary executrix, claims that Underhill wanted anything that was helpful to others to be published. See L. Menzies, Biography of Evelyn Underhill, TS unfinished, Underhill Collection, Archives, St. Andrews University Library, St. Andrews, Scotland, p. IX, 7.

9. C. Williams, ed., *The Letters of Evelyn Underhill* (London: Longmans, Green and Co., 1943), p. 29.

10. M. Cropper, *Evelyn Underhill* (London: Longmans, Green and Co., 1958), p. 6. Quoted from a letter of 5 Dec. 1892.

11. William Butler Yeats as quoted by Justin Kaplan in "The Naked Self and Other Problems," *Telling Lives: The Biographer's Art*, p. 46.

Chapter 1: Routes to the Unseen

1. E. Underhill, "The Possibilities of Prayer," *Theology* 14, no. 82 (14 Apr. 1927):195.

2. E. Underhill, "Our Two-Fold Relation to Reality," *The Hibbert Journal* 23, no. 2 (January 1925):224.

3. L. Menzies, Biography of Evelyn Underhill, TS unfinished, St. Andrews University Archives, St. Andrews, Scotland, is the best source for her early life. For details regarding her mother, her health, schooling, and lack of religious exposure, see pp. II, 2; IV, 9; II, 7. Although Menzies says Underhill went to Folkstone at age ten, there is no documentation to support this claim. Correspondence from Evelyn to her mother while at Sandgate begins in July 1888, when she was thirteen. Evelyn Underhill Collection (EUC) Archives, King's College, London, folder 27.

4. Ibid., p. II, 7.

5. M. Cropper, *Evelyn Underhill* (London: Longmans, Green and Co., 1958), p. 5. Emphasis added.

6. E. Underhill, "A Woman's Thoughts About Silence," 1892, EUC, folder 19.

7. Cropper, p. 5.

8. A. Underhill, *Change and Decay: The Recollections and Reflections of an Octogenarian Bencher* (London: Butterworth and Co., 1938), p. 211.

9. Menzies, p. II, 1.

10. Ibid., p. II, 10.

11. Ibid.

12. Ibid., p. I, 5.

13. Cropper, p. 5.

14. E. Underhill, "How Should a Girl Prepare Herself for a Worthy Womanhood," *Hearth and Home*, 27 July 1893, EUC, folder 19.

15. Ibid.

16. Cropper, p. 6.

17. Ibid.

18. "Speech by Evelyn Underhill at King's College, London, 1927," EUC, folder 57.

19. N. Marsh, *A History of Queen Elizabeth College* (London: King's College, London, 1986), p. 29.

20. "A Speech by Evelyn Underhill...," folder 57.

21. A. Underhill, p. 41.

22. Cropper, p. 13.

23. Menzies, p. II, 11.

24. "To Mrs. Meyrick Heath," 14 May 1911, in C. Williams, ed., *Letters of Evelyn Underhill* (London: Longmans, Green and Co., 1943), pp. 125–26.

25. Menzies, p. II, 19.

26. Ibid., p. II, 13.

27. Ibid., p. III, 11.

28. Ibid.

29. Letters of H. Stuart Moore to E. Underhill; Letters of E. Underhill to H. Stuart Moore, EUC, folder 28.

30. C. Armstrong, *Evelyn Underhill* (Grand Rapids, Mich.: Eerdmans, 1975), p. 27.

31. Menzies, p. II, 11.

32. Ibid., p. III, 9.

33. Letter from Alice Herbert to Evelyn Underhill, 16 Sept. 1904, privately owned. Found by John Mitchell.

34. Armstrong, p. 32.

35. E. Underhill, *The Grey World* (London: William Heinemann, 1902), p. 332.

36. Ibid., p. 93.

37. Ibid., p. 332.

38. Ibid., p. 140.

39. Ibid., p. 336.

40. Ibid., p. 146.

41. Ibid., p. 194.

42. Ibid., p. 204.

43. Ibid., p. 203.

44. Ibid.

45. Ibid., p. 338.

46. Ibid., p. 239.

47. F. King, *Ritual Magic in England: 1887 to the Present* (London: Neville Spearman, 1970), p. 112.

48. Armstrong, p. 33.

49. Ibid., p. 38.

50. A. E. Waite, *Shadows of Life and Thought: A Retrospective in Form of Memories* (London: Selwyn and Bount, 1938), p. 147.

51. E. Underhill, "The Ivory Tower," *Horlicks Magazine*, no. 2 (1904):211.

52. "To M. R.," 29 Nov. 1904, *Letters*, p. 51.

53. Ibid.

54. Ibid.

55. "To M. R.," 29 Aug. 1908, *Letters*, p. 81.

56. Menzies, p. III, 8.

57. Letter from E. R. Barker to E. Underhill, EUC, folder 33.

58. E. Underhill, *The Lost Word* (London: William Heinemann, 1907), p. 315.

59. Ibid., p. 316.

60. Ibid., p. 313.

61. Ibid., pp. 183–84.

62. Ibid., pp. 88–89.

63. Ibid., p. 89.

64. Ibid., p. 292.

65. Ibid., p. 269.

66. Ibid., p. 270.

67. Menzies, p. IV, 2, indicates that Underhill began collecting materials on mysticism in 1904.

68. Cropper, p. 29.

69. Diary entry of 4 Feb. 1907, quotes in Menzies, p. IV, 3.

70. Cropper, pp. 29–30. Originals not extant.

71. Quotes in C. C. Martindale, *The Life of Monsignor Robert Hugh Benson* (London: Longmans, Green and Co., 1916), 1:259.

72. Ibid., I, p. 260.

73. Menzies, p. IV, 3.

74. Cropper, p. 30.

75. Menzies, p. IV, 3.

76. Cropper, p. 30.

77. Ibid.

78. Letter from E. R. Barker to E. Underhill, 8 Apr. 1907, EUC, folder 28.

79. Cropper, p. 30.

80. Ibid., pp. 30–31. See Carol Gilligan, *In a Different Voice* (Cambridge, Mass.: Harvard University Press, 1982). Gilligan argues that the moral reasoning of women differs from that of men and that their judgments are based not on abstract rules of justice but on their concern for human relatedness and the suffering their choices might cause.

81. Menzies, p. IV, 4.

82. "To H. S. Moore," (1907), *Letters*, pp. 58–59.

83. Cropper, p. 31.

84. "Pascendi Dominici Gregis," *The Papal Encyclicals: 1903–1934*, ed. Claudia Carlen (Salem, N.H.: McGrath Publishing, 1981), pp. 72–79.

85. "To Mrs. Meyrick Heath," 14 May 1911, *Letters*, p. 126.

86. Ibid.

87. Martindale, 1:262.

88. Ibid., 1:263.

89. J. A. Herbert to E. Underhill, no date, EUC, folder 45.

90. "To H. S. Moore," 1 May 1907, *Letters*, p. 61.

91. "To M. R., " 29 July 1908, *Letters*, p. 80.

92. Ibid., 9 Oct. 1907, p. 69.

93. Ibid., 30 Dec. 1907, pp. 70–71.

94. Ibid.

95. Ibid., 16 Jan. 1908, p. 73.

96. Ibid., p. 72.

97. Ibid., 29 Aug. 1908, p. 81.

98. "A Defence of Magic," *Fortnightly Review*, 88 (November 1907):763–64.

99. Ibid., pp. 764–65.

100. Ibid., p. 763.

Chapter 2: The Work of the Borderland

1. Details regarding Underhill's house and daily life are taken from C. Armstrong, *Evelyn Underhill* (Grand Rapids, Mich.: Eerdmans, 1975); M. Cropper, *Evelyn Underhill* (London: Longmans, Green and Co., 1958); L. Menzies, Biography, TS unfinished, Underhill Collection, St. Andrews University Archives, St. Andrews, Scotland; *Letters of Evelyn Underhill*, ed. C. Williams

(London: Longmans, Green and Co., 1943). The ETERNITY plaque was not acquired until 1916.

2. Letter to E. Underhill from F. von Hügel, 9 Aug. 1924, von Hügel–Underhill Correspondence, St. Andrews University Archives.

3. E. Underhill, "The Cant of Unconventionality — A Rejoinder to Lady Robert Cecil," *National Review* 229 (January 1908):755.

4. "To Margaret Robinson," 17 Feb. 1909, *Letters*, p. 93.

5. Letters, 1907–1922. MS. E. Underhill to M. Sinclair. May Sinclair Collection, University of Pennsylvania, Philadelphia, Pa. The one exception is a letter from 1911 in which Underhill writes of having experienced evil.

6. "To J. A. Herbert," 16 Sept. 1911, *Letters*, p. 129.

7. "To H. S. Moore," 25 Apr. 1908, *Letters*, p. 74.

8. Letters from E. R. Barker to E. Underhill, Underhill Collection, King's College Archives, London (EUC), folder 33. These letters from 1906–7 show that Barker was an intimate of Underhill. There is no further correspondence with Barker after this period.

9. F. von Hügel to E. Underhill, 30 Oct. 1911, EUC, folder 46.

10. "To J. A. Herbert," 16 Sept. 1911, *Letters*, p. 129.

11. F. von Hügel, *Selected Letters*, 1896–1924, ed. B. Holland (London: Dent and Sons, 1928), p. 187.

12. Much has been written on von Hügel. See, for example, T. M. Loome, "The Enigma of Baron Friedrich von Hügel–As a Modernist," *Downside Review*, 92, nos. 302, 303, 304 (1974):13–34, 123–40, 204–30.

13. P. Thompson, *The Edwardians: The Remaking of British Society* (Bloomington, Ind.: Indiana University Press, 1975).

14. J. Macquarrie, *Twentieth Century Religious Thought* (London: SCM Press, 1983), pp. 169–81.

15. A. Quinton, "Thought," *Edwardian England, 1904–1911*, ed. S. Nowell-Smith (London: Oxford University Press, 1964), p. 286.

16. H. Davies, *Worship and Theology in England* (Princeton, N.J.: Princeton University Press, 1965), 5: 144–50. L. Johnson, "Modern Mysticism: Some Prophets and Poets," *Quarterly Review* 220 (January 1914):223.

17. "To Mrs. Meyrick Heath," (1913?), misdated, 1912, *Letters*, pp. 146–47.

18. E. Underhill, *The Column of Dust* (London: Methuen and Co., 1909), p. 65.

19. Cropper, p. 41. No citation given.

20. "To Margaret Robinson," 16 June 1908, *Letters*, p. 77.

21. "To Mrs. Meyrick Heath," 14 May 1911, *Letters*, p. 126.

22. "To Margaret Robinson," 12 Apr. 1910, *Letters*, p. 116.

23. "To Margaret Robinson," 16 June 1908, *Letters*, p. 77.

24. "To Margaret Robinson," 26 Sept. 1908, *Letters*, p. 83.

25. "To Margaret Robinson," 9 May 1908, *Letters*, p. 76.

26. "To Margaret Robinson," 16 June 1908, *Letters*, pp. 77–78.

27. "To Mrs. Meyrick Heath," 31 Mar. 1911, *Letters*, p. 122.

28. "To Mrs. Meyrick Heath," 16 Nov. 1911, *Letters*, p. 130.

29. "To Margaret Robinson," 13 Oct. 1909, MS. 5128, St. Andrews University Archives, St. Andrews, Scotland.

30. "To J. A. Herbert," May 1910, *Letters*, p. 118.

31. "To Margaret Robinson," 26 Sept. 1908, *Letters*, pp. 83–84.

32. "To Margaret Robinson," 29 July 1908, *Letters*, p. 78.

33. "To Margaret Robinson," Feast of the Visitation, 1909, *Letters*, p. 101.

34. "To Margaret Robinson," 12 Apr. 1911, *Letters*, pp. 123–24.

35. M. Decker, "A Hermeneutic Approach to the Problem of Mysticism," Ph.D. diss., Emory University, 1978, p. 42.

36. "To Mrs. Meyrick Heath," 19 Mar. 1911, *Letters*, p. 122.

37. "To Margaret Robinson," 1909, *Letters*, pp. 100–101.

38. "To Margaret Robinson," 1 Dec. 1909, *Letters*, pp. 106–7.

39. Decker makes a similar point. See also E. Fox Keller, *A Feeling for the Organism: The Life and Work of Barbara McClintock* (New York: W. H. Freeman, 1983) in which the author shows that Barbara McClintock's methodology is gender specific.

40. E. Underhill, *Mysticism: A Study in the Nature and Development of Man's Spiritual Consciousness* (London: Methuen, 1912), p. ix.

41. Ibid., p. 84.

42. Ibid., pp. 84–85.

43. Ibid., p. x.

44. Ibid., p. 28.

45. Ibid., p. 97.

46. Ibid., p. 86.

47. Ibid., p. 96. James's four marks are Ineffability, Noetic Quality, Transiency, and Passivity, from W. James, *Varieties of Religious Experience* (London: 1902), p. 380.

48. Ibid.

49. Ibid., p. 100.

50. Ibid., p. 107.

51. Ibid., p. 212.

52. Ibid., p. 502.

53. Cited in "In Memoriam; Miss Evelyn Underhill," *The Church Times*, 20 June 1941, EUC, folder 57.

54. Armstrong, p. 128.

55. "To My Dear ———," 27 Nov. 1911 in J. Chapman, *Spiritual Letters of Dom John Chapman* (London: Sheed and Ward, 1935), p. 244.

56. Letter from Methuen to Mr. James B. Pinker, 26 May 1909, EUC, folder 34. Pinker, Evelyn Underhill's agent, was also the agent of many of London's most prominent literati of those years.

57. E. Underhill to H. S. Moore, 21 Apr. 1911, EUC, folder 28.

58. E. Herman, *The Meaning and Value of Mysticism* (London: James Clark, 1915), pp. 7, 14–15, 23–29, 98–99.

59. Letter from Methuen to Mr. James Pinker, 10 June 1909, EUC, folder 34.

60. *Mysticism*, p. 27.
61. Ibid., p. 23.
62. Ibid., p. 21.

Chapter 3: The Cauldron of War

1. E. Underhill to F. von Hügel, 21 Dec. 1921, TS. Underhill–von Hügel Collection, St. Andrews University, Archives, St. Andrews, Scotland.
2. L. Menzies, Biography of Evelyn Underhill, TS unfinished, Underhill Collection, St. Andrews University, Archives, St. Andrews, Scotland, p. VI, 2.
3. The substance of this description of Underhill in 1916 was provided by Barbara Gnospelius née Collingwood and is recorded in M. Cropper, *Evelyn Underhill* (London: Longmans, Green and Co., 1958), p. 58.
4. "To Mrs. Meyrick Heath," 10 Feb. 1912, *Letters of Evelyn Underhill*, ed. C. Williams (London: Longmans, Green and Co., 1943), p. 134.
5. E. Underhill, "Bergson and The Mystics," *Living Age* 27 (10 Feb. 1912):511–22.
6. E. Underhill to M. Sinclair, 7 Nov. 1912, May Sinclair Collection, University of Pennsylvania, Philadelphia, Pa.
7. C. Armstrong, *Evelyn Underhill* (Grand Rapids, Mich.: Eerdmans, 1975), pp. 142–43.
8. E. Underhill, "An Indian Mystic," review of *Gitanjali* by Rabindranath Tagore, *The Nation*, 12 Nov. 1912, p. 321.
9. Ibid.
10. E. Underhill to R. Tagore, 19 Aug. 1913, Evelyn Underhill Collection (EUC), Archives, King's College, London, folder 31.
11. See *Imperfect Encounter: Letters of William Rothenstein and Rabindranath Tagore, 1911–1941*, ed. and with an intro. by M. Lago (Cambridge, Mass.: Harvard University Press, 1972), pp. 124, 156–60.
12. "To J. A. Herbert," (? 1913), *Letters*, p. 144.
13. H. N. Fairchild, *Religious Trends in English Poetry*, vol. 5 (New York: Columbia University Press, 1962), pp. 255–60.
14. E. Underhill, "Nature,"in *Theophanies: A Book of Verses* (London: J. M. Dent and Co., 1916), pp. 54–56. This book was dedicated to Hilda, an old friend at Appledore, who gave her the Eternity plaque in 1916. See Menzies, pp. viii, 28–29.
15. Ibid., "Dynamic Love," pp. 3–4.
16. Menzies, p. VI, 14.
17. E. Underhill letters, EUC, folder 28, and Menzies, p. XI, 3.
18. R. Woods, *Understanding Mysticism* (Garden City, N.Y.: Doubleday, 1980), p. 3.
19. E. Underhill, "St. Paul and the Mystic Way," *Contemporary Review* 546 (June 1911):694–706.
20. E. Underhill, "A Franciscan Mystic of the Thirteenth Century: The

Blessed Angela of Foligno," in *Franciscan Studies* by P. Sabatier (Aberdeen, Scotland: The University Press, 1912), pp. 88–107, reprinted in E. Underhill, *The Essentials of Mysticism and Other Essays* (London: J. M. Dent and Co., 1920).

21. E. Underhill, "Introduction," *One Hundred Poems of Kabir*, trans. R. Tagore (London: The India Society, 1914), pp. 1–18, reissued as *Songs of Kabir* (London: Macmillan, 1915); E. Underhill, "Kabir the Weaver Mystic," *Contemporary Review* 578 (1914):193–200.

22. *Songs of Kabir*, p. 45.

23. Ibid., p. 36.

24. E. Underhill, "Introduction," in *The Autobiography of Maharishi Devendranath Tagore* (London: Macmillan and Co., 1914), pp. ix–xlii.

25. E. Underhill, "Julian of Norwich," *St. Martin-in-the-Fields Monthly Review* 35 (May 1920):10–15, reprinted in *Essentials of Mysticism*.

26. E. Underhill, "Mysticism in Modern France," in *Essentials of Mysticism*, pp. 199–227.

27. E. Underhill, "Introduction," in *The Fire of Love or Melody of Love . . . of Richard Rolle*, ed. F. Comper (London: Methuen and Co., 1914), p. 194, pp. vii–xxv.

28. E. Underhill, "Introduction," in *The Confessions of Jacob Boehme*, ed. W. Scott Palmer (London: Methuen and Co., 1920), pp. xi–xxxv.

29. L. Menzies, p. VII, 12.

30. E. Underhill, *Ruysbroeck* (London: G. Bell and Sons, 1915).

31. E. Underhill, *Jacopone da Todi, Poet and Mystic, 1228–1306. A Spiritual Biography* (London: J. M. Dent and Sons, 1919). This excellent work is commended in *Jacopone da Todi, The Lauds*, edited and with an introduction by Serge Hughes (New York: Paulist Press, 1982), pp. 20–21.

32. E. Underhill, "Introduction," in *The Mirror of Simple Souls, The Porch* 1, no. 8 (1910):2–4; "The Mirror of Simple Souls," *The Fortnightly Review* 89 (February 1911):345–54, reprinted in *Essentials of Mysticism*. It has been subsequently determined that the *Mirror of Simple Souls* is the work of Marguerite Porete.

33. E. Underhill, *The Cloud of Unknowing*, ed. and with an introduction (London: J. M. Watkins, 1912), pp. 5–37.

34. E. Underhill, *The Mystic Way: A Psychological Study in Christian Origins* (London: J. M. Dent and Sons, 1913).

35. Ibid., p. 58.

36. "To J. A. Herbert," (? 1913), *Letters*, p. 144.

37. "To Miss Nancy Paul," 1913, *Letters*, p. 140.

38. "To J. A. Herbert," 30 Mar. 1913, *Letters*, p. 141.

39. Ibid., pp. 141–42.

40. Ibid.

41. Ibid.

42. Ibid., p. 143.

43. Ibid.

44. E. Underhill, *Practical Mysticism: A Little Book for Normal People* (London: J. M. Dent and Sons, 1914), p. 30.

45. E. Underhill, "The Education of the Spirit," *The Parents' Review* 28, no. 10 (October 1916):753–61, reprinted in *Essentials of Mysticism.*

46. E. Underhill, "The Place of Will, Intellect and Feeling in Prayer," *The Interpreter* 9, no. 3 (April 1913):241–56, reprinted in *Essentials of Mysticism*, p. 99.

47. Ibid.

48. "To Margaret Robinson," 29 Aug. 1908, *Letters*, p. 82.

49. *Practical Mysticism*, pp. 162–63.

50. Ibid., p. viii.

51. Ibid., pp. ix–x.

52. Menzies, p. VII, 2.

53. Armstrong, p. 159.

54. This is Menzies' surmise based on an article Underhill wrote for *The Saturday Westminster*, p. VII, 12.

55. Ibid.

56. E. Underhill, "The Prayer of Silence," *The Challenge* 3, no. 39 (11 June 1915):125.

57. E. Underhill, "Mysticism and the Doctrine of the Atonement," *The Interpreter* 10, no. 4 (January 1914):131–48, reprinted in *Essentials of Mysticism*, p. 43; "The Mystic and the Corporate Life," *The Interpreter* 11, no. 2 (January 1915):143–60, reprinted in *Essentials of Mysticism.*

58. E. Underhill, "Charles Péguy: In Memoriam," *The Contemporary Review* 592 (April 1915):472–78, reprinted in *Essentials of Mysticism.*

59. "Mysticism and War," *The Quest*, January 1915, pp. 207–19, published as a pamphlet by John Watkins, 1915; "Problem of Conflict," *The Hibbert Journal* 13, no. 3 (April 1915):497–510; "A Note on the Fight For Right Movement," in *The Training of the Combatant* by C. F. E. Spurgeon (London: J. M. Dent and Sons, 1916), pp. 21–28; "The Consecration of England," given in 1916 and published in *For The Right: Essays and Addresses by Members of the Fight For Right Movement* (New York: G. P. Putnam and Sons, 1918), pp. 232–42.

60. "Mysticism and War," p. 6.

61. "Non-Combatants," *Theophanies: A Book of Verses* (London: J. M. Dent and Sons, 1916), pp. 115–16.

62. A. Underhill, *Change and Decay: The Recollections and Reflections of An Octogenarian Bencher* (London: Butterworth and Co., 1938), p. 105.

63. Menzies, pp. VII, 29; VIII, 13.

64. E. Underhill to F. von Hügel, 21 Dec. 1921, Underhill–von Hügel Collection.

65. "To Margaret Robinson," *Letters*, 9 Nov. 1917, p. 147.

66. Menzies, p. VIII, 4.

67. *Jacopone da Todi*, p. 26.

68. This is her final interpretation of Jacopone da Todi given in "A Francis-

can Poet — Jacopone da Todi," in *Essays... of the Royal Society of Literature of the United Kingdom*, ed. G. K. Chesterton (London: Oxford University Press, 1926), NS. 6, pp. 63–64.

69. E. Underhill, "The Future of Mysticism," *Everyman*, 12, no. 301 (20 July 1918):336.

70. Ibid.

71. E. Underhill, "A New Reformer," review of *Christ, St. Francis and Today* by G. G. Coulton, *Saturday Westminster Gazette*, 17 May 1919, p. 16.

72. E. Underhill, "A Foster-Father of the Church," review of *Plotinus: The Ethical Treatises*, ed. Stephen MacKenna, *Saturday Westminster Gazette*, 1 September 1917, p. 10.

73. E. Underhill, "The Mysticism of Plotinus," *The Quarterly Review* 231, no. 4559 (1918):479–97, reprinted in *Essentials of Mysticism*, p. 130.

74. Underhill hints at some of these points in a review of *Mysticism and Modern Life* by John Buckman and *Mysticism and the Creed* by W. F. Cobb, *Harvard Theological Review* 9, no. 2 (April 1916):234–38.

75. E. Underhill, "Essentials of Mysticism," in *Essentials of Mysticism*, pp. 13–14.

76. Menzies, pp. VIII, 8–11. In 1920 Underhill, serving as one of the Entente's secretaries, urged Lucy Menzies, a deeply religious Scot with whom she had corresponded during the war years, to stop in Siena on her Italian tour and visit six poor women, including an English woman, a Miss Turton, who composed the nucleus of the Entente.

77. Ibid., p. VII, 11. She indicates that Underhill was an Anglican by 1921. F. von Hügel to E. Underhill, 29 Oct. 1921, St. Andrews indicates how happy he was that during the course of writing the Upton lectures that she "came out strongly and self-committingly for Traditional, Institutional, Sacramental Religion."

78. J. P. Jacks to E. Underhill, 13 May 1921, EUC, folder 45. Underhill was paid fifty pounds for the series.

79. E. Underhill, *The Life of the Spirit and the Life of Today* (London: Methuen, 1922), p. xix.

80. *Annual Reports of Manchester College*, Manchester College, Oxford, June 1922, pp. 8–9.

81. Menzies, p. VIII, 12.

82. Ibid., p. III, 13.

83. *Life of the Spirit*, p. xix.

84. Ibid., p. xvii.

85. Ibid., p. 169.

86. Ibid., p. 143.

87. Ibid., pp. 220–21.

88. E. Underhill to F. von Hügel, Summer 1922, Underhill–von Hügel Collection. She indicates that she had agreed to attend a retreat prior to coming under his direction.

Chapter 4: Seeking "Real, Permanent Life"

1. F. von Hügel to E. Underhill 5 Nov. 1921, von Hügel–Underhill Collection, St. Andrews University Archives, St. Andrews, Scotland.

2. J. Cordelier (E. Underhill), *The Path of Eternal Wisdom* (London: John Watkins, 1911), p. 89.

3. F. von Hügel to Mrs. Stuart Moore, 26 June 1916, Evelyn Underhill Collection (EUC), Archives, King's College, London, folder 46.

4. E. Underhill, "Finite and Infinite: A Study of the Philosophy of Baron Friedrich von Hügel," in *Mixed Pasture* (London: Methuen, 1933), pp. 209–28, and "Baron von Hügel as a Spiritual Teacher," in *Mixed Pasture*, pp. 229–33.

5. E. Underhill to F. von Hügel, 21 Dec. 1921, von Hügel–Underhill Collection.

6. L. Menzies, Biography of Evelyn Underhill, TS unfinished, St. Andrews University Archives, St. Andrews, Scotland, p. IX, 22.

7. Ibid., pp. xx, 21–22.

8. "To J.A. Herbert" (1913), *Letters of Evelyn Underhill*, ed. C. Williams (London: Longmans, Green and Co., 1943), p. 144.

9. "To Lucy Menzies," 28 Aug. 1924, *Letters*, p. 324.

10. Underhill, "Baron von Hügel as a Spiritual Teacher," p. 229.

11. Ibid., p. 230.

12. "To Dom Chapman," 9 June 1931, *Letters*, p. 196.

13. F. von Hügel to E. Underhill, late 1921, von Hügel–Underhill Collection.

14. Ibid.

15. Ibid.

16. Ibid.

17. Ibid.

18. E. Underhill to F. von Hügel, 21 Dec. 1921, von Hügel–Underhill Collection.

19. Ibid.

20. F. von Hügel to E. Underhill, end 1921, von Hügel–Underhill Collection.

21. Ibid.

22. Ibid.

23. Ibid.

24. Ibid.

25. Ibid.

26. For the history of the Retreat House see M. Avery, *Pleshey: The Village and Retreat House* (Bishop's Stortford: Ellis and Phillips Ltd., 1981).

27. For information on E. Underhill see Fay Campbell, "Evelyn Underhill: Conversion at Pleshey," *The Living Church*, 1 Mar. 1987, pp. 11–13.

28. E. Underhill to F. von Hügel, midsummer, 1922, von Hügel–Underhill Collection.

29. Ibid.

30. E. Underhill to F. von Hügel, midsummer, 1922, von Hügel–Underhill Collection.

31. Ibid.

32. E. Underhill to F. von Hügel, June 1923, von Hügel–Underhill Collection. Emphasis added.

33. C. Williams, "Introduction," *Letters*, p. 26.

34. E. Underhill to F. von Hügel, midsummer, 1922, von Hügel–Underhill Collection.

35. Ibid.

36. Ibid.

37. E. Underhill to F. von Hügel, 21 Dec. 1921, von Hügel–Underhill Collection.

38. E. Underhill to F. von Hügel, June 1923, von Hügel–Underhill Collection.

39. E. Underhill, Notebook, February 1923, EUC, folder 58.

40. E. Underhill, Notebook, 16 Feb. 1923.

41. E. Underhill to F. von Hügel, June 1923, von Hügel–Underhill Collection.

42. F. von Hügel to E. Underhill, 12 July 1923, von Hügel–Underhill Collection.

43. E. Underhill to F. von Hügel, 21 Dec. 1921, von Hügel–Underhill Collection.

44. Ibid.

45. E. Underhill to F. von Hügel, midsummer, 1922, von Hügel–Underhill Collection.

46. Underhill, Notebook, "Self-Examination."

47. Underhill, Notebook, 15 Feb. 1923.

48. F. von Hügel to E. Underhill, end of 1921, von Hügel–Underhill Collection.

49. Ibid.

50. E. Underhill to F. von Hügel, midsummer, 1922, von Hügel–Underhill Collection.

51. F. von Hügel to E. Underhill, 21 July 1922, von Hügel–Underhill Collection.

52. "To Margaret Robinson," 29 July 1908, *Letters*, p. 78.

53. F. von Hügel to E. Underhill, 9 Aug. 1924, von Hügel–Underhill Collection.

54. E. Underhill to F. von Hügel, June 1923, von Hügel–Underhill Collection.

55. Underhill, Notebook, January 1923.

56. Ibid., 26 Dec. 1923.

57. Ibid., 20 June 1924.

58. Ibid., 8 Feb. 1924.

59. Ibid., 15 Jan. 1924.

60. Ibid., 26 Dec. 1923.

61. Ibid., 16 Oct. 1924.

62. Underhill, Notebook, 13 Apr. 1924.

63. "To Lucy Menzies," 7 Oct. 1923, *Letters*, p. 317.

64. "To W. Y.," 11 Oct. 1925, *Letters*, p. 168.

65. "To W. Y.," 19 Mar. 1924, *Letters*, p. 152.

66. "To Lucy Menzies," 25 Jan. 1923, *Letters*, p. 312.

67. "To Lucy Menzies," 7 Feb. 1923, *Letters*, pp. 313–14.

68. "To Lucy Menzies," 27 June 1923, *Letters*, p. 316.

69. "To Lucy Menzies," 14 Dec. 1924, *Letters*, p. 320.

70. "To Lucy Menzies," 26 Jan. 1924, *Letters*, p. 320.

71. E. Underhill, "Degrees of Prayer," *The Mount of Purification* (New York: David McKay Co., 1962), pp. 161–79.

72. E. Underhill, "Some Implicits of Christian Social Reform," in *Mixed Pasture*, pp. 63–83.

73. E. Underhill, "Suggestion and Religious Experience," *Fortnightly Review*, 117 (March 1922):410–21.

74. E. Underhill, "Walter Hilton," *Mixed Pasture*, pp. 188–208; "Introduction," in *Scale of Perfection* by W. Hilton (London: John Watkins, 1923), pp. v–liv.

75. Underhill, "Walter Hilton," p. 189.

76. M. Cropper, *Evelyn Underhill* (London: Longmans, Green and Co., 1958), p. 115.

77. See "Retreat" by J. Townroe, *Study of Spirituality*, ed. C. Jones et al. (London: SPCK, 1986), pp. 578–81; J. Moorman, *The Anglican Spiritual Tradition* (London: Darton, Longman and Todd, 1983), p. 209; E. Underhill, *Worship* (London: Nisbet, 1936), p. 338.

78. Underhill, Notebook, 18 Mar. 1924.

79. Cropper, p. 116.

80. Underhill, Notebook, 18 Mar. 1924.

81. Ibid.

82. E. Underhill to F. von Hügel, June 1923, von Hügel–Underhill Collection.

83. Cropper, p. 120. Quoted from Barbara Gnospelius.

84. F. von Hügel to E. Underhill, 30 May 1924, von Hügel–Underhill Collection.

85. Underhill, Notebook, 13 Apr. 1924.

86. Cropper, p. 122.

87. "To Lucy Menzies," 1 Feb. 1925, *Letters*, p. 162.

88. Cropper, p. 133.

89. E. Underhill, "The Will of the Voice," in *Mixed Pasture*. pp. 84–94.

90. E. Underhill, "The Christian Basis of Social Action," in *Mixed Pasture*, pp. 95–112.

91. E. Underhill, "Christian Fellowship: Past and Present," *The Interpreter* 20, no. 3 (July 1924):171–81.

92. E. Underhill, "Our Two-Fold Relation to Reality," *Hibbert Journal* 23, no. 2 (January 1925):228.

93. E. Underhill, *Prayer* (London: Y.W.C.A., 1926). Previously, in November 1925, Underhill gave a retreat at Pleshey for the Y.W.C.A.

94. E. Underhill, *The Mystics of the Church* (London: James Clarke, 1925), preface.

95. "To Lucy Menzies," 2 Aug. 1924, *Letters*, p. 323.

Chapter 5: "Called Out and Settled"

1. E. Underhill, "The Authority of Personal Religious Experience," *Theology* 10, no. 55 (January 1925):13.

2. The major exceptions are her many reviews in *The Spectator* and her book *Man and the Supernatural* (London: Methuen and Co., 1927).

3. There is no evidence that she gave retreats for lay men.

4. M. Cropper, *Evelyn Underhill* (London: Longmans, Green and Co., 1958), pp. 138, 148.

5. E. Underhill, *The Spiritual Life: Four Broadcast Talks* (London: Hodder and Stoughton, 1937) reprinted (New York: Harper & Row, 1963), p. 36.

6. E. Underhill, "A Franciscan Poet — Jacopone da Todi," *Royal Society of Literature*, ed. G. K. Chesterton (London: Oxford University Press, 1926), N. S. 6, p. 64.

7. Ibid., pp. 64–65.

8. Ibid., p. 64.

9. Cropper, p. 188.

10. Ibid., p. 180.

11. Ibid., p. 163.

12. Ibid., p. 180.

13. C. Armstrong, *Evelyn Underhill* (Grand Rapids, Mich.: Eerdmans, 1975), p. 254.

14. Cropper, p. 161.

15. She wrote reviews for the *Spectator* for ten years and was religious editor for four, leaving in 1932 apparently after a strong Non-Conformist, Modernist editor took over. See "To E. I. Watkin," 11 June 1934, *Letters of Evelyn Underhill*, ed. C. Williams (London: Longmans, Green and Co., 1943), p. 233.

16. Cropper, pp. 141–43.

17. This appointment carried with it no official duties.

18. M. Ramsey, "Foreword," in C. Armstrong, *Evelyn Underhill*, p. x.

19. Cropper, p. 157. She continued to wear her mother's lace veils when in retreat.

20. Ibid., pp. 140, 157; O. Wyon, *Desire For God: A Study of Three Spiritual Classics* (London: Collins, 1966), p. 98.

21. Cropper, p. 158; L. Menzies, "Memoir," in *Light of Christ*, published with *Fruits of the Spirit* (London: Longmans, Green and Co., 1944), p. 20–21.

22. E. Underhill, "The Spiritual Significance of the Oxford Movement," *Hibbert Journal* 31, no. 3 (April 1933):401–12.

23. E. Underhill, "The Ideals of Ministry of Women," *Theology* 26, no. 151 (January 1933):37–42.

24. "To John Chapman," 9 June 1931, *Letters*, p. 195.

25. Ibid.

26. Ibid.

27. "To F. H.," 20 Mar. 1933, *Letters*, p. 210.

28. E. Underhill, *Worship* (London: Nisbet, 1936), reprinted (New York: Crossroad, 1982), pp. 316–17.

29. "To F. H.," 11 May 1933, *Letters*, p. 211.

30. This book contains revisions of a number of her articles including "The Authority of Personal Religious Experience," 1925; "The Two-Fold Relation of Reality," 1925; and "Possibilities of Prayer," 1927.

31. Cropper, p. 136.

32. E. Underhill, *Man and the Supernatural* (London: Methuen and Co., 1927), p. 21.

33. "To M. C.," 1932, *Letters*, pp. 205–6.

34. "To L. K.," 21 June 1934, *Letters*, p. 234.

35. *Man and the Supernatural*, pp. 131, 134. Although this book is dedicated to von Hügel, there are differences between them. See S. Smalley, "The Relationship Between Friedrich von Hügel and Evelyn Underhill, paper delivered at the London Institute for the Study of Religion, London, June 1975.

36. E. Underhill, "Christianity and the Claims of Other Religions," in *Essays Catholic and Missionary*, ed. E. R. Morgan (London: Macmillan, 1928), pp. 3–22.

37. E. Underhill, "Spiritual Life and Influence," in *Walter Howard Frere, Bishop of Truro: A Memoir* by C. S. Phillips et al. (London: Faber and Faber, 1947), pp. 175–82.

38. Ibid., p. 180.

39. E. Underhill, "Worship," in *Collected Papers* (London: Mowbray, 1946), pp. 73–92.

40. "To J. A. Herbert," 19 Mar. 1910, *Letters*, p. 112.

41. E. Underhill, "Introductory Note," *Mysticism and the Eastern Church* by N. Arsenieu (London: Student Christian Movement, 1926), reprinted (Crestwood, N.Y.: St. Vladimir's Seminary Press, 1979), pp. 13–15.

42. "To L. K.," 8 Feb. 1935, *Letters*, p. 243.

43. *Worship*, p. xiii. She also acknowledges the help of Dr. N. Zernov.

44. F. von Hügel to E. Underhill, 21 July 1922, von Hügel–Underhill Collection, Archives, St. Andrews University, St. Andrews, Scotland.

45. "To Y. N.," Ascension Day, 1935, *Letters*, p. 247.

46. E. Underhill, review, *The Spiritual Letters of Dom John Chapman*, ed. R. Hudleston, *Theology* 30, no. 180 (June 1935):369–73.

47. "Dear Mrs. . . . ," 28 Sept. 1931, *Spiritual Letters of Dom John Chapman* (London: Sheed and Ward, 1935), p. 107.

48. Only letters from 1931 survive, although correspondence apparently continued for another year. Chapman died in 1933.

49. Margaret Cropper was a friend, retreatant, a religious dramatist, and the first to publish a biography of Underhill. They met in 1931. Underhill dedicated *Mixed Pastures* to her.

50. Armstrong, p. 251. This letter of 8 Dec. 1932 to Margaret Cropper is not reprinted fully in her biography or in *Letters*.

51. Ibid.

52. Ibid., p. 252.

53. E. Underhill, Notebook, "Notes on Retreat, May 1926," Evelyn Underhill Collection (EUC), Archives, King's College, London, folder 58.

54. Ibid.

55. Ibid.

56. Notebook, "Notes made in Retreat, July 1928, Moreton."

57. Ibid. "Notes made in Retreat at Moreton, June 1929." The first reference is to "L.," Lucy Menzies, her close friend, who was apparently a very intense personality and very devoted to Underhill. Subsequently Underhill listed her personal relationship with L. M. as something that needed attention. See Flowered Notebook, "Notes for Reginald Somerset Ward, Oct. 1936," EUC, folder 47. The second reference to "C." is most assuredly Clara Smith, whom she mentions by name in Notebook, "Notes made in Retreat at Moreton, July 1928," and by abbreviation in Flowered Notebook, "Father Talbot's Advice," and Notebook, "Fruit of Retreat, 1933."

58. Notebook, "Notes made in Retreat at Moreton, June 1929."

59. Flowered Notebook, "Father Talbot's Advice" and "Bede Frost's Advice." No dates are given on these entries, but they both clearly refer to problems arising in or around 1929 and have to do with her possessiveness. The entries are not recorded in Underhill's handwriting but were probably copied by Marjorie Vernon with whom the Stuart Moores lived during World War II. They are arranged in the notebook prior to the 1933 entries, giving further support to the notion that they occurred between 1929 and 1933.

60. Notebook, "Notes Made in Retreat, May 1930, St. Mary's Abbey."

61. L. Menzies to Gillian (Wilkinson), 17 Jan. (no year), EUC, folder 37.

62. Interview with Renée Tickell née Haynes, May 1988, London.

63. Record Book, House of Retreat, Pleshey.

64. Notebook, "Notes Made in Retreat at Moreton," June 1929.

65. L. Menzies to Gillian (Wilkinson), 17 Jan. (no year).

66. Ibid.

67. Notebook, "Notes made in Retreat at Moreton," June 1929.

68. Flowered Notebook, "Reginald Somerset Ward's Advice, Michaelmas, 1933."

69. Notebook, "Notes Made in Retreat, May 1930, St. Mary's Abbey."

70. Ibid.

71. Flowered Notebook, "Easter . . . 1933."

72. (R. S. Ward), *A Guide for Spiritual Directors* (London: Mowbray, 1957), pp. 12–17, 38–39, 94–96.

73. Ward was aware of the limitations of the new science of psychology, which he believed should assist but not dominate spiritual direction. See *Guide for Spiritual Directors*, pp. 14, 38–39, 94–95.

74. Cropper, p. 1.

75. Ibid. This is confirmed by Arthur Underhill's *Change and Decay: The Recollections and Reflections of an Octogenarian Bencher* (London: Butterworth and Co., 1938), in which he makes very few references to his daughter.

76. Flowered Notebook, "Reginald Somerset Ward Advice: Later, 1933."

77. Flowered Notebook, "Reginald Somerset Ward's Advice, Michaelmas, 1933."

78. Notebook, "Reginald Somerset Ward, 19 June 1934."

79. "To L. M.," July 1929, *Letters*, p. 335.

80. "To L. M.," June 1932, *Letters*, p. 204.

81. "To G. F.," 1932, *Letters*, p. 208.

82. "To G. F.," 16 Aug. 1933, *Letters*, p. 214.

83. "To A. B.," 1 Aug. 1927, *Letters*, p. 174.

84. "To M. C.," 1932, *Letters*, p. 206.

85. "To M. R.," 29 July 1908, *Letters*, p. 78.

86. "A. B.," 22 Oct. 1927, *Letters*, p. 177.

87. See E. Underhill, *Mount of Purification* (New York: David McKay Co., 1960), p. 61, where she urges "attachment in detachment" and then "detachment in attachment," p. 64.

88. Most reviews treated two or three books; consequently the total number of books reviewed for the nine-year period, 1926–1934, is in excess of four hundred.

89. Her preference for Ruysbroeck was stated in 1911. See, "To Mrs. Meyrick Heath," 19 Mar. 1911, *Letters*, p. 122.

90. E. Underhill, "St. Francis and Franciscan Spirituality," in *Mixed Pasture* (London: Methuen, 1933), p. 156.

91. Ibid., p. 163.

92. "To M. C.," 19 Feb. 1932, *Letters*, p. 201.

93. She wrote mostly reviews for the *Spectator;* however, she also did a few essays.

94. E. Underhill, "A Franciscan Hermitage," *Spectator*, 11 Feb. 1928, p. 183.

95. Armstrong, pp. 261–63. There is an obvious diminishing of reliance on Lévi, Machen, Waite, Bergson, and Eucken; increased weight is given to Otto, Maritain, and Poulain.

96. E. Underhill, *Mysticism*, 12th ed. (New York: New American Library, 1974), pp. ix–x.

97. Miss Daphne Martin-Hurst, who attended Underhill's retreats, indicated that the retreats had no more than this number. Oxford, 22 May 1986.

The record books of the House of Retreat, Pleshey, confirm this with a few exceptions.

98. Record Books, House of Retreat, Pleshey.

99. E. Underhill, *Fruits of the Spirit* (1942), reprinted with *Light of Christ* (1944) (London: Longmans, Green and Co., 1956), pp. 1–2.

100. E. Underhill, "Need of Retreat" (1932), reprinted in *Light of Christ*, pp. 102–7.

101. Cropper, p. 159; L. Menzies, "Memoir," in *Light of Christ*, pp. 12–16, 22.

102. Cropper, p. 159; Menzies, "Memoir," pp. 12–16, 22; Armstrong, pp. 265–67; Wyon, pp. 93–96. *Concerning the Inner Life*, given in 1926, was published the same year; *House of the Soul*, given probably in 1927, was published in 1929; *The Golden Sequence*, given probably in 1930, was published in 1932; *Mount of Purification*, given in 1931, published in 1960; *Light of Christ*, given in 1932, published in 1944; *School of Charity*, given in 1933, published in 1934; *Abba*, given in 1934, published in 1940; *Mystery of Sacrifice*, given in 1935, published in 1938; *Fruits of the Spirit*, given in 1936, published in 1942. Retreats published while she was alive were usually dedicated to friends: *Concerning the Inner Life* was dedicated to Gwendolyn Greene; *House of the Soul*, to Rosa; *Golden Sequence*, to Lucy Menzies; *School of Charity*, to Pleshey; *Abba*, to B. B. G.; *Mystery of Sacrifice*, to Marjorie Vernon. EU did not dedicate any book to Hubert.

103. E. Underhill, *The Golden Sequence: A Four-Fold Study of the Spiritual Life* (London: Methuen, 1932), reprinted (New York: Harper & Row, 1960), pp. 12, 36.

104. E. Underhill, "Philosophy of Contemplation," Counsell Memorial Lecture, 1930, in *Mixed Pasture: Twelve Essays and Addresses* (London: Methuen, 1933), pp. 1–2; "Inside of Life," Radio Broadcast, 1931, in *Collected Papers* (London: Mowbray, 1946), pp. 120–22.

105. E. Underhill, *Concerning the Inner Life*, 1926, published with *House of the Soul*, 1929 (Minneapolis, Minn.: Seabury Press, 1984), pp. 93–94.

106. E. Underhill, *Abba. Meditations Based on the Lord's Prayer*, 1940, published with *Fruits of the Spirit* and *Light of Christ*, pp. 3–4. Although *Abba* was given in 1934, the retreat was rewritten in 1939. See "To M. C.," 3 Oct. 1939, *Letters*, p. 278.

107. *Golden Sequence*, p. 152.

108. Ibid., p. 152; *Concerning the Inner Life*, p. 118.

109. *Golden Sequence*, p. 173.

110. Ibid., p. 75.

111. *Mount of Purification*, p. 11.

112. *Concerning the Inner Life*, p. 134.

113. Ibid., pp. 94–95.

114. E. Underhill, "The Spiritual Life," address to Harrow Masters, published in *Mixed Pasture*, p. 61.

115. *Concerning the Inner Life*, p. 106.

116. Ibid., p. 105.

117. Ibid., p. 122.

118. E. Underhill, "The Meaning of Sanctity," *Spectator*, 23 Jan. 1932, reprinted in *Mixed Pasture*, p. 42.

119. Ibid., p. 35.

120. E. Underhill, *School of Charity: Meditations on the Christian Creed* (London: Longmans, Green and Co., 1934), p. 47.

121. *Concerning the Inner Life*, pp. 150–51.

122. *School of Charity*, p. 32.

123. *The Spiritual Life: Four Broadcast Talks*, p. 95.

124. *Golden Sequence*, p. 104.

125. *Mount of Purification*, p. 16.

126. Ibid., p. 10.

127. Ibid., p. 64.

128. Ibid.

129. *Golden Sequence*, p. 114.

130. Ibid., pp. 62–63.

131. *School of Charity*, p. 14.

132. *Concerning the Inner Life*. The whole of this book is devoted to this subject.

133. See E. Underhill, "The Spiritual Life of the Teacher," 1934, and "The Teacher's Vocation," 1927, printed in *Collected Papers*, pp. 200–217 and 182–99.

134. *Abba*, p. 30.

135. Ibid., pp. 34–35.

136. "To Conrad Noel," 1 Mar. 1933, *Letters*, p. 209.

137. Ibid.

138. *The Spiritual Life: Four Broadcast Talks*, pp. 90–91.

139. *Light of Christ*, p. 66.

140. *The Spiritual Life: Four Broadcast Talks*, p. 36.

141. Cropper, p. 184.

Chapter 6: Not Thy Gifts But Thyself

1. This retreat was revised and published later as *Mystery of Sacrifice: A Meditation on the Liturgy* (London: Longmans, Green and Co., 1938).

2. M. Cropper, *Evelyn Underhill* (London: Longmans, Green and Co., 1958), p. 190. Quoted from a letter. No source given.

3. Ibid., pp. 187–88. Quoted from a 1935 letter to Lucy Menzies.

4. E. Underhill, "Worship," *Collected Papers* (London: Longmans, Green and Co., 1946), pp. 73–92.

5. E. Shackle, review of *Mysticism*, in *Christian Parapsychologist*, September 1988, p. 1.

6. E. Underhill, "Education and the Spirit of Worship," *Collected Papers*, p. 226.

7. Ibid., p. 231.

8. "Worship," p. 92. Emphasis added.

9. E. Underhill, *Worship* (London: Nisbet, 1936), p. 251.

10. Cropper, p. 194.

11. E. Underhill, *The Fruits of the Spirit* (London: Longmans, Green and Co., 1942).

12. "The Priest's Life of Prayer" and "The Life of Prayer in the Parish," *Collected Papers*, pp. 140–81.

13. Cropper, p. 193.

14. "What Is Mysticism?" *Collected Papers*, pp. 122–39.

15. *The Spiritual Life: Four Broadcast Talks* (London: Hodder and Stoughton, 1937).

16. "To M. C.," 19 Feb. 1932, *Letters of Evelyn Underhill*, ed. C. Williams (London: Longmans, Green and Co., 1943), p. 201.

17. "To G. F.," Sept. 1937, *Letters*, p. 260.

18. "To M. C.," 27 Sept. 1937, *Letters*, p. 261.

19. "Education and the Spirit of Worship," p. 240.

20. Ibid., p. 229.

21. Cropper, pp. 208–9.

22. Ibid., p. 209.

23. She began to do book reviews for *Time and Tide* in 1937. *Eucharistic Prayers from the Ancient Liturgies* (London: Longmans, Green and Co., 1940) was a compilation of prayers that developed out of *Mystery of Sacrifice*.

24. "To L. M.," Eve of Annunciation, 1938, *Letters*, p. 339.

25. "To L. M.," Trinity VI, 1938, *Letters*, p. 340.

Chapter 7: Precursor of a World to Come

1. M. Caedel, "Christian Pacifism in the Era of Two World Wars," in *The Church and War*, ed. W. J. Sheils (London: Blackwell, 1983), p. 404. See also D. Greene, "Evelyn Underhill and Her Response to War," *Historical Magazine of the Protestant Episcopal Church* 55, no. 2 (June 1986):127–35.

2. "Death Certificate of Arthur Underhill," Evelyn Underhill Collection (EUC), Archives, King's College, London, folder 51.

3. E. Underhill, *Eucharistic Prayers from the Ancient Liturgies* (London: Longmans, Green and Co., 1939), and "Introduction," in *Letters of Direction: Thoughts on the Spiritual Life* by Abbé de Tourville (London: Dacre Press, 1939), pp. 7–10.

4. "To Nesta De Robeck," St. Stephen, 1940, *Letters of Evelyn Underhill*, ed. C. Williams (London: Longmans, Green and Co., 1943), p. 298.

5. Sister Mary of St. John to Evelyn Underhill, 23 Feb. 1939, EUC, folder 45.

6. A. Norman, "Evelyn Underhill and Her Prayer Group," EUC, folder 57, and A. Norman, "The Story of the Fellowship of St. Faith: Its Origin and Development," privately owned.

7. Underhill's description of meditation and some of her guided meditations used in retreats were published posthumously under the title *Meditations and Prayers* (London: Longmans, Green and Co., 1949).

8. "Letters to the Prayer Group," in *Fruits of the Spirit* (London: Longmans, Green and Co., 1956), pp. 43–72.

9. "Easter, 1941," "Letters to the Prayer Group," p. 69.

10. "To S. T.," 12 Aug. 1940, *Letters of Evelyn Underhill*, ed. C. Williams (London: Longmans, Green and Co., 1943), p. 292–93.

11. I have found one instance in which she actually signed her letter "Your affection(ate) mother, ESM" on a letter of 5 Mar. 1940 to Daphne Martin-Hurst. Letter is privately owned.

12. "To Daphne Martin-Hurst," 1 Feb. 1940 and 5 Mar. 1940. Letters are privately owned.

13. "To K. N.," 3 May 1941, *Letters*, pp. 306–7.

14. "Easter, 1941," "Letters to the Prayer Group," p. 71.

15. M. Cropper, *Evelyn Underhill* (London: Longmans, Green and Co., 1958), p. 237.

16. "To L. M.," 3 Oct. 1939, *Letters*, p. 278.

17. The original, apparently never published, was called "A Service of Prayer for Peace," TS, EUC, folder 58. "A Service of Prayer for Use in War-Time" (London: Christian Literature Association, 1939), is different in tone.

18. "To Mrs. Merrix," 7 Nov. 1940, EUC, folder 56.

19. C. Armstrong, *Evelyn Underhill* (Grand Rapids, Mich.: Eerdmans, 1975), p. 288.

20. "To G. F.," 1 Nov. 1937, *Letters*, p. 262.

21. Cropper, p. 214.

22. E. Underhill, "A Meditation on Peace" (London: Fellowship of Reconciliation, 1939).

23. E. Underhill, "Prayer in Our Times," TS, EUC, folder 57, and "The Spiritual Life in War-Time" (London: Christian Literature Association, 1939).

24. Cropper, p. 214.

25. "To E. I. Watkin," 28 Dec. 1939, *Letters*, p. 283.

26. "To Maisie Spens," 31 Dec. 1939, *Letters*, p. 283.

27. "To E. I. Watkin," 12 Jan. 1940, *Letters*, p. 285.

28. "To L. K.," 20 May 1940, *Letters*, p. 288.

29. "To Maisie Spens," All Saints, 1940, *Letters*, pp. 296–97.

30. "To L. K.," 1941, *Letters*, p. 304.

31. "To C. S. Lewis," 13 Jan. 1941, *Letters*, p. 301.

32. "Will of Evelyn Maud Bosworth Moore," 1 May 1940, EUC, folder 44.

33. All unspecified assets went to Hubert Stuart Moore, but on his death allotments were made from the Wife's Fund, a certain portion of his estate.

34. "To Mrs. Holdsworth," 6 Oct. 1940, *Letters*, p. 294.

35. "To M. C.," Trinity IV, 1940, *Letters*, p. 291.

36. "To Geoffrey Curtis," 18 Jan. 1940, *Letters*, p. 285.
37. "To Maisie Spens," 22 June 1940, *Letters*, p. 289.
38. Cropper, p. 228 quotes from a letter from Dorothy Swayne.
39. E. Underhill, "Letter," *Time and Tide*, 20 July 1940, p. 757.
40. "To Mrs. Merrix," 7 Nov. 1940, EUC, folder 56.
41. Cropper, p. 229 quotes from a letter to Maisie Fletcher.
42. Cropper, p. 231. E. Underhill, "Postscript," in *Into the Way of Peace*, ed. Percy Harill (London: James Clarke, 1941), pp. 187–92. This chapter was dated incorrectly in *Evelyn Underhill: A Modern Guide to the Ancient Quest for the Holy*, ed. D. Greene (Albany, N.Y.: SUNY Press, 1988).
43. "Postscript," p. 191. She quotes from de Tourville's *Pensées Diverses*, p. 29.
44. T. S. Eliot, "Four Quartets," *Collected Poems, 1909–1962* (New York: Harcourt, Brace and World, 1963), p. 208.
45. "To Mildred Bosanquet," 12 May 1941, *Letters*, p. 308.
46. "To E. I. Watkin," 27 April 1941, *Letters*, p. 305.
47. "To M. C.," Trinity 1941, *Letters*, p. 310.
48. Sister Mary of St. John to Evelyn Underhill, Christmas 1940, EUC, folder 45.
49. E. Underhill, "Thomas à Kempis," *Time and Tide*, 1 Mar. 1941, pp. 172–73. Cropper says she used this prayer at all of her retreats, p. 237.
50. E. Underhill, "Lenten Fare," review of *Readings in St. John's Gospel* by W. Temple; *The Love of God* by Dom Aelred Graham; *Christian Discourses* by Søren Kierkegaard, *Time and Tide*, 10 Feb. 1940, pp. 141–43.
51. "To L. M.," Ascension Day, 1941, *Letters*, p. 340.
52. "To Gil," 4 June 1941, EUC, folder 32.
53. "To C. D.," 5 May 1941, *Letters*, p. 307.
54. "Death Certificate of Evelyn Maud Bosworth Stuart Moore," General Register Office, London. In describing her death Armstrong quotes from a paper given to him by a Mrs. A. J. Swainston of London who found a handwritten description of what appeared to be the last hours of Underhill. The note indicated that Underhill was ill for four weeks, but in the end was radiantly happy. I have not seen this paper and therefore am unable to validate its authenticity. Cropper, p. 232, indicates that she had one week of increased illness.
55. Her will specifically requests that her funeral have no mourning, no flowers, no lugubrious hymns.

Afterword

1. U. Holmes, *What Is Anglicanism?* (Wilton, Conn.: Morehouse-Barlow, 1982), p. 69; V. Pitt, "Clouds of Unknowing," *Prism* 3, no. 3 (June 1959):7–12.
2. *The Life and Letters of Father Andrew*, ed. by K. Burne (London: Mowbray, 1948), p. 238.

3. S. Katz, "Introduction" and "Language, Epistemology and Mysticism," in *Mysticism and Philosophical Analysis*, ed. S. Katz (New York: Oxford University Press, 1978), pp. 2, 22–74.

4. M. Thornton, "The Cultural Factor in Spirituality," in *The Great Christian Centuries to Come*, ed. C. Martin (London: Mowbray, 1974), p. 183; K. Leech, *Soul Friend* (New York: Harper & Row, 1980), pp. 81–82; U. Holmes, *A History of Christian Spirituality* (New York: Seabury Press, 1981), pp. 148–49; D. Steere, "Introduction" in *Spiritual Counsels and Letters of Baron von Hügel* (New York: Harper & Row, 1961), pp. 13–34. Steere is sympathetic and appreciative of Underhill but sees her work as largely derivative from von Hügel.

5. T. S. Eliot, MS. Aff. 90, 91. Cited in H. Gardner, *The Composition of the Four Quartets* (London: Faber and Faber, 1978), pp. 69–70; L. Gordon in *Eliot's New Life* (New York: Farrar, Straus, Giroux, 1988), says that as a graduate student Eliot read and took copious notes on *Mysticism* soon after its publication in 1911, p. 95. *The Secular Journal of Thomas Merton* (Garden City, N.Y.: Doubleday, 1969), pp. 268–69; T. Merton, *The Seven Storey Mountain* (Garden City, N.Y.: Doubleday, 1970), p. 146. A. Watts, *In My Own Way: An Autobiography, 1915–65* (New York: Random House, 1972), pp. 179, 193. For Underhill's influence on Charles Williams, see J. Heath-Stubbs, *Charles Williams* (London: Longmans, Green and Co., 1955), p. 13.

6. R. Woods, "Introduction," in *Understanding Mysticism*, ed. R. Woods (Garden City, N.Y.: Doubleday, 1980), pp. 1–15.

7. M. Furse, "Mysticism: Classic Modern Interpreters and Their Premise of Continuity," *Anglican Theological Review* 60, no. 2 (1978):189–90; H. Egan, *What Are They Saying About Mysticism?* (New York: Paulist Press, 1982), pp. 40–50.

8. H. Davies, *Worship and Theology in England* (Princeton, N.J.: Princeton University Press, 1965), 5, pp. 145–47; D. Greene, "Evelyn Underhill and Her Response to War," *Historical Magazine of the Protestant Episcopal Church* 55 (June 1986):127–35; J. Horne, *The Moral Mystic* (Waterloo, Ontario: Wilfrid Laurier University Press, 1983), pp. 77–84; Egan, p. 48.

9. J. Booty, "Christian Spirituality from Wilberforce to Temple," in *Anglican Spirituality*, ed. W. Wolf (Wilton, Conn.: Morehouse-Barlow, 1982), p. 92.

10. J. Baker Miller, *Toward a New Psychology of Woman* (Boston: Beacon Press, 1976), p. 83; C. Gilligan, *In a Different Voice: Psychological Theory and Women's Development* (Cambridge, Mass.: Harvard University Press, 1982), p. 156.

11. C. Bynum, *Holy Feast and Holy Fast: The Religious Significance of Food to Medieval Women* (Berkeley, Calif.: University of California Press, 1986), pp. 23–30. D. Weinstein and R. Bell, *Saints and Society: The Two Worlds of Western Christendom, 1000–1700 A.D.* (Chicago: University of Chicago Press, 1986), pp. 220–38.

12. V. Saiving, "The Human Situation: A Feminine View," in *Womanspirit Rising*, ed. C. Christ and J. Plaskow (San Francisco: Harper & Row, 1979), p. 26, and C. Christ, *Diving Deep and Surfacing* (Boston: Beacon Press, 1980), p. 19.

13. In August 1988 the House of Deputies of the Episcopal Church of America revised its Calendar of the Church Year to include Evelyn Underhill, defining her as theologian and mystic.

INDEX